A FINAL GIRL'S GUIDE TO
THE HORRORS OF DATING

A FINAL GIRL'S GUIDE TO
THE HORRORS OF DATING

RORY UPHOLD

First Edition
Copyright © 2025
By Rory Uphold/Blue Lakes

Ebook: 979-8-9997401-0-6
Paperback: ISBN: 979-8-9997401-1-3

All rights reserved. No part of this publication may be reproduced, distributed, or transmitted in any form or by any means, including photocopying, recording, or other electronic or mechanical methods, without the prior written permission of the publisher, except in the case of brief quotations embodied in critical reviews and certain other noncommercial uses permitted by copyright law.

Cover Design: Chris Steward and Daniel Kiyoi
Editors: Rea Frey & Jennifer Chesak
Formatting: Elaine York, Allusion Publishing, www.allusionpublishing.com

For anyone brave enough to still believe in love.

This book is dedicated to:

The daughters of the witches they could not burn.
And to the coven that has supported me through thick and thin—
thank you for showing me what unconditional love looks like.

TABLE OF CONTENTS

A Note i
Welcome to Hell 1

ACT I 5

Serial Killers 7
Poison 15
Werewolves 31
Comedic Break 47
Bed Death 49
The Ick 61
Viruses 73
A Hint of Danger 95
Witches 97
Zombies 111
Demonic Clowns 121

ACT II 125

Monsters 127
Vampires 145
Flying Monkeys 167
Dark Night of the Soul 171
Spells 175
The B Story 187
Time is Running Out 189
Aliens 195
Ghosts 211
Serial Killers: The Sequel 225

ACT III 231

Dicksand 235
Sluts Get Cut 253
Body Count 261
Funerals 263
The Graveyard 275
They Always Come Back 277
Scorched Earth 279
Maybe I'm a Monster Too 285
Final Girls 295

Works Referenced 299
Acknowledgments 303
About the Author 307

A NOTE

This is a work of creative nonfiction. While the stories in this book are true, I've taken a few creative liberties because lawsuits are expensive. Names and identifying details have been changed to protect the guilty—and to keep my lawyer from having a panic attack. That said, trust me when I tell you Waldo was ugly, that detail is 100% accurate.

WELCOME TO HELL

◆

Raise your hand if you're a final girl.

A final girl, in case you didn't know, is a popular horror trope. She's the movie's sole survivor, the last one standing to confront the killer, and the only one left to tell the story. A final girl is the character who lives in the end. Think Jaime Lee Curtis in *Halloween*. (We *love* her!) In horror movies, a final girl is female but for the purposes of this book, final girls can be anyone. As long as you have a will to make it to the end of your romantic journey, you, too, are a final girl.

In a world where ghosts and zombies have replaced the proverbial white knights of fairy tales past, today's romantic prospects feel less like a nineties rom-com and more like a horror comedy. Even the words we use to talk about love are horrific: heartbroken, lovesick, strung along; or falling in love, ending it, love bombing, suffocating, ghosting—you get the idea. And sometimes the stakes feel like life or death. If you've ever felt the pain of rejection or the adrenaline that comes with watching those text bubbles as you wait for a response from the person you like, then you know that the pursuit of love is not for the faint of heart. And modern dating is a horror show! So, who better to help navigate readers through the pitfalls of "dicksand," "bed death," and the dreaded "ick" than a final girl? They have seen it (and survived it) all!

And so have I.

I'm Rory Uphold, a self-proclaimed final girl. I'm a resilient woman with a black belt in break ups, a PhD in rejection, and well over ten thousand hours clocked in the hellfire of digital dating. I've had my heart ripped out so many times, it's honestly a medical miracle that it still beats. And I've seen more skeletons in closets than I'd care to admit, which makes me the perfect person to help others navigate the perilous and often ruthless landscape that is modern love. And while I've spent years immersed in this horrifying new world, I'm aware that not everyone is as familiar with terms like "flying monkeys" or "dickmatization." So I created a funny and frightful roadmap through the horror show that is finding love in today's bleak digital landscape.

This book is filled with cringe-worthy, jaw-dropping, never-before-shared stories about the many horrors I've encountered while single and coupled, as well as the survival skills I've cultivated as a final girl. (Obviously I've had plenty of great relationships too, but my "failures" offer more lessons.) Want to survive to see the end credits in a very difficult dating world? Yeah, me too! And somehow, after fourteen million first dates and a whole lot of monsters slaughtered, I'm still freaking alive—and falling deeper in love with myself.

So learn from my mistakes.

This book is for the girl who still believes in love despite the many plot twists and jump scares that have been thrown her way. It's told from my (mostly) straight perspective, so the stories will feature heteronormative relationships, but in no way does that mean this book isn't inclusive of everyone.

My hope is for readers to use this book not only as a guide but as a companion to navigate their own romantic journeys. It's the book I wish I'd read in my twenties to avoid a whole lot of heartache, dating mistakes, and one guy named Jack. But most importantly, this book is a love letter to myself. The one thing a final girl needs for surviving the third act is trust in herself. Without self-love, "happily ever after" does not exist, right?

So, welcome to hell, aka modern dating. Let's survive together.

ACT I: YOU IN DANGER, GIRL

SERIAL KILLERS
♦

Final girls are not born; they're made. They're forged in fire and forced to become the heroes of their own story.

I never set out to be a final girl. In fact, I was on track to live out all my rom-com fantasies, but life had other plans.

My origin story starts when I was twenty-five and madly in love with Jack the Ripper. (Of course, he wasn't *actually* Jack the Ripper, as I am not over one hundred years old, but he was still a killer in his own right.)

To me, he was just Jack, the cute older boy I grew up with. He was dark haired and brooding, wickedly smart, and idiosyncratic. Jack made me laugh harder than anyone I knew, and he made me feel like I was the most beautiful woman in every room. I was living proof that "love finds you when you least expect it."

Three years earlier, Jack sent me a DM out of the blue to ask me out on a date. We had not spoken since I was a freshman in high school, but he informed me that he was moving back to LA and wanted to know if I was available. I was, and from that first date forward, we were basically inseparable.

He was everything I'd ever wanted—smart, funny, weird, athletic, artistic—and he made me feel like I could stop time in his presence. He was thoughtful and kind, not only to me but also to my friends and family. Jack was always giving me compliments and thinking of nice ways to show me he loved me. We had the kind of love that made me relate to fairy tales.

We'd been talking about getting married when he finished his residency, and we had developed a loose timeline. At the time, I often marveled at how wrong I was. I'd always thought I'd be the type of woman to collect wild dating stories, an assortment of boyfriends, and lots of life experience before settling down, but here I was, ready to spend the rest of my life with Jack. Knowing that I'd never sleep with anyone else or that I'd never go on another first date was weird, but those things seemed like easy tradeoffs for a life with a man I loved.

This is what I was discussing with my father as we drove for two hours to Jack's family reunion. My parents and I were about to meet his great grandparents and a ton of his extended family, family that I probably wouldn't see again until our wedding.

When we pulled up to a large Spanish-style house, Jack was outside waiting for us. He wore the new blue suit my mother had bought him for the occasion. In fact, she'd bought him three, but who was counting? We spent the rest of the evening blending our families, and I felt like the luckiest girl in the world.

Nine days later, Jack called me.

"I think we should take a break." His words stabbed me straight through the heart.

My first reaction was shock. My fingers and toes went numb as I struggled to make sense of what he'd just said.

A break? What is he talking about? We have tickets to Africa for Christmas in nine months. Why would we take a break?

Jack mumbled something about my being in entertainment and him not wanting to live in LA and that one day he hoped I could see that this was for the best. He twisted the knife around, and my heart shredded into a million pieces. Then he hung up, leaving me to bleed out in my living room, *alone*.

I was too stunned to scream or call for help, so I sat there as the life slowly drained out of my body.

Eventually my eyes began to well and suddenly I was sobbing on the floor. Hot tears and snot streamed down my face as I grabbed my left breast. I was acutely aware of the sharp pain emanating from the void where my heart used to be. I had been fatally wounded. The girl I was ten minutes ago was not the girl I was now. She was gone and so was the life she'd thought she had. Jack had ended that.

I cried until I physically could not shed another tear.

Then I had a choice to make: I could succumb to my wounds, or I could try with every fiber of my being to survive. The thought of living without Jack felt overwhelmingly awful, but he wasn't coming back. So I promised myself something:

Whatever life you thought you were going to have with Jack, it's going to be better—much better.

And it was there, in a puddle of my own heartbreak, that I decided to fight against the immense horror thrown my way. I may have been powerless in my breakup, but I told myself that I got to control how I wrote the ending of my love story—because it was my life and I'd be damned if I let Jack ruin it.

I didn't know it at the time, but this was a pivotal moment. Every horror movie has a scene where the final girl demonstrates an ironclad will to survive and the movie becomes hers. Much like the scream queens before me, I did not choose my set of circumstances, but I was going to do everything in my power to overcome the fresh hell I found myself in.

In another version of this story, I would have refused to accept Jack's breakup. I'd call him a hundred times before showing up at his house, begging him to get back together with me. I know someone reading this has done this before, and I don't blame you. Heartbreak is traumatic. Even an amicable breakup is torture. Maybe it's not *The Texas Chain Saw Massacre*—level horror, but sometimes it sure feels that way. So I understand why people go to great lengths to avoid that kind of pain.

But if Jack and I had gotten back together, we never would have been the same. He broke my trust when he broke my heart, and I wouldn't have been able to forget that. Getting back together would have meant settling for a kind of love that was less than what I'd wanted, and even at my lowest, I knew I deserved better.

If you only take away one lesson from this book, be sure it is the understanding that you must believe in yourself. You will never make it to the end of the proverbial movie if you don't think that you can, and this goes for both rom-coms and horror flicks. If you do not trust that you are worthy of love or that it's out there and possible for you, those thoughts become self-fulfilling prophecies.

That's not to say that you won't face difficulties. The aftermath of my breakup with Jack was not pretty—then again, most scary movies aren't. I was heartbroken. I struggled with basic tasks like eating, sleeping, and focusing. Studies have shown that the human brain reacts to a breakup like it does to withdrawal.[1] (Not well!) Love really is like a drug, and when we lose it, we can suffer immensely.

I found myself ruminating on three years' worth of memories, desperate to understand what happened.

When did he lose interest? Did I do something to make him fall out of love with me? When did he start faking it? How did I not know?

The not knowing was the worst part. I had so many questions and zero answers, and I couldn't ask Jack, because he re-

---

[1] Drake Baer, "Heartbreak Looks a Lot like Drug Withdrawal in the Brain," The Cut, February 17, 2017, https://www.thecut.com/2017/02/why-heartbreak-getting-dumped-feel-so-bad.html.

fused to speak to me. He'd cut me out of his life so swiftly and seamlessly, like a surgeon removing a tumor, that I had a hard time imagining I wasn't at fault.

A voice inside my mind kept peppering me with questions: *Did I do something? Am I not attractive to him anymore? If it wasn't my fault, why is he refusing to speak to me?*

Jack consumed as much of my mental energy now as he had when we were together. It was like we'd never broken up, and that needed to change. I needed to detox him from my life.

I didn't know it at the time, but one of the main things that allows people to move on is understanding *why* a breakup occurred. Since I wasn't going to get an answer from him, I tried to come up with reasons of my own.

We broke up because I deserve someone much better. The man you fell in love with is not the real Jack, and the Jack that exists now is not who you want to be with.

This is what I told myself, repeatedly, because intellectually I knew it was true. Unfortunately, I had trouble believing it.

My mind would often shift toward other thoughts.

Was it something I said? Something I did? Maybe I was too much for him? Or . . . maybe I'm not enough?

I wanted to forget him the way he forgot me, but even the act of getting dressed caused my brain to drift.

Does he think about me when he puts on the Red Wing boots I bought him for his birthday? He loves those boots. Does he even wear them anymore? I wondered.

Mostly, I wanted to know how it was so easy for him to walk away and never look back while I fought through the struggle daily.

Three months later, in another moment of weakness, I got my answer. I was looking at his Twitter when I clicked a link and discovered his secret Tumblr. Why this man had a Tumblr account in the first place is a topic for another book. The account was full of photos with him and "Jill," his new girlfriend. I instantly felt the color drain from my face. My eyes darted across the photos, putting the pieces together: Jack had been cheating on me.

Based on the timestamps, Jack had introduced Jill to his mom just a few weeks after he'd dumped me, and they'd moved in together about a month after our split. While I was bawling my eyes out, he was already *living* with another woman. The truth was both validating and harmful.

On the one hand, Jack was not the guy I thought he was. He was the kind of guy who allowed my mom to buy him clothes, knowing that he was cheating on me; the kind of guy who told me he loved me but clearly didn't respect me; and the kind of guy who insisted on my family coming to his reunion, knowing that we would never see these people again. He was not the kind of person I wanted to spend my life with, and knowing that reaffirmed my belief that the breakup was for the best. Someone better was out there for me.

On the other hand, this revelation birthed a new fresh hell, a monster so evil that it would follow me for years to come: my inner demon. The inner critic that had been planting seeds of doubt from the moment Jack broke up with me had suddenly spawned into a supernatural entity whose sole mission seemed to be to tear me down.

Almost immediately, I heard its demonic voice echoing from a dark corridor in my mind.

What does she have that you don't?

I tried to ignore it, but the voice only got louder.

How could you have missed this, Rory? If you knew Jack so well, then how did you miss that he was cheating on you? Maybe you're not as attentive as you think? Maybe that's why he left you.

I wanted to prove the little voice in my head wrong, but it had a point.

Jack had had my whole heart, but it wasn't enough—he wanted someone else. Based on his silence the last three months, I had feared that I was easy to walk away from, but now I had the photographic evidence to prove it. I was, in fact, replaceable.

It felt like being stabbed all over again.

However, this time I was determined to get over him. I started by retraining my brain. Anytime I found myself thinking about Jack, I redirected my thoughts to something else. I committed myself to a mantra:

This is happening to show me that I deserve so much better, and better is coming.

I repeated it several times a day. I got into therapy and threw myself into work, and any time I felt sad, I'd bury my grief by doing something that would better myself. Healing became a competition, and even though Jack may have moved on first, I was determined to get the last laugh. I told myself that Rory 2.0 was going to be unstoppable. Was this healthy? No, but it worked.

Days passed, and just as I would have from a nonfatal stab wound, I eventually healed, but I was also left with gnarly scars. All my romantic doubts and limiting beliefs took the shape of a demonic figure that lurked in the depths of my mind. The pain that Jack inflicted was etched into my psyche and buried in my cells, and my inner demon used my pain as fuel to torment me for years to come. I may have moved on, but I'd failed to heal the most broken parts of myself.

It would take a decade, two more cheaters, and a whole lot of heartbreak before I figured out how to vanquish my inner demon—but I wouldn't give up.

Like the many final girls before me, I would persevere. I'd keep pushing forward, not knowing what or who was around the corner, because deep down I still believed in love. No matter how many hits I took, I would get back up—because that is what icons are made of.

A FINAL GIRL'S GUIDE TO THIS BOOK

In the following pages, you will read about my decade's-plus romantic journey and the various lesson's I've collected along the way. Each chapter culminates with a guide where I recap what I've learned surviving that horror or monster. Depending on where you are in your life, the lessons I learned at twenty-five might feel obvious or they might feel revelatory; and the lessons I learned at thirty-five might feel relatable or you might not be there quite yet. As general rule of thumb, take what resonates and ignore what doesn't—because your journey will be unique to you.

POISON

◆

Shiiiit.

I'd just caught a glimpse of myself in the mirror, and I looked like a drowned poodle. I was covered in so much flop-sweat that my hair was stuck to the sides of my face in the most unflattering way.

Why did I say yes to this?

In fairness, this was not an average first date.

Tonight I was going out with Thomas, a man I'd met a couple of years ago because we ran in the same social circles. We'd immediately hit it off as friends, but I was happily in love with Jack at the time, so our chemistry was friend chemistry and I didn't know if it would translate into anything more. I had never considered Thomas as a romantic prospect, and that should have been a huge red flag, but I was at a place in my life where red flags looked like decorative tapestries in my house of bad decisions. You see, this was also my first *date* post-Jack, and I was delusional about moving on.

I'd like to take you out on a real date next weekend.

I read Thomas's text and blushed. We'd been texting for weeks, so I should have seen it coming, but I was still reeling from my breakup and lost in the fog of heartache. I felt a rush of excitement, the kind that comes with possibility and potential before the truth begins to flesh out the reality of a person.

Ok, sounds fun.

Great. Friday? I'll make a reservation and pick you up at 8.

For a moment I felt giddy, but the feeling was quickly eclipsed by a second one: fear. Thomas already knew he wanted to date me. Meanwhile, I felt safe edging with flirtation from behind the thick barrier of my iPhone. I'd been single long enough to realize that the dating landscape was barren AF, but I was still mildly terrified at the thought of sleeping with someone new. Plus, there was something claustrophobic about knowing that no matter how this date went, I wasn't going to be able to "unmatch" or "block" my way out of seeing him again.

I heard the little demon in my mind saying, *Don't fuck this up or you'll regret it.*

And now I had a little more than sixty minutes to pull it together, but my anxiety sweat 'stache was making it impossible to apply my foundation. I needed to calm down.

I'll open a bottle of wine, I thought. *To take the edge off.*

I pulled out a perfectly chilled bottle of Rombauer Chardonnay. As I sunk my comically large bottle opener into the blue metal layer covering the cork, I promised myself, *Just one glass so you can stop freaking out.*

Drinking and dating are a couple as iconic and toxic as Romeo and Juliet. The combo has been romanticized and normalized, and yet we all know that alcohol is bad for us. Maybe your relationship with alcohol is great, but for many people, drinking is a crutch. It helps us move through awkward situations and calms our nerves, or it gives us a temporary (albeit manufactured) sense of freedom and joy. But it's literally poison. You really must get the balance just right with drinking or you will end up à la Romeo and Juliet. (That's meant as more of a metaphor for embarrassment, but obviously you *can* drink yourself to death.) Booze has been my partner in crime for a lot of the dumb mistakes of my life, romantic or otherwise, and tonight would be no exception.

After I said yes to Thomas, I immediately began to overthink it. The demonic voice in my head was like an announcer commentating a sporting event: loud and annoying.

If Jack can move on, you should be able to move on too.

Thomas is the kind of guy your parents would approve of, so don't mess this up.

If you play your cards right, Thomas could be your last first date and you'll never have to deal with any of this ever again.

In the week leading up to our date, I had determined that, on paper, Thomas checked almost all my boxes. Even though he was not my type per se—he was shorter, rounder, and balder than I would have liked—Thomas was smart and stylish, and that counts for something, right? He was the type of guy whose appeal was equal parts sardonic charm and seemingly having his shit together. I'd been "talking to" a lot of guys who slept on futons, but Thomas had health insurance and multiple pairs of matching socks. I decided that Thomas was the type of person I *should* be dating.

There was just one thing I wasn't sure about: our sexual chemistry. Now that I was single, would I want to kiss him? Would the bald thing freak me out? Would he be good in bed? Based on absolutely nothing but my own mental math, I had concluded that the only thing standing between me and years of domestic bliss with Thomas was what would happen in the bedroom. I'd been ticking through his characteristics like items on a grocery list as if I were shopping for a husband meal I'd be cooking up later that night. The only thing left to discover was whether we had that *spice*, that sexual spark. And no amount of mental gymnastics was going to help me figure this out. I'd have to stretch those muscles IRL.

I decided that I'd have to fuck him on our first date—because that's a super rational conclusion that a very stable and sane person would jump to. No wonder I was sweating.

I took a sip of my Chardonnay. Thick buttery goodness. I was seven swigs away from a new perspective. I swished the fruity nectar of a forty-something-dollar bottle around in my mouth like it was the antidote to all my problems. And in that moment, *it was*. I felt dopamine rushing through my brain like an EDM beat about to drop. 5, 4, 3, 2: Instant calm. My mind quieted and my face stopped sweating. I was ready to roll up my sleeves and paint my face. Michelangelo once said—and I am paraphrasing here—that his job was to chisel away at the marble to let the sculpture free, and I relate to that. I feel like I am a model trapped in the body of an average woman and every swipe of mascara brings me closer to my true essence. Getting ready is an art. So is drinking.

In my personal experience, the key to drinking while dating is being aware of *why* you are drinking. I was too busy worrying about being late that I never stopped to ask myself why I was having such an intense reaction to a first date. Maybe then I would have realized my body was quite literally telling me, *Stop, this is not what you want to do.*

I longed to be over Jack and ready for love again, but I was neither of those things. Instead, I was trying to force myself into liking a guy I knew was good for me on paper to circumvent the tremendous amount of pain I still found myself in. I wanted to be over Jack, and I wanted to move on as quickly as he'd moved on. I thought that if I could fall in love with Thomas, then I could close the door on Jack. Problem solved. Except I wasn't attracted to Thomas, and I wasn't ready. You can't circumvent heartbreak by throwing yourself into another relationship, but that was exactly what I was trying to do. So instead of relishing the excitement of a first date, I was throwing back wine to stop myself from spiraling.

Shout out to all the final girls who are dating sober, especially the ones doing it in their twenties—I don't know if I would have had the courage to do this. While I don't identify as an alcoholic, nor have I ever *needed* to stop drinking, I have reexamined my relationship to booze over the years. I grew up in world where drinking was glamorized—it was something that sophisticated women did at lunch and my favorite rockstars did on stage—and I never questioned why. Regardless of your relationship with alcohol, it never hurts to ask yourself what you're hoping to achieve by drinking? Had someone asked me this before my date with Thomas, I probably would have said, *Everyone drinks on dates—it's what you do, and it's fun.* Then again, I wasn't ready to pull back the layers of what my drinking masked.

Two and a half Chardonnays and a full face of makeup later, I was *reeeeeeeeady* for this date. By the time Thomas picked me up, I'd traded all my nerves in for a healthy dose of liquid courage. Whatever fears I had an hour ago were drowning in white wine. Thomas opened the door of his BMW, and I crawled in without a care in the world. I liked that he had money. His financial status made me feel like he was safe and had his life together—which is ironic because I grew up with a lot of trust-fund babies who received BMWs for their sixteenth birthdays and many were a mess.

All of LA's best sushi can be found in places that look like you'd have a better chance of contracting crabs than eating them raw. We pulled into a shitty strip mall and walked into one of those spots that required a reservation despite no one else being in the restaurant. A tall and serious-looking waitress removed the "reserved" sign from our table. I was impressed by Thomas's effort. Making a reservation takes maybe two minutes, but even then my bar was so low. Thomas took control of ordering everything—a move that can go either way for women—but I loved it. I love assertive men, and so far we were off to a great start.

See, this is the type of guy you should be dating.

Unfortunately, I found myself staring at his bald head. A lot. Normally Thomas sported a hat or a beanie, which he wore well, but tonight his head was naked. I never realized how much I valued hair until I thought about the fact that I might end up with someone who didn't have it. I tried to picture my fingers grazing the stubble on his head.

Am I really this shallow?

Surely I could get over his lack of hair. I forced myself to stop thinking about his head and recommitted to the conversation.

"So wait, where did you grow up again?" I asked.

Clearly Thomas had not noticed my eyes surveying his dome. "On a dairy farm in Michigan."

Several bottles of sake later, I realized that the lights had dimmed in the restaurant, which could only mean one thing: I was *drunk*. Everyone has their drunk-tell and mine is lighting. It took years, and a lot of awkward conversations about "who turned the lights down," to figure out that when I cross the threshold between regular drunk and call-all-of-my-exes-and-order-three-pizzas drunk, the lighting changes. Of course this sushi restaurant hadn't randomly dimmed the lights in the middle of dinner; my inebriation had. Apparently, chasing half a bottle of white wine on an empty stomach with sake and some small pieces of raw fish *will* get you hammered.

As soon as I came to this realization, I stopped drinking and started pounding water.

This is perfect. By the time we get back to my place, I'll have sobered myself back to buzzed and I'll be ready for bonetown.

I'm pretty sure this is not how drinking works, or attraction, but even if I could reverse engineer my inebriation, Thomas had other plans.

Thomas, ever the gentleman, had organized a very cute date that involved us going to a separate restaurant for their lauded chocolate soufflé. Did you know that it takes most restaurants forty-five minutes to cook a soufflé? Let me break that down for you: That's enough time for at least one more drink, if not two. What a baller move this was. It automatically ensured another hour of our date, but it also threw a real kink in my plans. And not the fun kind of kink I was hoping for.

A spry waitress with new-to-LA energy came to take our order, and I snapped into performance mode. She was like a cop car pulling up behind me, forcing me to stay on my best behavior.

"I'll have an espresso martini, please." I hoped that the caffeine might counteract the booze.

"Whiskey neat," Thomas said.

As he handed our menus to the waitress, I wondered if I would remember any of this the next day. I sat up a little straighter, determined to nail the part of a sober date. I could tell that Thomas was pleased with himself. He had one of those shit-eating grins that men get right before they think they're going to get laid. I blinked and Thomas looked blurry. I blinked again and he came back into focus.

My inner voice cheered me on like a manipulative mean girl right before she sets you up to fail:

You can do this.

You're probably wondering why I didn't just tell him that I'd killed half a bottle of wine pre-date. Several reasons. One: If we *did* have sexual chemistry, I didn't want him to judge me for my drinking. Two: I also didn't want to let him know I was nervous or give him any sort of indication that I might be interested in him, because if we did *not* have chemistry, I wanted to be able to crab walk my way out of that situation and claim "just friends." The fact that I was still debating our chemistry this far into the date should have raised alarm bells, but then again, I was drunk.

"So . . . *Jack*. What happened there?"

The mere mention of my ex sent shock waves through my body. Suddenly I was sober.

"What do you mean?" I tried to force a smile to cover my uneasiness.

"Did he lose his mind or something, or did *you* break up with *him*?" Thomas chuckled to himself, as if Jack were a joke that we could laugh about.

"Oh, well, uh, I guess he lost his mind."

The waitress was back with our drinks; I was grateful for her interruption.

Thomas held up his whiskey. "To Jack, for being an idiot."

Suddenly, I felt my heart in my throat. I clinked his glass with mine before throwing back several gulps. I hated that I still missed Jack. I took another sip, hoping that this one would push my heart out of my throat and back into my chest where it belonged.

"Someone was thirsty." I looked down at my glass, which had one sip left in it.

Fuck. So much for sobering up.

Several hours later, we *finally* made it back to my place. We were at the finish line. The only thing left to do was make a move or give Thomas the opportunity to make his. I asked if he wanted a drink—because that's the polite thing to do when people come over to your home.

I handed Thomas his whiskey as I took a sip of my water. Suddenly, I felt five hours' worth of liquids hitting my bladder at once. I *really* needed to pee. I excused myself and walked down my extremely long hallway, past my dining room, my kitchen, my bedroom, and my office until I finally reached my bathroom.

Slightly winded and still very drunk, I plopped my ass down on the toilet and peed for an eternity—long enough for me to forget why I was in the bathroom in the first place. This is a nice way of saying I peed so long that I forgot that Thomas was in my living room. Instead, my drunk brain connected the bathroom with bedtime, and I went right into my nightly routine. We're talking floss, zit cream, a high pony with a scrunchie, the whole shebang. On a sober night, this takes about ten minutes, but who knows how long it takes when I'm hammered.

I can only imagine that Thomas thought I was droppin' a deuce; meanwhile I was busy toning and moisturizing before turning off lights. I walked into my bedroom and pulled out the least sexy, most comfortable pair of oversized sweatpants and Jack's old shirt. The long-sleeved, worn-in waffle knit was like wearing a hug from the past. It comforted me. (Note that I unconsciously chose to sleep with a relic of my ex over the human man sitting in my living room.) Then, I promptly fell asleep.

Yes, I fell asleep with Thomas in my living room. But that isn't even the worst part.

Who knows how long he waited before venturing down my dark hallway, trying to figure out which door led to my bedroom. Was it five minutes? Was it fifty? I just remember waking up to a dark figure in my doorframe, backlit by the lights I'd previously turned off, and Thomas saying, "Are you fucking serious right now?"

My drunk brain must have connected the white man standing in my doorway with gaslighting because that's exactly what I did next. I tried to convince him that this situation was actually *his* fault because "I'm such a lightweight" and "I just couldn't keep up with the drinking."

Thomas was not having it. "Wow, *okay*, so I should just go then?"

A thought crossed my mind, and before I could filter it, I blurted, "Actually if you could turn off the lights and lock the door on your way out, that would be uhhhhhmazing."

Thomas stood there for a second, staring at me in my zit cream and my oversized sleepwear, and then he turned off my lights.

I'm not saying people shouldn't drink on dates. That is a choice that only you can make, but I would challenge you to think about the ways in which you negatively self-soothe. We all have our poison. For some it might be drinking; for others it's sex, shopping, or even perfectionism. I'm talking about the things you do to dull your anxieties, tune out your thoughts, or numb your emotional wounds. Rejection sucks. Hurt sucks. Feeling too seen or not seen at all sucks. Most of us are either running away from pain or running toward pleasure as often as we can. Over time, each of us develops coping mechanisms to help us avoid our negative feelings. Have you ever stopped to think about what your pain points are and what protective mechanisms you've built to avoid them?

I was bullied as a kid, and one of the ways I survived was by pretending like I didn't care. I realized if I never let the people who were bullying me know that I was hurting inside, they wouldn't know they had any power over me. This manifested unconsciously in my romantic life as I found myself downplaying rejections or pretending like I wasn't as hurt as I was. In revisiting this story about Thomas, I see myself ignoring my instincts in the hopes of willing myself out of grief. I wanted to be over Jack, so I threw myself into dating before I was ready.

However, the walls we build to protect us when we are younger generally become the same walls that imprison us when we're older. When people think you're okay or that nothing ever bothers you, they don't know how to support you. Speaking from personal experience, this can be isolating. It took me years to learn how to be vulnerable with my romantic partners, because I was so used to pretending like everything was fine, which is a recipe for disaster.

Not everyone reacts to being bullied the way that I did. Maybe you realize that you only like people until things start to get serious and then, for whatever reason, you get turned off around the three-month mark. Behind the fear of intimacy is the fear of facing ourselves. Unconsciously, we may feel safer avoiding closeness with others than looking at our own shortcomings.

Or maybe you're the type of person who can't ever seem to find anyone who meets your standards. To be clear, I'm talking about someone who has a laundry list of reasons why "no one" is right or good enough. Perfectionism is often a way to set expectations so high that no one ever meets them, which means you never have to try and therefore never have to fail. Staying single and frustrated can be more familiar (aka safer) than opening yourself up to the potential rejection that comes with falling in love. These coping mechanisms might help us avoid short-term hurt, but they lead to long-term disappointment. The sooner we address the walls we erect, and the pain behind them, the sooner they can start to come down.

As I've gotten older, I've realized that the trick is to sit with the uncomfortable feelings, to acknowledge them and to give them space. And when I do that, I'm able to move through discomfort faster and healthier than I would if I'd tried to avoid it. Ultimately, most of our vices are ways of avoiding vulnerability, being seen, or addressing our baggage. So take a minute to think about the ways in which you dodge your feelings and whether your methods are serving you.

I no longer try to quiet my nerves when it comes to dating. I listen to them and lean into what they're trying to tell me. If I'd listened to my nerves before my date with Thomas, three things would have been apparent: I wasn't over my ex, I was desperately hoping that Thomas would magically heal the hole in my heart, and I was simply not attracted to him. I *wanted* to be attracted to Thomas, and I spent a lot of energy trying to convince myself that I *could* be, because I liked him as a person, but my body was telling me otherwise. And while I tried to manufacture a spark with some Chardonnay and a healthy buzz, that ultimately backfired.

I've heard plenty of stories about people suddenly finding platonic partners attractive, but I think these instances are rare. Yes, we should give people a chance, but I have yet to wake up and suddenly feel attracted to someone I previously felt zero heat with. So while some people believe that chemistry is something you can develop and build on over time, I'm of the mind that you can't force chemistry—you either feel it or you don't.

You also can't *think* your way into chemistry. Just because Thomas had most of the qualities I was looking for in a long-term partner didn't mean I was attracted to him. A lot of people make this mistake. They marry the person they think they are supposed to be with or the person who feels safe, ignoring the lack of magnetic pull. Now, don't get me wrong, I'm not suggesting that you marry the person you have the wildest one-night stand with, but I do think attraction matters—and booze can often create a false sense of intimacy.

I thought that buzzed Ror would have a better shot at hitting it off with Thomas because it was easier to disrobe the many layers of my armor, both literally and emotionally, when I was drinking. Bonding over cocktails has generally led me to a false sense of connection, but sharing my whole life story over several rounds of drinks could not compensate for the fact that we were still strangers. I was hoping that a little white wine would loosen me up so I'd be able to feel a spark with Thomas, leave the dating game behind me, and sail off into the sunset with a man who'd take care of me. L-O-L at my problematic train of thought.

A FINAL GIRL'S GUIDE TO DRINKING & DATING

Drinking is a sensitive topic that people have varied opinions about. Some would *never* date a person who's sober, while others would *only* date a person who's sober.

These are *my* rules as someone who considers herself a casual drinker.

- A first date is a vibe check. It's an assessment, and it's hard to properly assess someone if you're drunk. I stick to one to two drinks, depending on how long the date is, and I regularly don't drink at all.
- Never take shots on a first or second date.
- Never take shots if you're planning on hooking up for the first time.
- Never take your eyes off your drink.
- If you don't want to kiss them when you're sober, don't kiss them when you're drunk.
- If you think you're more fun, confident, or sexy when you're drunk, focus on inner work. Body confidence should not come from a bottle or a can.
- Sober sex is hotter than drunk sex. It requires confidence and intimacy, both of which are sexy and hard to fake. Sober sex is like fucking with the lights on—it's a yes for me.
- Make sure 50% or more of your quality time is spent sans booze.
- Under zero circumstances should you argue with your partner if one of you has been drinking. I don't care how mad you are. Come up with a catchphrase. Tell your partner you love them and that you'll discuss in the a.m., and then do that when you're both sober.
- Beer goggles are like rose-colored glasses—it's very hard to spot red flags.

- Don't text, swipe, or post past two drinks. It's not cute, it's not chic, and your odds of embarrassing yourself increase by 100%.
- If you do something dumb when you're drunk, you have twenty-four hours to feel embarrassed about it and then you must shake it off. Shame will not change what happened, and continuing to punish yourself accomplishes nothing.
- Never drink and drive. No exceptions. (If your date sends a car for you, give them a nearby public address until you've established that they're trustworthy.)
- And don't forget to add electrolytes to your hangover hydration.

My secret to drinking and dating is staying in the barely buzzed zone. Anything past that and I'm likely to regret it the next day. If I go over my tequila soda quota—two for those of you counting—I am bound to overshare, both verbally and physically. I've slept with some literal gargoyles because I was too lazy to get a ride home, too horned up to think about whether I was into the person, or too drunk to care that in the morning I would be waking up next to Quasimodo.

Alcohol is like that one friend you have that eggs you on in situations she would never participate in herself. She's the girl who tells you the DJ's been eye fucking you all night so you should absolutely flirt back by dancing on top of the nearest banquette, then posts the video of you falling off. She's the friend who tells you to *get ittttt girl* when she sees you going home with a literal two, then she shits on you at brunch for banging a random uggo. She's also the friend who reminds you of every single rejection the second you've had one too many cocktails, then she shames you the next morning for publicly crying. In other words, alcohol is the ultimate frenemy. So watch your back, babes.

For those of you wondering, no, we did not go on a second date.

But that was the last time I pregamed.

WEREWOLVES

◆

Werewolves, or lycanthropy, have been a horror staple harkening back to seventeenth-century fairy tales. They're shapeshifters known for their lack of self-control, beastly impulses, and raw, testosterone-fueled strength. Sometimes they are the victims of the tale, but regardless of where the villainy lies, werewolves are known for their "terror by night." And this is a story about the night my friend David turned into a werewolf.

Despite our decade-plus friendship, I'd never been to his house. This was probably a sign, but I'd known David for years, and in the same way that I don't know the names of the streets I grew up on, I wasn't looking for signs when I was hanging out with David. He was familiar and trusted, so signs were irrelevant.

When I stepped into his foyer, I was immediately greeted by dark wood floors, an arched doorway, a wrought iron staircase, and a healthy dose of old Hollywood charm, which was appropriate given his lineage. David was classic old Hollywood. He was an LA native who'd married into one of the most famous film families. He seemed to know everyone but never made a big deal about getting me on the list for the last Daft Punk show or snagging me VIP passes to Coachella. He was a stoner who moved through life with the kind of ease that money and privilege afford, and he was fucking fun. Also, since he was twenty years my senior, I looked up to him.

As I toured his Hollywood Hills home, I passed emerald furniture, gallery walls, and knickknacks from trips to India and Paris. His house felt very *him*: expensive but relaxed, eclectic, eccentric, and slightly falling apart.

"So where are the French people?" I asked.

David was throwing a last-minute party for some "crazy artist friends" who were visiting from France. We'd just left a show at the Hollywood Bowl, and I'd been convinced to keep the party going by coming to his house to meet this wild cast of characters.

I trailed behind him in a dimly lit hallway, and a piece of art caught my eye.

"I don't know, I thought they'd be here by now."

I examined the multicolored scribbles on butcher paper, trying to decipher if I was looking at a framed piece from one of his kids or some museum-worthy artist. With David, it would be one or the other. His vibe was high/low, which I adored. In a city full of pretentious assholes, I loved that David was almost fifty and still rocking Vans and long shaggy hair.

"You wanna drink?" he called out from another room.

"Sure—hey, who made the squiggles piece?"

"Amelia. Sick, right?"

Amelia was his youngest of two and the kind of child who made me reconsider my no-kids policy. Even at six, she knew how to roast me to my face in a way that few adults could.

I took a couple of steps before stopping again. An orange and green bird made from two sloppy circles and a white triangle took my breath away.

"Damn, Amelia is like really fucking talented."

I leaned in closer to examine the childlike surrealism. The way she'd accented her work with black chicken-scratch stars felt both whimsical and calculated. I was in awe.

David chuckled from the kitchen. "The one with the stars is Joan Miro."

"Oh." I forced a laugh to try and cover my embarrassment.

Miro was one of my favorite artists, and I suddenly felt young and unsophisticated for not recognizing his work. I lightly touched the frame, hoping to soak up some of the talent via osmosis before sauntering into the kitchen. I did my best to seem unfazed by my naivete.

Two tumblers with ice sat on his kitchen bar.

"I'm out of mixers, so you want tequila or tequila with water?"

I rolled my eyes, "*Tequila*, David."

"Atta girl. Don't worry, it's smooth."

He grabbed a bottle of Clase Azul and poured a giant glass.

"Whoa dude, easy."

I was visiting LA from New York, where I had just moved to, so I was borrowing my parents' Suburban, which was hard enough for me to drive sober. Driving it drunk seemed like a dangerous, dumb, and impossible task.

"You don't have to drink it all," David said, handing a full glass to me.

We clinked drinks, and I tried not to wince while taking a small sip.

"Oh yeah, that's good," I lied.

David was like a cool uncle I wanted to impress. We'd met through my parents when I was thirteen and he was thirty-three, but we were always into the same art, the same music, and consequently the same parties. I was the kind of kid who adults would refer to as "ahead of her time" or "an old soul," and David seemed eternally youthful. I'd initially left LA for boarding school, so I'd see David sporadically on breaks, but after I graduated and moved back, David took me under his wing, showing me the ropes. He knew all the up-and-coming DJs and where all the after parties were. Even though I'd recently moved to New York (to work with a Grammy-winning music producer) I came back to LA often and I'd regularly catch up with David.

"You wanna smoke?" He handed me a pre-rolled joint.

I thought about it for a second. "Eh, I get weird around strangers when I'm stoned."

"I'm hardly a stranger."

I chuckled. "No shit, I'm talking about the Frenchies."

"Oh, right." David said as he put the joint back into its carton.

I wandered over to the fridge to inspect the collage of photos he had taped to the stainless steel.

"So, when *are* they coming?" I asked.

Most of the photos were of his kids, Amelia and Bobby, but some of them were family photos that included his ex-wife. I'd never met Zoe, whom everyone referred to as "Z", and I was surprised by her photos. Amelia was a towhead with blue eyes, but David's ex looked like Morticia Addams. She was stunning in a severe way, with jet-black hair and seemingly black eyes. She and David had been separated for five years, but they hadn't formally divorced, because David called that "a headache we're both putting off." He talked about her so infrequently, I was shocked to see photos of her on his fridge.

"Yeah, they should be here any minute. Let me text them."

The sound of David's footsteps walking away snapped me out of my forensic accounting of his family photos. I followed him out to a giant wooden deck with expansive views of the hills. I set my drink down on the railing before leaning against it to take in the view.

"The moon looks insane tonight," I said.

It looked extra big and comically close, bathing the deck in a soft light. The set designer of whatever simulation we were in had gotten a little overzealous when he'd cut out the circle for the sky.

"Brrr." I shivered and shoved my hands into the pockets of my leather jacket.

For an August night it was uncharacteristically cold. David squared up to me, rubbing his hands across my arms to create friction. It reminded me of how my dad used to warm me up as a child during Christmas in the mountains. Despite David's efforts, I could feel the hairs on the back of my neck as goosebumps formed.

I looked up at the sky again.

Ahhwooooo. A wild howl echoed throughout the canyons.

I went to turn back to David, but as I did, he grabbed the sides of my face with both of his hands, pulling me in for a kiss.

My heart stopped and my stomach sank. I closed my eyes out of instinct and self-protection.

What the fuck is happening?

Panic coursed through my adrenaline-filled veins. My mind flashed on all the moments that had led up to this kiss: the concert, the car ride, the kitchen.

What signs did I miss? Why is he kissing me? Wait, is this my fault?

Questions flew through my mind faster than I could answer them.

Out of shock, I kissed back, hoping that at any moment, my brain would catch up with what was happening and I would think of a plan, an exit strategy, really *anything* to get me out of this.

Dear God, how am I going to get out of this?

I wanted to run or to barf, but I was too scared to do either. Every cell in my body wanted to flee, but I was afraid of the repercussions. David wasn't some random stranger; he was my parents' friend and someone I was going to see in the future.

Plus, he was *my* friend—or so I thought. I didn't want things to be weird between us, but life had shown me that men don't take rejection very well.

What will happen to our friendship if I turn him down?

In my innocence, I hadn't realized that whatever relationship we once had had changed the second that David kissed me. I was afraid of ruining a dynamic that he had already shifted. I was negotiating against myself. Maybe if my prefrontal cortex had been fully developed, I would have realized this and pushed him off me like I wanted to.

What should I do? screamed the voice in my head.

No one answered back. Apparently, the demonic voice inside my mind was only there when I needed bullying, not when I needed rescuing.

I pulled back, hoping we could go back to talking, but when I opened my eyes, I was terrified by what stood in front of me. In a flash, the person I'd known since I was a child became unfamiliar. There, backlit by the full moon, was the silhouette of a wolf.

I blinked hard, willing my eyes to refocus on the figure in front of me.

His metamorphosis had been swift; in a matter of seconds, David had transformed from someone I'd trusted into a werewolf. His bright yellow eyes bulged out of his head. I wanted to scream and run, but I was frozen in fear. I couldn't move. I could barely even breathe.

He took one look at me, licked his lips, and confessed, "I've been waiting years for this. You're so fucking hot, Rory."

My blood went cold. This had been his plan all along. I'd been caught off guard but he'd premeditated it. Any hope I had for an easy exit flew out the window. I didn't know how to respond, so I grabbed my tequila and gulped. I was terrified.

David must have seen my drinking as a green light, because the next thing I knew he was leading me by the hand back down the dimly lit hallway and up the stairs to his bedroom. With every step, I prayed that the French people would burst through the door, but deep in my heart I knew they weren't coming. There weren't any French visitors and there wasn't a party. Who throws a party without mixers? The writing had been on the wall; I was just too naive to read it.

I felt like Little Red Riding Hood being led into her grandmother's house by the Big Bad Wolf. Only there was no woodsman coming to rescue me.

So when I crossed the threshold into his bedroom, I resigned myself to the fate in front of me: This was happening. I didn't know how to stop it, so I decided not to resist. The sooner "it" was over, the sooner I could leave and put this all behind me. I tried to tell myself that it was just sex and that it wouldn't be a big deal. *You've hooked up with strangers; you can certainly get through this.*

I walked into his obscenely large bedroom, which held two king-size beds.

"Uh, what's with the beds?" I asked.

He barely acknowledged the giant purple velvet monstrosity in the corner of the room.

"That's Zoe's, for when she's in LA," David said. He threw me onto his bed and climbed on top of me.

What the fuck?

Who keeps a king-size bed in his room for an ex?

I didn't have time to unpack this, because the second my head hit the pillows, David began tearing off my clothes. I felt like prey being ripped at by a predator. He flung my belongings around the room: My figurative red cape floated through the air before crumbling into a pile. I was dissociating, but David was foaming at the mouth, ready for what was about to happen next.

David took a finger and dragged his nail across the outline of my body. I shuddered. He saw the goosebumps forming on my skin, and it turned him on. His eyes flickered with a golden hue, burning into me. He grabbed my tits with his paws before burrowing his head between them like a feral dog looking for a bone.

His erection dug into my leg as he leaned in for a kiss. I closed my eyes, praying one last time for a miracle, for my own silver bullet, but when I opened them, David was moving down my body. He spread my legs open and sniffed around before he removed my cotton undies. I stared at the ceiling as he lapped me up, and with every slurp, I dissociated further.

My survival instincts kicked in, and I told myself that this wasn't happening to me; this was happening to Little Red Riding Hood, whom I just so happened to be playing tonight. It was a game, and it would be over shortly. The situation reminded me of when I was in Africa on safari. As a former vegetarian who faints at the sight of blood, I was only able to watch lions ripping apart their prey if I was photographing it. The act of playing a role helped to distract me from what was actually happening, and tonight I was doing the same thing. So I would assume the role of a concubine for the next few hours; then I'd leave, and I'd figure the rest out later.

I let out a manufactured shrill moan to signal that I had climaxed. David watched and grinned, revealing sharp teeth that glistened in the dark. He felt proud of himself. I could tell by the way he puffed out his chest and unbuttoned his pants. Now it was his turn.

I braced myself.

David slipped off his boxers, I was shocked. His dick did not match his personality or the animal that was about to mount me. It was small and sad, like a hot dog or piece of string cheese. I was momentarily relieved. I knew that he could fuck me as hard as he wanted to and I'd never feel a thing.

And I was right.

As David inserted himself into me, I watched as his face contorted. He threw his head back, as if to howl at the moon, but no sound came out. I looked at his old-man body writhing on top of me in ecstasy, and I felt numb.

He looked down at my naked body with hungry eyes.

"Tell me you're mine," he commanded.

"I'm yours," I said, never breaking eye contact.

By this point, I was fully committed to my role. I was going to survive the Big Bad Wolf if it was the last thing I did.

He thrust in and out of me, undulating like a wild beast trying to devour its dinner. But that wasn't enough. He was insatiable and wanted every part of me, including my mind.

"I'm gonna put a baby in you."

"Mmmhmmm," I moaned back, terrified by the admission. No one had ever said this to me, and I'd spent most of my life fearing an accidental pregnancy.

"Tell me you *want* me to put a baby in you," he demanded.

I looked David dead in the eyes and pretended to beg, "Put a baby in me."

He thrust harder, and I'd never been more grateful for my birth control than I was in that moment.

This went on for hours.

David unloaded on me, not just physically but psychologically. He told me he was in love with me, that he'd always been in love with me. He made me promise to run away with him and get married. He wanted to spend the rest of our lives together, with me bearing his children. The more deranged his requests became, the less personal the situation felt. I looked over at the empty bed of his ex-wife and couldn't help but feel like she was in the room with us.

Werewolves are cursed creatures, and David was no exception. Whatever happened between him and Zoe had left an indelible mark on this man-beast, and I was bearing the brunt of it. Hurt people *hurt* people, and I resolved not to take on his curse. I almost felt bad for him. I thought that he was this wise and cool older male figure, but now I was seeing the truth. I looked back at David, and suddenly he looked less like a werewolf and more like a pathetic street dog desperate for someone, *anyone*, to love him.

Eventually David wore himself out and he fell asleep.

This wouldn't have happened if I had a boyfriend, I thought.

Suddenly, I really missed Jack. I wanted to call him. I wanted him to swoop in like Superman and rescue me, but I knew that neither of those things were going to happen.

Think about something else.

David seemed serious when he'd made me promise that we were going to run away together, so I was afraid to accidentally wake him, and the beast, up. I lay next to him, wide eyed, accompanied by the rhythmic sounds of his snoring, counting down the seconds until daybreak. I needed the light to be able to locate my clothes without causing a commotion, and at 5:02, that is exactly what I did.

Finally, I could see the smattering of my clothing that had been thrown about the night before. I took a deep breath.

You can do this, Rory.

I sat up, ever so slowly, watching David to make sure he wasn't stirring. I swung my legs over the side of the bed and quietly stood up. I held my breath and took soft but deliberate steps, collecting my clothes as fast as I could.

Half naked, I fled the room, bolted down the stairs and out the front door.

My bare feet hit the cold pavement. Two-hundred more feet and I would be in the safety of my parents' Suburban.

I thrust my keys into the ignition the way that David had thrust himself into me, with a desperation.

My phone was on 15% battery, a historic low for me, but I dialed my best friend anyway. I floored the Suburban down the windy canyon road, watching David's house get smaller in my rearview mirror.

After three rings, she picked up.

"Hello?" said a groggy voice on the other end.
"Something bad happened last night."

◆ ◆ ◆

Addendum

David called me a few weeks later, but I refused the call.

So he texted me.

Hate to put this in a text but wanted to tell you sooner rather than later. One of my partners tested positive for chlamydia and I was with her before I was with you so you probably have chlamydia.

I lost it.

I did not have chlamydia, but I used the opportunity to unload some of the vitriol I was feeling. Plus, I took a tiny bit of solace knowing that David was seeing other people, plural. It meant that he wasn't singularly focused on me, and that gave me relief.

We saw each other about a month and a half later at one of his events. I wanted to attend to make sure things weren't awkward; I would occasionally have to see him around my parents, and I couldn't bear the thought of them knowing. I pretended like nothing had ever happened between us—and it's been like that ever since. Granted, our friendship ended that night. I never see him without my parents present, but no one has ever suspected anything weird between us.

In fact, I never spoke about that night for years.

I buried it deep down in the depths of my body to normalize a situation that should never have been normalized. I kept it a secret so that I wouldn't have to deal with other peoples' opinions. I would tell myself that it was just a bad hookup—it wasn't a big deal, and to forget about it. Eventually that worked. This allowed me to move on without ever really processing it.

As time went by and I became more vocal about sex and my sexual experiences, I would describe this night as "the one time that I had sex and didn't want to, but it wasn't rape." I was always very quick to clarify that it wasn't rape, because I had gone along with it. I saw that night as unfortunate but something I'd participated in. I'd decided to have sex with David, making it *my* choice and not something I was forced into.

A friend of mine asked me, "What was it about that night or that person that made you not want to have sex?" And that's when I found myself telling them the full story. It was the first time I'd shared the details of that night with anyone other than the two people I'd called immediately after. My friend listened intently before finally saying, "Rory, it sounds to me like you were groomed."

I still grapple with this.

I often think about his kids and how I watched them grow up. The age gap between his son and me is about the same as it is between David and me, I would never in a million years think about having sex with his son—or anyone his age for that matter. It makes me sick thinking about it, and yet that's what David did to me.

Still, I didn't see myself as a victim.

But when I started writing this book, I discovered that I have a pattern of unconsciously trying to give myself control in situations where I feel powerless. As I noted in the previous chapter, this often shows up in the form of minimizing my feelings.

Long before Jack and my journey as a final girl, I had a "friend" who had a habit of making moves on my boyfriends. I'd just broken up with one when she asked if it would be okay if she dated him. I told her absolutely not, and she did it anyway. I was devastated and livid, but I quickly buried it. I see now that convincing myself I didn't care and that it wasn't a big deal was easier than admitting that I had absolutely zero recourse and zero power in the situation. Instinctually, I defaulted to downplaying my pain to give me some sense of control. I couldn't stop her from the choices she made, but I could control whether I let them bother me.

Similarly, I was afraid of what would happen if I rejected David. When he kissed me, going along with what he wanted felt easier than facing the reality that this person I'd trusted had tricked me into coming to his home so he could have sex with me. I went along with what happened that night, but I only did it to protect myself. Pretending I was in the driver's seat and choosing to go along with what David wanted felt safer than facing the reality that I was, in fact, being taken advantage of. Blaming myself was easier than feeling like I had been violated; seeing the night as a mistake I'd made was simpler than admitting to myself I'd been victimized.

If I could go back in time, I would do everything differently, but that's the benefit of hindsight and experience. I am older and wiser and far more confident saying no to men, but that took time. In a do-over, I would stop that man the second he kissed me—in keeping with my own wants. I'd like to think that this would have stopped the rest of the night from happening, but of course I will never know.

A FINAL GIRL'S GUIDE TO AGENCY

+NO. (Is a full sentence.)
While I don't blame myself, or anyone who has been in a similar situation, I am offering insight into how I could have potentially prepared myself for a different outcome.

Many of us have been socialized to be easygoing, to not take up space, and to be likable. so saying no might feel uncomfortable or even foreign to some people. Saying no to certain things, like signing up for charities when solicitors stop you outside the grocery store, may seem easy, but letting down friends or a romantic partner may feel harder. This is why practicing saying no to both little and big things can help.

Everyone is going to have a different relationship with saying no. Start small and work your way up. You can start in low-stakes settings, like when a cashier asks you if you'd like your receipt or if a server asks if you want to see a dessert menu. If you really struggle with saying no, you may wish to find a therapist or a trusted friend to role-play with. This might sound like overkill, but in the same way that actors use repetition to memorize lines, you can use role-playing and muscle memory to help you get more familiar with saying no.

Eventually you can work your way up to saying no to your friends or coworkers. Maybe you turn down drinks after work or say no when a friend asks you for an imposing favor. For me, I used to stress out over telling friends no when they asked to borrow clothes. For whatever reason, I'd get super nervous, cave, lend out my clothes, and inevitably regret it. I'd lose items I loved, or they would come back stretched or stained. Now, with plenty of practice, I don't think twice about saying no to lending clothes.

Next, start to look at your social life and your commitments and ask yourself if you really want to do the things that you say yes to. Practice checking in with yourself and then saying no to the things that aren't in alignment with what you want. The more comfortable you get with saying no to people you're afraid to let down, the better you will be at saying no in other high-pressure situations.

At the time, I did not have a lot of experience saying no to people I admired and looked up to, but now I would shut a situation like the one with David down in a heartbeat.

+Reclaiming Your Agency.

I'm not going to pretend to be an expert on sexual violence, so please know that my words come only from the perspective of a two-time sexual assault survivor and not a credentialed therapist. I have, however, had the benefit of speaking to a ton of experts on the subject, especially Nicole Bedera, PhD, and I'd love to share some of the things I've learned from her about reclaiming one's agency after assault.

Sexual assault, harassment, rape, or coercion are emotional and psychological injuries. Some are also physical. Regardless, one of the biggest injuries results from our loss of agency, of wanting something to stop happening to our person and not being able to stop it. What most people don't realize is that what happens *after* the assault can inform how traumatic that event is.

Bedera, in her book *On The Wrong Side*, writes, "The impact of sexual violence is shaped by what happens after."[2] I find this quote hopeful; regardless of how little control you had during an unwanted experience, you *can* give yourself control afterward. How do you do that?

Your recovery will depend on two things: correctly blaming the right person (aka not yourself) and giving yourself agency in as many aspects of your life as possible.

I don't care if you were blackout drunk and naked in a frat house: It's not your fault. It takes a real creep to make a move on someone who can't consent. I don't care if you feel stupid and dumb for not seeing the warning signs: It's still not your fault. Consent is not a hard concept, so let's, as a society, stop making excuses for the people who want you to believe that it is. Self-blame will not help you heal.

The second piece of recovering from a psychological injury is giving yourself agency and cultivating a support system that will also encourage this. In the same way that you might practice saying no, constantly checking in with yourself and asking yourself what you want or need in any given situation, and then

---

2 Nicole Bedera, *On The Wrong Side: How Universities Protect Perpetrators and Betray Survivors of Sexual Violence*(Univ of California Press, 2024).

giving it to yourself, will help you heal. Whether you want eggs or waffles for breakfast or whether you want to press charges, you get to reclaim your agency and autonomy.

I encourage anyone who is interested in learning more about recovering from sexual violence to look up Bedera and her books.

In the aftermath of my experience with David, I unknowingly followed a lot of Bedera's advice. While I still wrestle with correctly blaming the infracting party, I did get to unleash on David when he texted me, and I think that helped. Even if I couldn't say, "I never wanted to kiss you," I did get to say, "You put my health at risk." And he apologized. We both walked away from that situation feeling like David had fucked up—even if he didn't fully understand the reason. Moving forward, I was careful about who I told, which gave me a sense of control, and when I eventually saw David again, it was on my terms.

Unfortunately, most women I know or speak to have lived through a similar situation, which is why I felt compelled to share this story. Nothing compounds grief like isolation, so at the very least, let me remind you that you are not alone.

COMEDIC BREAK

◆

Even in the scariest movies, the final girl normally has a comedic break with her friends and few moments of reprieve.

After Jack, I threw myself into therapy and into a new career. I was transitioning away from music—where I'd had a record deal—into film and television, and my breakup became the inspiration for my first film. Thomas and David looked like tiny specs in my rearview mirror as I cruised down the single highway.

I had a thriving friend group that planned random costume parties and charades nights and celebrated every holiday—even Bastille Day. I was a part of both a ramen club and film club, where we regularly got together and never watched the movie.

I may have been single, but I never felt alone.

When my film started getting into festivals, I met a ton of new friends, collaborators, and my next long-term boyfriend. Chris was the kind of guy who got along with everyone, and for the next few years I'd coast, horror free.

And then the comedic break would come to an end.

BED DEATH

◆

"Ror, we haven't had sex in like six months."

His words hung in the air like a bad fart searing my nostrils. It wasn't a lie, but the shame of the truth still stung.

After two and a half years, Chris and I were breaking up. I knew the conversation was coming, but I'd been avoiding it in the same way that I'd been avoiding sex for the last six months. Our relationship, which once felt fiery and full of passion, was now nothing more than a pile of cold ash.

Three years earlier, I was at a stuffy Hollywood party when I spotted a tall, dark, handsome man across the room. He was wearing beat up Converse and a vintage tee with a tailored suit. Somehow he looked effortlessly cool and unpretentious in a room full of people trying too hard. I watched him laugh with a group of similarly cool-looking guys, and I panicked at the thought of walking up to them, but I knew if I didn't force myself to say hello I would spend the rest of the night regretting it. So I took a deep breath and hoped for the best.

"Hey, I'm Rory." Admittedly not my best opener, but Chris's face lit up in a way that set my nerves at ease.

"Chris." He held out his hand for me to shake before introducing me to the rest of the guys. "And this is Adam, Marco, and Jake."

"Are you guys enjoying the party?" Suddenly I was like a chaperone at a middle school dance.

Jake, fully tattooed up to his neck, answered before anyone else could. "It's funny you should ask that, Rory, because we were actually about to take off."

I chuckled. "I guess that's a no."

"But you should come with us." His invitation caught me off guard.

"Yeah," Chris said, "you should come." He smiled at me and that was it.

I am absolutely going to go with them.

If it had been up to me, Chris and I would have started dating that night, but he was fresh off a breakup and not ready to jump into something new.

"Obviously I like you, Rory. And I wish that I was ready." Chris averted his eyes before staring at his feet. For all his swagger, he was extremely shy and conflict avoidant. "But I need some time to process. I thought we were going to get married and . . ." His voice trailed off and I didn't press it.

I already knew the story. His ex, Melissa, had moved out of their house without warning and into a new place with the man she'd been cheating on him with. Chris found out when he came home and half the furniture was gone. The situation was traumatic, and even though a couple months had passed—it had still only been *a couple months.*

Plus, if anyone understood the time needed to recover from being cheated on, it was me. So I continued to date other people, and Chris and I kept hanging out as friends, but the attraction between us only grew. By the time we started dating, we'd been "hanging out" for five months and I'd already been to Vegas and

Nashville with him, met all his friends, and seen him cry. I'd already fallen in love with Chris.

Maybe that's why I didn't notice that our sex was sorta *meh*.

Five months of sexual tension meant that our first kiss left me floating. I spent our first year drenched in dopamine and oxytocin, walking on sunshine. Every time Chris held my hand, I got chills. Everything was perfect.

Until it wasn't.

On a morning like any other, the light streamed through Chris' bedroom window. He wrapped his arm around my body and pressed his boner into the small of my back. We had a routine. He would snuggle up behind me like a big spoon, I would slip off my pajama bottoms, and he would fuck me from the side—a nice way to start the morning.

Except on this day, I realized I was bored.

Maybe this was the moment the honeymoon phase officially ended or maybe I'd just experienced this position one too many times, but for whatever reason, this morning I found myself thinking:

This can't be the only sex I have for the rest of my life.

This was the initial kiss of death. The first kernel of doubt. The original spore of mold that would ultimately rot our relationship from the inside out.

I liked our morning routine because it was the only time I'd reliably orgasm, but on this morning, something clicked in my brain: I was only getting off because of my manual stimulation. It wasn't that this position worked for *us*; it was that I had my back turned to Chris so I felt more comfortable masturbating. This revelation was disheartening and all-consuming.

Moving forward, anytime we would have sex, I was acutely aware of what it wasn't. It wasn't like the sex with my ex, and it wasn't like the sex I'd been having when I was single. It felt stale and anticlimactic, *literally*.

Chris was on the smaller side of what I'd been used to, and in my naivete, I thought that his small stature meant that we were doomed. At the time, I didn't realize all the other ways—outside of penetrative sex—I could have incredible orgasms. Maybe if I had been with someone who was more open or sexually adventurous, or if I had been brave enough to express my unhappiness, we could have worked on this. Instead, I was too self-conscious and too afraid of hurting Chris's feelings to properly express myself, and as a result, my frustrations only grew.

Eventually, I started to avoid sex.

I did this unconsciously at first. I'd get resentful and turned off and avoid sex for a couple of days—until I felt guilty or panicked about losing Chris—and then I would try to hype myself up into feeling attracted to him. I was playing a weird game of mental tug-of-war.

I tried drinking more, thinking that might help. It didn't.

As time went on, each sexual experience left me more unsatisfied, and sex began to feel like a chore—something I had to do as opposed to something I *got* to do.

Then, I started to avoid sex consciously.

I'd go to bed before he did so I could pretend to be asleep by the time he crawled in. I'd punt it to the next morning and then bound out of bed with the energy of a toddler. I'd fake stomachaches, PMS, headaches—you name it. And when I'd used up these excuses, I got really into lifting at a gym near my apartment. I would book morning classes so that spending the night at my place instead of Chris's made sense.

I always thought that Chris was going to call me out and that one day he would ask me why we weren't having sex, but he never did. I guess that was part of the problem. Chris was endlessly chill, which I loved, but his demeanor meant we never discussed uncomfortable topics unless I brought them up. His conflict avoidance was so extreme that eventually I stopped making excuses and Chris stopped trying to initiate sex.

The antidote was obviously communication, but again, I didn't know how to broach the conversation without hurting Chris's feelings, and I was afraid we'd break up. My inner demon chimed in.

Chris isn't like other guys. He's one of the good ones, and you don't want to lose that, because good guys are rare.

This wasn't a lie, but it also wasn't entirely true either. Yes, Chris was a good guy, but my fear of getting hurt was holding me back from speaking up—well, that and I didn't know how to fix our problem, so I chose to avoid it all together.

Days turned into weeks turned into months, and suddenly we were being plagued by an invisible toxin that was slowly killing our relationship. The original spore was now a constellation of black mold that enveloped the bed entirely. Six months and one romantic trip to France later, I was finally confronted with the truth: Chris and I had fallen prey to bed death.

Originally coined "Lesbian Bed Death" by sexologists Pepper Schwartz, PhD, and Phillip Blumstein, PhD, in 1983, the term was widely criticized as being homophobic and inaccurate, since couples of all kinds deal with bed death—and lesbians tend to have higher rates of sexual satisfaction than their bisexual or straight female counterparts.[3]

So what exactly is bed death? It's a slang term for what happens when the sex dies and then the relationship dies, and it's a phenomenon plaguing every type of couple. In fact, sex and intimacy issues are one of the top reasons why people get divorced. And while Lesbian Bed Death might not be a real thing, after six frigid months, Chris and I found ourselves in his living room digging a grave for the relationship we once loved.

"I don't know what happened or how we got here," I choked out through tears.

My words weren't a lie, but they weren't entirely true either. I knew we had a problem—that was obvious—but I couldn't fig-

---

3 "Infographic: Debunking 'Lesbian Bed Death,'" October 27, 2022, https://blogs.iu.edu/kinseyinstitute/2022/10/27/infographic-debunking-lesbian-bed-death/.

ure out how I'd once been so enamored with someone who now felt like a roommate. How could I love someone as much as I still loved Chris but not want anything to do with him sexually? It would take me years, and several partners, to fully understand.

I was too young in my sexual journey to know how to vocalize my dissatisfaction, and I was way too ashamed to tell my boyfriend that I wasn't getting off. Growing up, I felt like sex was one of those things we were all supposed to be naturally great at—yet no one ever taught us how. I wanted to be effortlessly desirable like all the women in my favorite love scenes. In movies, women orgasm within minutes, if not seconds, and it's always through penetrative sex. I never voiced my discontent, in part because I didn't want to draw attention to the fact that maybe something was wrong with *me*. Why wasn't I able to orgasm uncontrollably at the drop of a hat? I was afraid to speak up and ruin what we had, when in the end our mutual silence led to our downfall. This fear also kept me from talking about the situation honestly with friends who might have been able to help me understand that we needed to incorporate more foreplay or try other things.

Instead, I was still faking orgasms, and I was faking it for him just as much as I was for me. I wanted to seem like the kind of girl who was in touch with her sexuality because, again, that was hot. I also wanted him to feel good about sex because I knew that he was trying his best. And then sometimes I'd fake it just because I wanted it to end.

Back then, I surrendered almost all my sexual agency over to my partners. I was Goldilocks, testing out different seats at the sexual table, trying to find someone who would fit "just right." (More like Goldicocks.) Sex felt like something that did or didn't work, as opposed to a team effort where both partners come together to create an experience that's mutually beneficial.

I barely understood my own body, but I was somehow hoping that my partner would magically know how I liked to be touched. Chris never asked me what I was into or what felt good, and we rarely talked about the intimate parts of our relationship. Chris and I had communication problems; specifically, we never communicated. He was oddly reserved regarding sex, which made me feel like I needed to be as well.

The thought of asking him to finger me harder or to incorporate toys felt mortifying, partially because I didn't realize that I would like these things or that they were very normal aspects of female pleasure. (I was significantly older when I learned that 80% women don't orgasm from vaginal penetration alone).[4] There's also an element of risk in advocating for yourself. What if you are shot down? But sex isn't just about getting physically naked; it's also about getting *emotionally* naked. It requires a lot of vulnerability to share your fantasies, to talk about what turns you on, and to ask for what you want. Without taking these risks, we are never going to reap the reward of regular satisfaction. At the time, it seemed easier for me to find someone new than to have these vulnerable conversations.

Even today I have girlfriends who get squirmy when I talk about sex, and I feel kind of sad for them because I know what's on the other side of overcoming that discomfort. And yes, I realize it's possible that they may feel comfortable talking about it with their partners and not me, but I have a sneaking suspicion that they don't. The same goes for my friends who pretend like their sex lives are always amazing—never dipping or evolving. I used to be like them. I would pretend like Chris and I were always having hot sex; meanwhile, I was repressing my frustrations to the point where I'd recoil at the thought of Chris trying to make a move.

---

[4] Debby Herbenick et al., "Women's Experiences With Genital Touching, Sexual Pleasure, and Orgasm: Results From a U.S. Probability Sample of Women Ages 18 to 94," Journal of Sex & Marital Therapy 44, no. 2 (July 5, 2017): 201–12, https://doi.org/10.1080/0092623x.2017.1346530.

Sex is meant to evolve and change, but that also means both parties need to be honest with themselves and with each other to evolve and change together. A great example of this was my relationship with Phil.

Years after Chris and I broke up, I was at a Los Angeles Philharmonic concert when my eyes kept landing on a hot brunette—whom we're calling Phil. I decided that I wanted to date him, so I did. *Twice*—once for five months and then again for seven months. And both times could not have been more different.

The first time around, our sex life was *soooo* boring and very routine. We would make out for a little bit before inevitably ending up in missionary—*Every. Single. Time.* Imagine me lying on my back like a dead person and him rocking back and forth on top of me—that was basically it. Outside of the rhythmic creaking of the bed, we were silent. *Silent!* Maybe we had side sex a couple of times, but that was as wild as it got. When we eventually parted ways, I did not find myself missing our intimacy.

A couple of years later, Phil and I got back together, and from our very first kiss, I could tell something had changed. First off, we felt connected, which made everything more intimate and electric. Second, we didn't jump straight into sex. Instead we made out and rolled around and talked about what we were both into. We communicated and became emotionally naked before we ever took off our clothes. As a result, our sex was consistently great. Maybe this is TMI—welcome to my personality—but I got used to having multiple orgasms every time.

So what changed? I was more open and freer than I had been the first time we were together. Maybe I was older and more confident in my skin, or maybe I'd just gotten used to being explorative and communicative in bed. Either way, we were different people having extremely different sex—and we talked about it often. I remember lying next to Phil one afternoon when I asked him, "How was it *sooooooo* bad before and now it's like mind-blowing?"

Phil just laughed.

"I'm serious," I said. "I don't understand how we can be doing *this* when it used to be so boring."

Phil took a second to think about it, then said, "I always felt like you weren't that into it, and I wasn't really sure what to do."

"Interesting." My turn to laugh. "Yeah, I wasn't."

"Plus I was going through a lot back then, and I'm not sure I was really as open or available as I pretended to be," he said.

We concluded that our "bad" sex resulted from several factors. Phil wasn't sure what I liked, and he didn't sense a green light from me in terms of experimenting. In turn, I felt like he wasn't exciting or invested in my pleasure, and that made me less interested in sex.

Plus, Phil wasn't emotionally available, and that complicates intimacy. Outside of the bedroom, Phil treated me well and appeared to want a girlfriend, so I never imagined he might have put up some walls. In our first relationship, we never talked about sex. We didn't ask each other about boundaries and turn-ons or how we prefer to climax. We were just two people fumbling in the dark (literally and metaphorically) versus two people interested in discovering all the ways we could achieve pleasure together.

My dual experiences with Phil forever changed the way I think about sex. I used to think that people were compatible or not and that was it. Now I know that sex is something that can 100% be improved upon if both parties are attracted to each other and willing to be curious and communicative. Again, sex isn't something that's set in stone; it ebbs and flows and evolves, and it's something you can improve.

I went from being the girl who sometimes got off to the girl who almost *always* gets off—multiple times—due to *my* changed relationship with sex.

I am exponentially more open about what I'm into and what I need from a sexual partner. And men find this hot. Maybe this is because of the guys who I attract or the way I express my needs, but I've yet to be with someone who balks at my desires or feels threatened by toys. The men worth fucking want you to get off, and empowering them to make that possible is sexy. Trust me!

I often wonder what would have happened had Chris and I been able to talk about our sex life in a constructive way. I don't think we would have worked it out, but I'll never know. And, ultimately, I don't regret what happened, because we had a beautiful relationship and a great life together. And for someone else, that might have been enough to stay.

Sex is only as important as it is *to you*—and my experience with Chris taught me that a fulfilling sex life is important to me. For some people, intimacy is less about sex and more about feeling close, so sex isn't a huge priority for them, and that's okay. There's no right or wrong answer here, only what is right *for you.*

After Chris, I never went longer than a handful of dates before making sure that I was sexually compatible with someone. That's not to say that we had to knock it out of the park on the first try, but I wanted to know that I liked the way a person kissed and that anatomically we were a match. Sex is a polarizing topic, and I think when it comes to having it, the only person you should be listening to is yourself: When do *you* feel comfortable having it? Because that's when you should do it—as long as the other person consents, of course.

Part of navigating our own romantic journeys means learning what we do and don't like and what we will and won't compromise on, both romantically and sexually. Once you know these things, the key is communicating them to your partner and holding true to your boundaries. My relationship with Chris rotted from the inside out, and while I'm not 100% sure that we would have gone the distance, I am certain that talking about our issues would have led us to a resolution faster.

Through bed death, I was able to breathe new life into my relationship with sex—and for that, I am grateful.

A FINAL GIRL'S GUIDE TO TALKING ABOUT SEX WITH YOUR PARTNER

+QUESTIONS TO ASK YOURSELF & YOUR PARTNER

- What's your definition of great sex?
- Is there somewhere you like to be touched that I don't know about? Or, where, and how, can I touch you that would turn you on?
- Do you have any favorite toys or positions?
- Do you watch porn and if so what kind?
- What's something you'd want more of in our sex life?
- Is there anything I could do to help you in terms of being able to enjoy sex more?
- Where's one place you've always wanted to have sex but haven't?
- What's your favorite post-sex activity and why?
- What are your nonsexual turn-ons?
- What's the best dirty dream you've ever had? (Let this be an icebreaker into discussing top fantasies.)
- What's the best thing about our sex life?
- Post-sex: So tell me, what was your favorite part of what just happened?

+TIPS FOR TALKING TO YOUR PARTNER ABOUT SEX

- Don't have this conversation during sex and don't spring it on them without advanced warning; instead set a time to have a conversation about sex, outside of the bedroom and where you won't be distracted.
- Use "I" Statements not "you" statements (e.g., "I feel like . . ." vs. "When you do this, it makes me . . .")
- Start the conversation off by saying something like, "We are on the same team, and the goal of this conversation is to bring us closer together."

THE ICK

If you've never heard of "the ick," it's an invisible monster destined to kill boners and romantic relationships. It's as illusive and deadly as an assassin— lurking in the shadows of your mind, striking when you least expect it, eliminating any and all attraction on the spot.

Originally coined by the 1997 TV show *Ally McBeal*,[5] the ick gained popularity thirty years later when a *Love Island* contestant named Olivia Attwood started using it.[6] However, the ick didn't enter the zeitgeist until 2020, when it became a new buzzword and a viral trend on TikTok. So, what exactly *is* the ick?

It's a horrifying phenomenon that happens when you're suddenly cringed out or even repulsed by a person you once fancied. The ick typically attacks during the early stages of a relationship before people fall in love and learn to overlook smaller flaws. However, it can also afflict long-term partners who get temporarily turned off by their significant others. In

---

5 Ally McBeal, season 1, episode 15, "Once in a Lifetime," written by David E. Kelley, Nicole Yorkin, and Dawn Prestwhich, directed by Elodie Keene, aired on Feburary 2, 1998, on FOX.
6 Love Island, season 3. Producers Mandy Morris, et al., aired July 7, 2021–August 15, 2021, on CBS.

keeping with its shapeshifting nature, the ick can be a protective response, but it can also be a sign of self-sabotage.

Sometimes, the ick is in reaction to red flags or subtle warnings, like the way a person treats restaurant staff or speaks about their exes. It can attack after your date is being overly needy or aggressive, both of which are signs of deeper issues. Other times, it's your toxic patterns looking for a reason to dip. Finding yourself repelled because of a person's shoes, how they hold a fork, or the way they say a certain word is likely about you and your baggage. I've found myself catching the ick on a few occasions, but the most notable one was mid-coitus. Here is the story of my worst ick.

I was sitting in the back of a Toyota Camry, headed to the valley at 9 p.m. on a Thursday, hoping I wouldn't regret it. I'd left my friends and a reliably fun situation to meet up with a stranger from Tinder. All I really knew was his name, Bobby, and that he looked cute enough to meet on a Thursday, but not cute enough to risk meeting on a Friday or a Saturday.

Post-Chris, I was enjoying my newfound singledom. After six frigid months, I was eager to explore my sexuality and see what LA's bachelor scene had to offer. One might say I was in my fuckgirl era, where I was telling people I wanted a boyfriend but all my actions were suggesting otherwise. I was generally talking to at least three guys and never seriously interested in any of them. Yet I was cautiously optimistic that Bobby, despite living in the Valley, could be the guy who would make me want to clear the roster.

Bobby was waiting for me outside the bar when my Uber pulled up. I immediately clocked that he was cuter in person. He had sandy blond hair that curled at the ends and bright blue eyes that crinkled when he smiled. He was familiar in a comforting way. I couldn't put my finger on who he reminded me of, but the familiarity made me feel close to him. Because of this, I really wanted to like him.

Unfortunately for me, Bobby was from a tiny town in the middle of nowhere and the son of two preachers—an automatic disqualification for the role of boyfriend. Judge me all you want, but I do not want small-town preacher in-laws. I don't want to fight about politics on Thanksgiving or spend Christmas Eve at church. I want to be close with my in-laws, and I have spent enough time around ultra-religious family members to know that we mix about as well as oil and water. A difference of opinions is one thing, and cool with me, but I draw a hard line when anyone tries to impose their beliefs on other people's lives. Suffice to say, Bobby's family would never be *my* family.

I sat across from Bobby, but a wall had gone up. I was no longer interested in investing in him long term. He was out of the potential boyfriend bucket, but that didn't mean he was out of the hookup category. I was always looking for safe hookups, which meant someone who seemed responsible with their sexual health but also someone with whom I felt emotionally safe. I put on my detective hat for the rest of the date, trying to suss out Bobby's level of emotional intelligence and candor.

Two and a half hours later, Bobby and I were in the back of a car headed to his place. We kissed our way into his apartment and up his stairs, where I discovered that time travel was, in fact, real. I plopped onto his bed and was promptly transported to 1980. To this day, Bobby's the only man I have ever fucked on a waterbed—I didn't even know that waterbeds still existed.

"Woah," I said, trying to steady myself on the ever-moving "mattress" beneath me.

Bobby laughed. "Yeah, it takes a second to get used to."

He sat down next to me, and a wave of water lifted my side of the bed up.

I chuckled. "It's kinda fun." This was a stretch, but I was trying to be a good sport.

Bobby pulled me close for a kiss, and I tried to forget that I was basically making out on a raft in the San Fernando Valley. He was a good kisser, which helped tune out my intrusive thoughts—that is, until either one of us made a big movement.

I was straddling Bobby when we inevitably reached the point where our clothes started to come off. He slowly lifted my dress above my head before throwing it on the floor. I unbuttoned his shirt from the bottom up. When I finally reached the top button, I leaned in to give him a kiss. I gently pulled away, running my hands through the insides of his shirt. Bobby sat up to help me take it off, but in doing so he shifted the water underneath us, and I ended up headbutting him instead.

We both grabbed our heads before bursting into laughter.

"That's it—you're taking your pants off on your own," I said.

Bobby laughed. "Deal."

We were off to a weird and rocky start, so imagine my surprise when several minutes later I was having one of the most intense orgasms of my life. Bobby, unlike all the men who had preceded him, had found my G-spot. And he fingered me in such a way that I squirted all over his waterbed. A first for me! I was into it. This was a different kind of release, one that left me floating above my body.

I needed a second to find words, but when I did, I confessed.

"That was crazy! I've never done that before."

Bobby's eye's widened. "I don't believe that."

"I swear on my life that has *never* happened to me before." I wasn't lying.

"Me either," he said.

"What? I don't believe *that*."

How can that be possible? I thought.

"I swear on my life, I have never made a woman squirt before," Bobby held his hand up in the air as if to testify, which I am assuming was a nod to his religious upbringing.

"Damn, that's crazy," I said while lying in a puddle of my own making. This was also crazy but I was way too relaxed to move or care.

I looked over at Bobby, and I'm honestly not sure which one of us was enjoying it more. I've since come to realize that men get a certain satisfaction when they know they're the first at something. It boosts their ego, and I could see that Bobby was thoroughly pleased with himself.

And if you think it's lost on me that the first time I squirted was on a waterbed, you would be wrong. That, my friends, is what we call irony and divine comedic timing.

Eventually, Bobby grabbed me a towel. We had sex. And I got up to do my obligatory after-pee.

I switched on the bathroom light—and JUMP SCARE!—what lay before me was like a scene out of the movie *Hostel*. I was standing in the grossest bathroom I had ever seen. We are talking dirt and grime and hair and mold. I thought about not peeing and risking a UTI, because holding it seemed more sanitary than peeing in this bathroom. I didn't bother washing my hands, because I knew I wasn't going to be touching the crusty-looking dish towel that hung before me. It was officially time to go.

I walked out of the bathroom and began looking for my clothes.

"That was fun," I said, "but I should probably take off 'cause I have to be up early tomorrow."

This wasn't a lie, but I knew damn well I would have stayed longer had there not been a science experiment growing in the bathroom.

I couldn't find my socks. After a few minutes, Bobby turned the lights on, and I had to physically turn away to conceal my horror. Turns out, the bathroom was not an anomaly. The carpet, which I am assuming started off beige, was a gray-brown and looked like it had never seen a vacuum, much less a proper cleaning. The floor was dotted with several dark stains where I can only imagine a pet had relieved itself. I needed to find my socks quickly or I was going to catch a staph infection.

I left, and by the grace of whomever, the only thing I caught that night was an Uber out of there.

I never planned on seeing Bobby again (because *Duh!*), so when he reached out, I told him that work was intense and I wasn't in a place to be dating. I thought that was going to be the end of it, and for a moment, it was.

Then my roster thinned out, and he randomly texted me.

What's up?

I'd tried to recreate my waterbed experience with a couple of other guys but had come up dry (pun very much intended). I lacked the understanding of what had happened with Bobby and why it had been so pleasurable for me, so I was at a loss trying to explain it to other men. I found myself fantasizing about squirting again, so when Bobby's text popped up, I decided to reply.

I figured he could come to *me*, which he did, and thus began eight months of sporadic hookups. Bobby became the guy that I would booty-text when literally all my other options were unavailable. Knowing I would never end up with this person was freeing. It allowed me to try whatever sexual thing I felt like trying without feeling embarrassed. I'm not saying our arrangement was healthy; I'm just saying it's what happened. He was like my sexual R&D guy. And while he might have been my last resort, he was also reliably consistent.

◆ ◆ ◆

Fast forward eight months.
I texted him after 11 p.m.
Come over.

Bobby responded almost immediately.

See you in thirty.

At this point in our "relationship" I didn't even bother tidying my apartment. I brushed my teeth and changed my underwear, and then I had twenty-five minutes to kill. Do not ask me what possessed me to do the thing I did next (because I will never know), but I decided to take a couple of bong rips.

A couple of bong rips? Who was I? A 22-year-old frat boy? I was almost thirty.

I hadn't owned a bong since I was a teen, but a month earlier I needed one for a video shoot and I felt weird throwing it away, so I held on to it. And on this fateful eve, I decided to use it. At this point in my life, I was probably smoking weed one to four times a year, max, so this move was especially wild on my part. And I wasn't trying to quiet my nerves or dissociate; I was just bored.

I lit a densely packed bowl like I was Snoop Dogg before pulling hard on the mouthpiece. The bong water bubbled up inside the chamber—a harbinger of how the ick would bubble up inside me a few hours later. I blew out the smoke, blissfully unaware of what was coming.

By the time Bobby walked into my apartment, you could have called me Boeing because I was high as fuck and struggling to hold it together.

Bobby eyed me, then the bong on my dining room table. "Uh, are you okay?" he asked.

"Oh yeah," I lied.

"Were you ripping that by yourself?"

"Mmmhmm."

He looked at me suspiciously. "Okay, Ror."

I offered him a drink, which he accepted, saying, "I guess I need to catch up."

I would have told him there was no way in the world he was going to catch up, but I was too stoned to get the words out. Instead, I handed him a half glass of tequila, with lime and ice.

We pretended to hang out and catch up for the obligatory twenty minutes or so until enough time had passed that we could transition to my bedroom. That's the funny thing about hookup culture; there's usually an awkward dance before clothes come off. I don't know why; we both knew exactly what was about to happen.

Inside my room, shirts and shoes went flying, and before I knew it, we were rolling around making out. I'd love to be able to tell you about the sex, but the trauma of what happened next has left a big blank spot in my mind—as if my body decided to protect me from those memories. What I do know is, at a certain point, Bobby flipped me onto my back into the missionary position. I looked up at him as he was grinding in and out, when suddenly I realized who he looked like.

Eight months of casually hooking up, and it was *during sex* that it finally clicked. Maybe it was the lighting, or the bong hits, or the combination, but in that moment, I realized Bobby was the spitting image of my cousin Reggie.

I physically gasped, absolutely gobsmacked by the revelation.

Bobby stopped. "Is everything okay?"

"Yeah," I said before fully processing.

It wasn't okay.

No one wants to fuck their cousin. Especially not me. And sure, Reggie was my step-cousin, so not blood related, but it didn't matter. The legal technicality did not undo a lifetime of family memories. Just because Reggie and I hadn't spent meaningful time together since we were kids—which is probably why the resemblance didn't immediately jump out at me—the thought of sleeping with my cousin was enough to make my stomach turn.

Bobby kept gliding in and out of me, completely unaware of the horror unfolding in my mind. I tried to focus on the fact that I was with *Bobby,* but all I could see was my cousin. In an instant, everything was different. I closed my eyes, but it didn't help; I was still repulsed. Even now as I type this, I'm wincing at the thought of sex with Reggie. (Also, Reggie if you are reading this, I am *so* sorry.)

I tried to push through.

Think about someone else!

But it was too late. I'd already caught the ick, and it had taken over my body like poisonous gas infiltrating every corner of my mind. I couldn't unsee my cousin, and my vagina was drying out faster than the Colorado River.

"I'm sorry. You have to stop."

Bobby looked confused.

"I'm so sorry, but I can't do this anymore." I said.

"Uh, okay." Bobby paused. "Do you need a break? Do you need some water? What's happening?"

He had a lot of questions, understandably.

"I don't know how to say this, so I'm just going to say it. I just realized that you look like my cousin and it's really freaking me out."

Bobby laughed. It took a second before he realized I was serious.

"Wait, so you want me to stop, like completely?"

"Mmmhmm, yeah."

Bobby tried to process this information. "Okay."

"I'm really sorry," I said.

And, I meant it. I was sorry. I was also terribly grossed out. I needed Bobby to get out of me, get off me, and get away from me, ideally as fast as possible.

He awkwardly pulled out, dismounted, and pulled the condom off his dick, utterly confused about what had just happened. I buried my head in my pillow, trying not to throw up. I listened to Bobby's footsteps as he walked to my trash can then back to me, and then I forced myself to face him.

He sat on the edge of my bed.

"So, should I go?"

I felt instant relief but did my best to play it cool.

"I guess that makes sense. I'm probably going to pass out anyway."

Bobby stared at me in disbelief before he got dressed.

The ick was so bad that I never recovered. Despite his many texts over the following years, I never saw Bobby again. In fact, I did my best to forget that we'd ever met. That night traumatized me for a long time, and I never told Reggie. I mean, until now. I also never touched another bong.

Some people come into your life for a reason, a season, or a lifetime. Looking back, I think Bobby came into mine (*wink*) to help teach me about my body and new ways that I liked to experience pleasure. Through him, I became comfortable with a part of myself that I hadn't realized existed, and after him, I was better at expressing the ways in which I like to be touched. His excitement around my squirting made me feel powerful and grateful for my body. I've since heard from other women who were made to feel weird or ashamed in these situations, and I imagine that shame has lingering effects. Perhaps unconsciously, Bobby created a safe space for me to explore sexually, and it set the tone for my erotic future.

Why the ick? Ultimately, I don't think I was ever that into Bobby. While I'm grateful for our time together, I think my body finally wanted me to stop sleeping with someone I wasn't genuinely attracted to. This is not to say that I ever felt bullied into having sex—because I didn't. Bobby was always polite and great about consent (even when I wanted to stop mid-act). I would reach out to Bobby when I needed a release or when I wanted to feel close to someone (anyone!), which is not the same as reaching out because you want to spend time with that person.

Whether this is true, I always felt like Bobby wanted something more than what we were doing, and that made me a little uneasy because I knew that I did not. I intentionally kept him at arm's length, and at a certain point, I think my subconscious was like, *Enough. Move on!* I've had other fuckbuddies since Bobby, but they were always guys I genuinely liked or felt really attracted to. Sometimes, that led to getting my feelings hurt, and other times it worked out great, but it never resulted in the ick, and that's telling.

Wherever Bobby is, I hope he's happy and that he learned to clean his bathroom!

A FINAL GIRL'S GUIDE TO AVOIDING THE ICK

Knowing whether the ick is happening to you as a form of protection—or if it's your baggage self-sabotaging—is hard. So let me ask you some questions:

- Do you get the ick often?
- Have you caught the ick more than twice in the last six months or more than twice with your last four dates?
- If your date does something nice for you or shows that they're into you, does it ever give you the ick?
- Do you find yourself ick-ing out over smaller things like the way someone walks, texts, or dresses?
- Do you get the ick when your date shows genuine emotions?
- Does talking to your friend about the person you're dating ever lead to your catching the ick?
- Is your level of ick disproportionate to the size of the thing or event that's causing it?

If you answered yes to one or more of these questions, you might want to explore the ways in which you could be emotionally unavailable. Perfectionism—or in this case, being hypercritical—is a form of avoidance. The ick is a way to keep your distance—because if you never get close, you can never get hurt. Or maybe you just simply aren't into them and it's best you stop wasting everyone's time.

VIRUSES

I can still remember the heat on my cheeks and the knot in my seventeen-year-old throat as I bravely approached the checkout at the CVS where I was buying my first pack of condoms.

Why am I so embarrassed?

I could barely make eye contact with the older lady behind the counter.

What is she thinking? Will she ask me for an ID?

Thoughts swirled in my brain.

I loved my boyfriend, and we'd been together for over a year, but the thought of talking about my sex life with strangers, even tangentially, made me want to melt into a puddle.

Could you blame me? I grew up in the 2000s, where all my pop idols were either half naked, gyrating against their mic stands, or wearing purity rings (or in some cases both). Magazines were littered with articles about pleasing men, from, "Tease Him and Please Him!" to "The Brazilian: Is He Secretly Busting for You to Have One?" At the time, advertisers regularly used the objectification of women to sell everything from food to cars and clothing. Bubble gum misogyny reached a fever pitch just as I was coming into my sexuality, and it was confusing as hell.

On the one hand, sex was everywhere, but on the other hand, being a slut was a cardinal sin. Religion, politicians, society, and sex-ed were all telling me that my virginity made me valuable. "Why would a man buy the cow if he can get the milk for free?" was an adage I heard a lot growing up; never mind that women were the cows bought and sold by men in this scenario.

If you'd never kissed a boy, you were a freak, but if you'd kissed too many boys, then you were a whore—but no one ever told you how many proverbial kisses was considered *too* much. For Monica Lewinsky, it was one blow job, for Janet Jackson it was one nipple, and for Charlotte Weathersby, it was dating three guys on the varsity soccer team before my entire school labeled her a slut and treated her as such. I watched iconic women fall from grace for the same reasons I watched others ascend: *sex*. Society instilled two truths in my brain: I needed to appear sexy, but I couldn't let people know if I was having sex (or ever talk about it), because if I flew too close to the sun, I'd get burned. It felt like a real lose-lose situation to me, but what did I know? I was only a teenager.

As if walking the tightrope between being a prude and being "run through" wasn't difficult enough, most of my sexual education came in the form of fearmongering. I'm lucky because I grew up in a sex-positive house with medical parents and never had to shake the stigmas that come from growing up in sex-negative or sex-avoidant households. And yet, when I think about learning about sex, the thing I remember the most is stress.

Once a year I would gather with all my female classmates and we would sit through an hour-long sexual education lecture designed to scare the shit out of us. I learned all the ways in which sex might lead to death, pregnancy, or worse: herpes. We would look at slides of chlamydia and genital warts and silently hope to never be the kind of person who got a sexually transmitted infection (STI), for they were the marks of a dirty person. It seemed like STIs were the potential punishment for having sex—and *that* was the gamble.

Nearly a decade went by before I stopped worrying I had AIDS any time I had unprotected sex. Never mind that you don't contract AIDS; you contract HIV. AIDS was my biggest anxiety and one I carried with me for way too long. All of that "education," and I was still clueless. Suffice to say, I grew up with a lot of shame around sex, and it took me years to undo it. So imagine my horror when in 2016 my gyno informed me that I had my first STI.

◆ ◆ ◆

THE OUTBREAK

"Please call the office to schedule a follow-up to discuss your results," said the message in my medical chart.

My heart dropped.

I scanned my results. My eyes paused on several red exclamation points next to the word: POSITIVE.

Panic rose up in me like a flood. Adrenaline filled every nook and cranny of my body as I tried to make sense of what was happening and how bad it was. My Pap smear had come back abnormal, which, ironically, wasn't that abnormal for me. In the past, the lab would double-check my swab, I'd be cleared, and I'd go about my business. But this time was different. This time I was positive for the human papillomavirus, aka HPV. More specifically, type 16 and "other high-risk strains."

It felt like a death sentence. Remember, I'm dramatic.

I was infected. And even though I'd had HPV for weeks, or maybe even months, and never felt any different, *knowing* that I had it somehow made it worse. I felt tainted. The virus had invaded my body and mutated the cells on my cervix, but now that I was armed with the knowledge of its existence, it also infected my thoughts.

You're one of the dirty ones, whispered the demonic voice in my head.

Once I recovered from the shock of my diagnosis, my mind shifted.

Who the fuck gave me HPV?

I ran through my mental Rolodex.

It was a busy year.

After my brush with bed death, I'd set out on a quest to understand all the ways I liked to be pleasured. My sexual awakening had been met with eager participants.

Was it the sexy businessman? The brother of that famous actor? Maybe it was the guitarist with the neck tattoos?

Bobby and I had always used protection, but even condoms don't 100% protect against HPV.

I wanted someone to blame, someone other than myself, because I was embarrassed. No matter how much deprogramming I thought I'd done, this felt like karma—as if the world were like, *See, this is what you get for sleeping around!* It felt like I'd been branded with three scarlet letters: HPV. And even though my rational brain knew this was insane patriarchal rhetoric, I still felt dirty and disappointed in myself.

HPV was one of the permanent ones: a virus I could never outrun. It would follow me forever (I see you David Robert Mitchell), and a quick internet search told me that the specific strains I had were also of the lethal variety—if left untreated, I could quite literally die. All those years worrying about AIDS, and it never occurred to me that I could be taken out by HPV. God bless America's sexual education! The same internet search let me know that almost 90% of sexually active people will contract HPV in their lifetime.[7] Though nowadays, the HPV vaccine offers protection against the virus, so we may see that percentage change in the future. The general sentiment online seemed to be that everyone gets HPV and it isn't that big of a deal. In fact, I was pretty sure I was the only one out of my friends who *didn't* already have HPV, and my hyperbolic response garnered several eye rolls from friends.

"Literally everyone has HPV, Rory. I'm honestly shocked it took you this long," my friend Melissa responded when I bravely admitted to my newfound STI.

The more people I told, the better I felt. Melissa was right, it seemed like everyone had HPV. Well, nearly everyone born before June of 1980—and *me*.

"Wait, did you not get the vaccine?" my friend Rhiannon asked me.

I shook my head no. I hadn't. Which is very unlike me.

"Weird. My gyno *made* me get it. Either way, I don't think it's a big deal." She trailed off, clearly less pressed about this diagnosis than I was.

Why didn't I get the vaccine?

The vaccine came out in 2006 and, at the time, was recommended for women ages nine to twenty-six.[8] So I should have gotten it, but no one asked me if I wanted it or told me it was important, so I never got it—a great metaphor for what women's healthcare is like in general. You have to advocate for yourself because the people whose job it is likely won't be doing it for you. By the way, now the vaccine is recommended for all genders, and you can get it up to age 45.[9]

---

7 Geraldine McQuillan, Deanna Kruszon-Moran, Laurie E Markowitz, et al. "Prevalence of HPV in Adults Aged 18–69: United States, 2011–2014." NCHS Data Brief, no 280. (Hyattsville, MD: National Center for Health Statistics, 2017), https://www.cdc.gov/nchs/products/databriefs/db280.htm.
8 Lauri E Markowitz and John T Schiller, "Human Papillomavirus Vaccines," The Journal of Infectious Diseases 224, no. Supplement_4 (May 18, 2021): S367–78, https://doi.org/10.1093/infdis/jiaa621.
9 Jane J. Kim et al., "Human Papillomavirus Vaccination for Adults Aged 30 to

My doctor, much like my friends, was unfazed by my new diagnosis. She even suggested I could "wait and see" if the cells changed into precancerous cells. That sounded a lot like, *Hey why don't you walk down that dark hallway to investigate the creepy sound you heard and we can see what happens!*

"Oh, I am absolutely not trying to die this way," I said.

She chuckled, but I was only half joking.

"It's very hard to die from HPV-related cervical cancers under medical care," she said.

I nodded along but figured I would be consulting with my own team of experts, aka my mom, dad, and sister who all have medical degrees. They unanimously agreed that "wait and see" was not an option I'd be exploring. Instead, we decided I should opt for cryotherapy, which is where my gynecologist kills off the abnormal cells by freezing them with liquid nitrogen. Plus, cryo sounded like the antidote in a sci-fi movie about a killer virus, so I was down.

Let's kill this motherfucker!

Then my sister warned me: "Heads up, Ror, it's painful, like v*ery* painful. You should ask them to numb your cervix. And you'll definitely want to take some painkillers ahead of time."

And just like that, I became infected with a second affliction: fear.

◆ ◆ ◆

THE DREAD

I asked around to see if anyone else I knew had gone through something similar, and their answers only added to my growing anxieties. I knew it was going to be bad, but everyone's version of bad is different. When I got my wisdom teeth out, friends told me it would be brutal. So when I ended up back at the oral surgeon's with three dry sockets and he asked me, "How are you even standing?" I told him, "Everyone said it was supposed to be awful, so I thought this was normal." Not having context for my upcoming procedure somehow made the situation seem worse.

Meanwhile, I felt totally disconnected from my body. This virus was multiplying inside of me, infecting my cells and maybe, just maybe, trying to kill me. Walking around carrying this secret made me feel gross and undesirable. My inner demon kept reminding me I was tainted, and the thought of having sex with anyone, even with myself, made me squirm. Rationally, I knew this was stupid, but outrunning societal stigmas and sexual repression is hard. I decided to bottle up my feelings, push them down as far as I could, and just get to the surgery.

◆ ◆ ◆

THE BATTLE

The day of my procedure, I was nervous. I grabbed a latte, hopped in an Uber, and pregamed a Vicodin I had laying around at home.

I sat in an empty room with my legs dangling off the side of the exam table. Within a few minutes, I was covered in goosebumps and enough anxiety sweat that my butt stuck to the thin piece of tissue paper. I wondered if all the other women sitting in paper gowns were also freezing or if it was just me.

Eventually, my gynecologist walked in, and I explained that I was nervous about the pain.

"Oh, it's really fast. It's not a big deal." She clacked away on the computer, business as usual.

"Can you numb my cervix just to be sure?" I asked.

Without looking up, she told me, "We don't do that here."

To which, I'd like to take this opportunity to say, *Hey, renowned university that shall go unnamed—GO FUCK YOURSELVES*. Not providing numbing is barbaric, especially when a patient asks for it.

She stopped typing. I'd like to think she sensed my unease, but who knows.

"It's really not that big of a deal. A lot of patients just feel mild discomfort, maybe a little cramping, and some don't even feel anything at all." She said it with such assurance that I almost believed her.

Regardless, I accepted her answer because she was in a position of authority and because I didn't fully understand what was to come. I thought I was asking for something that would be considered special treatment. I didn't realize that many countries view the United States' handling of some standard procedures as stuck in the dark ages.

The procedure was hell. The best way to describe the pain is *blinding*, like I was being stabbed and electrocuted at the same time, but from *inside* my uterus.

"Ahhhhhhhhhhhgh," I groaned, as I gripped the sides of the table.

The nurse who was helping my doctor looked at me like I was crazy.

I gritted my teeth. "Holy shit, how long is this again?"

"You're about halfway through the first half," my gyno responded cooly.

A burning sensation emanated like hot lava from my cervix all the way to my throat, where I was sure I was going to vomit. Suddenly chills washed over my body like a warning of worse things to come. I tried to focus on my breathing like I'd seen pregnant ladies in movies do, but I couldn't. I wanted to jump out of my skin. The waves of pain kept rolling in faster and stronger, threatening to drown the proverbial ship that was my body. I could feel myself giving up.

"I don't think I can do this anymore!" I shouted.

"You've got this!" the nurse said back. She was trying to be encouraging, but it took everything in me not to scream, *No I don't!*

My doctor kept going.

I squeezed my eyes shut, trying to contort my body in a way that would better absorb the shock waves of pain radiating between my legs.

"Almost there." My doctor pulled the metal wand from inside me. "Okay, done. We have a five-minute break before we start part two."

I was covered in flop-sweat and gasping for air. I couldn't see myself, but somehow I knew that I looked gray. The color had left my body and so had any hope I had for the "mild discomfort" version.

"This is normally a very easy process," my doctor said. I'd like to think she was trying to be reassuring, but it felt like gaslighting. "Most patients just feel period cramps."

I wanted to explain that I used to end up on the bathroom floor vomiting from extreme period pain, but my five minutes were up and it was time to start.

"I really don't think I can do that again," I pleaded.

My doctor motioned for the nurse. "Gina, can you grab her one of the heating pads?"

The nurse opened a drawer and retrieved a sandwich-sized plastic rectangle and snapped it a few times.

"Here," she said, handing me a heating pack to hold over my uterus. "This should help."

It did not.

How in the world was an instant heat pack supposed to help me with surgical pain? That's like losing a leg and then trying to be gracious when someone offers you a Band-Aid.

The second time was even worse. I felt like I might black out from the pain, but it hurt too bad to speak, so I just pushed through.

"Okay we're done!" The nurse was already cleaning up when my doctor wheeled herself back from between my legs. "See, that wasn't so bad."

I was too weak and too sick to my stomach to tell her to fuck off, so I gave her a half smile.

"Okay, so you might experience some cramping, watery or abnormal discharge, and maybe even some light bleeding for the next two to three weeks. No tampons, baths, pools, sex, or anything going inside your vagina for two to three weeks. And if you experience fever, excessive pelvic pain, or excessive bleeding, you need to call us immediately, because it could be an infection."

I blinked back.

My doctor was already up and taking off her gloves. "Okay, take your time getting up."

And with that, the women left the room. I was alone.

◆ ◆ ◆

THE AFTERMATH

I felt like I had been defiled in a way that words could have never prepared me for.

I went to sit up but struggled. The room spun. I tried to fight through the vertigo with slow deep breaths, but I just grew even more hot and woozy. I wanted to curl up into the fetal position and teleport to my bed. Through sheer will and the promise of my apartment, I managed to slip my black cotton dress over my head without my legs folding. I reached for my Vans but stopped myself. I needed to sit down or I would collapse. I was shaking. "You're just cold," I said, pulling on my jean jacket.

I requested my Uber so I could minimize the amount of time I'd spend in public feeling like I might keel over at any second. The app let me know I had five minutes until Ronald, my driver, would arrive. I took another deep breath before standing up.

You got this.

My Vans finally on, I marched out of the exam room with the confidence of a stoned teenager thinking she was pulling off sober well enough to trick her parents. I knew I wasn't okay, but I didn't want to seem weak. So I opened my eyes a little wider, relaxed my arms at my sides, smiled, and took deep breaths.

Just get to your Uber. You can fall apart in the car.

I hustled out of the office and into the main corridor toward the exit. I wanted to take the stairs because the elevator took too long. My sole mission in life at that moment was to sit down (in my Uber) as fast as humanly possible. I was about two feet away from the door to the stairs, which was sandwiched between the door of the ladies' room and the door to the elevators, when the wheels fell off.

Suddenly, the hallway went dark. I took two more steps before reflexively reaching my hand to grab the circular metal handle belonging to the stairwell door, but it wasn't there. I looked down at the door where the handle should have been, but my vision blurred. I thought that maybe I'd just missed. I reached out again, hoping to feel the cold metal in my palm, but I only swiped air.

What happened to the handle? I thought.

With two hands, I patted down the door like I was a blind person feeling for braille. Instead of a handle, all I felt was the smooth finish of a metal door and more confusion.

What I failed to consider was that I was fainting.

Instead of giving up, I got even closer to the door. With my nose to the wall, I ran my hands up and down, searching for clues like I was in an escape room with sixty seconds left on the clock. I imagine I looked like a horny teenager feeling up her date for the very first time.

I wondered if this was some elaborate prank and if someone had removed the handle as a joke. I was just about to walk through that logic, when a heaviness overwhelmed my body. I needed to sit down.

Unaware of what was happening and committed to playing it cool, I held up my phone as I slid down the wall into what I thought was a squat. I figured no one would look twice at someone checking their phone even if they were on the floor. I sat on airport floors, so why not on a hospital hallway floor? Again, it had still not occurred to me that I was blacking out.

In fact, my concern was with Ronald, my Uber driver. He was probably 3.5 minutes away, and I was going to take at least three minutes to make it down four floors and eight sets of stairs. So I had thirty seconds to figure out where the goddamn stairs had been moved to or I was going to be late. This was the motivation I needed to get back up.

Unfortunately, I woke up to a woman hysterically screaming, so I'm not sure I'm the most reliable narrator. See, I was confident that I'd slid down the wall with a casual effortlessness, but based on what I now know, I think I probably slammed into the door, ricocheting backward, before my legs buckled and I dropped to the ground.

"Haaaaaaaaaalp! She just went down! Haaaaaaalp!" a woman's voice echoed through the hallway. I was not immediately aware that I was the "she" in this situation.

Then I felt the tight grip of a woman with long acrylic nails wrap her hand around my forearm.

"You just went down. I saw you hit the floor. We gotta get you help!"

I managed to lift my head up long enough to tell a horrified woman with long box braids that I was "alllllll good." I could see that my answer had made her nervous by the way her face contorted, so I forced myself to stand up. I was acutely aware of the fact that I was causing a scene and was definitely going to be late to meet Ronald.

"Sorry, I've got to get to my Uber, but I can't find the stairs, which is weird because the door should be right here." I pointed at the stairwell door and watched the woman's eyes widen.

"Baby, this is the *bathroom* and you just *fainted*."

I wanted to reassure her, but I was still focused on Ronald and how he was probably waiting for me, so I decided to make a move for the stairs.

I took two more steps and magically woke up on my back, twenty feet in the opposite direction.

Again, this woman's screaming rattled me back to consciousness.

"She was up and then she was down! Then she was up and then she was dooooown!"

I felt the familiar grip of acrylics digging into my arm.

Why is she still holding my arm? I wondered.

"Y'all she went downnnnnnn!"

I blinked my eyes open, only to be greeted by a semicircle of strangers staring down at me.

My box braid savior shook my arm. "And then she was oooooout."

I was slowly starting to put the pieces together. My savior kept on screaming, in what I can only imagine was a trauma response, but as my vision became clearer, I had trouble hearing her muffled voice, as if I were only able to concentrate on one sense at a time.

My eyes blinked in and out of focus until they settled on a face at my twelve o'clock.

I blinked hard, and suddenly a handsome man with flowy brunette hair and kind brown eyes stared back at me. His light-blue collared shirt was tucked into navy slacks and held in place with an understated leather belt. Coincidentally, this was my high school uniform. I wondered if maybe I was dreaming.

And then he opened his mouth. "Ma'am? Can you hear me?"

Ma'am? Who the fuck is he calling ma'am?

I was immediately convinced that I was not dreaming, because I never would have written dialogue like that, not even in my subconscious.

"Mmmmhmmm," I responded.

"Great. I'm Dr. Davidson." I noticed the medical identification tag hanging around his neck. He ran his fingers through his hair, pushing back the strands that had fallen into his face as he leaned over me. He smiled, revealing a dimple that I immediately dubbed my north star.

Wait a second . . . Is this a meet-cute?

I scanned his hands for a wedding ring: nothing.

Score!

Even in my hazy state, I knew this would make for an incredible story. I'm the only non-medical person in my family, so how wild would it be to tell people that I met my hot doctor boyfriend when he unexpectedly saved my life? I mean, I never thought I'd end up with a doctor, mostly because I'm never around them—and because my dad, a doctor, told me that a lot of them have a God complex and that sounds exhausting. But maybe this hot doc was different. Maybe he was one of the good ones.

My reverie was, again, cut short.

"Ma'am, are you okay?"

I wanted to find something cute to say, something to let this man know that this was potentially *his* meet-cute as well, but then I felt a breeze. And not just any breeze.

Why is air blowing on my belly button?

Suddenly, I was acutely aware of the carpet touching the undercarriage of my butt. I felt the familiar pang of embarrassment, as this could only mean one thing.

Without breaking eye contact, I said, "Is my dress above my waist right now?"

I watched as the hot doctor glanced down at my body before quickly resuming eye contact.

"Yes, yes it is."

I held his eye contact, mortified about the granny panties I was wearing because I needed full coverage for the dead HPV cells and weird gyno jelly mixture that was currently leaking out of me. And in what might have been my most deadpan response ever, I said, "Then I don't think I'm okay."

Before he could respond, the savior lady took this as an opportunity. "I told her she was *not* okay!"

I was still lying on the carpet, half naked, with her nails digging into my arm, when my savior explained to the hot doc that I had been trying to find the pull handle for the stairs on the push door to the bathroom, when she saw me hit the ground. *Hard.* This was when she started calling for help. She also noted that I said I was okay but she knew I wasn't. Apparently, I'd ping-ponged off the walls before dropping my phone and fainting *again.*

She never did explain how I managed to get my dress to fly up above my belly button, but I do believe that was an act of kindness and her sparing me the extra humiliation.

The nurse from earlier appeared, and the people from the semicircle dispersed. I took the opportunity to pull my hemline back down to my knees where it belonged, and I watched as the hot doc told the nurse about my twinning blackouts.

The nurse turned back to me, and I could tell that she was pissed.

Why the fuck is she pissed?

I was the one who'd just flashed a bunch of random strangers and gave my savior PTSD.

Then, in a not-so-shocking twist, the hot doc told me to "take it easy" before walking away without so much as a first name or an Instagram handle.

I had no time to dwell, because the nurse grabbed me by the elbow like a mom about to ground me for embarrassing her in front of her friends.

She ushered me back into the office, handed me a juice box and some graham crackers, and placed me by the scale, where everyone could watch me recover. It felt punitive—mostly because she kept scolding me for "leaving before I was okay" and for "not saying something."

It worked. I felt bad.

I was also annoyed. I'd spoken up several times in the exam room, but the nurse and doctor had shut me down. When I'd noted that the pain was too much, they'd told me that most women are fine and that I was the anomaly, as if to say I was weaker than average. This was the message they'd conveyed to me during the procedure, so I'm not sure why I would have assumed that in the aftermath I'd be treated any better? I didn't have the energy to fight with the nurse, and I didn't feel like having to find another gyno, so instead I kept apologizing.

Then I remembered: RONALD! *My Uber driver.*

I looked down at my phone, which had numerous Uber notifications. Ronald had sent me several messages before canceling the ride, and Uber let me know I would have to pay for it. That felt fair. Not karmically, but literally, like poor Ronald. I wish he could have known how hard I'd tried to be there.

Eventually my blood pressure recovered, and I felt normal again.

I got up to leave, the nurse eyeing my every move, and I walked out of the office. Before I took to the stairs, I stepped back, looking at all three doors. I couldn't believe that I had confused the bathroom door with the stairwell. I had been out-of-my-mind fucked up, and suddenly I felt bad for myself.

I looked over at where I'd fainted the second time, and I was floored by how far away I'd landed. I pictured myself stumbling like a drunk person walking diagonally.

I spent the rest of the day in bed with a heating pad on my stomach, trying to dull the pain.

◆ ◆ ◆

THE ANTIVIRAL

My HPV diagnosis served as a huge lesson in personal agency. Obviously, I had a lot to learn about sex—not simply how I liked to have it but also about the *actual* risks involved with being sexually active. The truth is, I didn't get a vibrator until my mid- to late twenties. I didn't realize that I could squirt until I was almost 30. Maybe you had it easier than me—I hope you did—but my journey with pleasure involved a lot of unraveling of what I thought sex was *supposed to be* and then a slow discovery into what I *wanted it to be*.

While female pleasure seems to have finally entered the social consciousness, STIs still remain a taboo topic. No one wants to talk about them, despite the fact they are a real aspect of many people's lives. For instance, up to 80% of people in the United States have some form of herpes, whether sexually transmitted or not, yet it is still so stigmatized.[10] The shame around STIs created a dating culture that seemed to encourage ignorance and silence around the topic of sexual health—making it easy for me to stay oblivious.

I'd never inquire about how many partners someone currently had or when they were last tested. Instead, I'd casually ask if someone was "clean" and choose to believe them when 100% of the time people responded with yes. I simply hoped I'd get lucky and dodge whatever was out there rather than have uncomfortable conversations, namely, a conversation about condoms and sexual health.

---

10   Michael Ray Garcia, Stephen W. Leslie, and Anton A. Wray, "Sexually Transmitted Infections," StatPearls–NCBI Bookshelf, April 20, 2024, https://www.ncbi.nlm.nih.gov/books/NBK560808/.

While I grew up with a fear of STIs, I was also conditioned to think that condoms were lame and a turnoff for men. (I also grew up thinking that blue balls were a real thing, so please, cut me some slack!) I felt weird being the one to insist on using a condom—because no one likes a buzzkill. Obviously, lots of guys brought them or were quick to say yes, but some guys would balk or push back and make me feel like I was ruining the party.

For years, I told myself that *I* didn't like the feel of condoms. (I've since found a brand I love). I had been convinced I didn't like them, but even if I had loved them at the time, I would have felt too small to insist on my sexual safety.

I know I'm not the only woman who's put someone else's pleasure above her health, but I do want to be the one to encourage you to stop.

I may have lost my virginity at seventeen, but I didn't truly come into my sexuality until I began to own my sexual agency a decade later. The journey required me to be vocal about my desires and boundaries, which helped me get comfortable taking up space and making my satisfaction and safety a priority. As I got more comfortable with saying no, I got better at advocating for myself in a way that still felt sexy and playful. As a result, I started having safer and more satisfying sexual encounters.

I see my cryo experience as an extension of my sexual journey. I lacked agency in that situation because I was uneducated; I trusted someone in an authoritative position, and I wasn't comfortable making my well-being someone else's problem. Not to mention, I knew nothing about advocating for myself regarding pain management and gynecological procedures.

In the years since my HPV diagnosis, millions of women have taken to social media, podcasts, and newsletters to share their horrific stories with ignored pain. For centuries, women have been bullied into staying silent about their medical experiences, gynecological or otherwise. We've been collectively gaslit into thinking we're the only ones in agony when, in reality, we are not. The medical industry is inherently misogynistic, even if the people who treat us aren't intending to be. They are trained in institutions that don't adequately test on women and whose curricula have been questioned for blind spots.[11] Gynecology has a pain problem, and only recently have women (and allies) started speaking up about it.

I already felt like a difficult patient. I'd been scared and thought I was being dramatic when I'd requested additional care and was shot down. So when my procedure was over and I was feeling wobbly and weird, I didn't tell anyone, because I didn't want to seem like an even bigger problem. My care team had indicated that other women handled cryo better than me, so I was trying to do my best not to draw attention to myself. I was already ashamed of having HPV in the first place; the last thing I wanted was to be seen as histrionic and a pain in the ass.

In reality my pain was so bad that it caused my blood pressure to plummet, triggering a vasovagal reaction, which caused me to faint. I now know this is quite common, especially with cervical pain.[12] Go figure. Maybe if I had known that I wasn't such an outlier, I would have felt safer speaking up, but that is how shame works.

Shame is the ultimate virus. It burrows into the deepest parts of us and festers until one day you realize you're paralyzed. It keeps us suffering in silence and holds us back from growing. People say, "You're only as sick as your secrets," and I would venture to bet that it's the *discomfort* around those secrets seeing the light of day and not the secrets themselves that keep people sick. The good news is that the antidote to shame is vulnerability, self-

---

11   Margaret Waltz, Anne Drapkin Lyerly, and Jill A. Fisher, "Exclusion of Women From Phase I Trials: Perspectives From Investigators and Research Oversight Officials," Ethics & Human Research 45, no. 6 (November 1, 2023): 19–30, https://doi.org/10.1002/eahr.500170.
12   Willbroad Kyejo et al., "Cervical Vasovagal Shock: A Rare Complication of Incomplete Abortion Case Report," International Journal of Surgery Case Reports 97 (July 25, 2022): 107455, https://doi.org/10.1016/j.ijscr.2022.107455.

love, and acceptance. Once I confronted the parts of myself I felt embarrassed about, my whole world shifted.

I now know I'm not going to have sex with someone who isn't enthusiastic about wearing a condom, and I'm always going to discuss STIs and recent sexual health tests. It's not embarrassing; it's *empowering* to care about my health and pleasure. Sure, at first, insisting on someone wearing a condom (who I could sense didn't want to) was a bit nerve-racking, but now it's second nature. I am so clear about my boundaries that I can easily walk away from anyone who doesn't respect them, because disrespect is no longer attractive to me. I will also never see a doctor who doesn't believe that the cervix has nerves or that cervical pain isn't real.

I never thought that testing positive for HPV would lead me down a rabbit hole of confronting internalized misogyny and sexual repression, but that's exactly what happened. And through an extremely painful and embarrassing experience, I learned to embrace my autonomy.

Every time I advocate for myself now, I think about the next girl who might be less bold, and I hope that my bullishness helps her out. Whether for an equitable sexual experience or a gentler medical experience, I'm not just advocating for myself, I'm advocating for the women around me. So the next time you're feeling shame creeping in to silence you, think about the girl who's about to faint in granny panties and help her out; stand a little taller and get a little louder.

A FINAL GIRL'S GUIDE TO SEXUAL HEALTH

- Do you have a brand of condoms that you like, and do you have a way to carry them when you're on a date or in a situation that might turn sexual?

- In the event you get nervous or feel uncomfortable, do you have a script you can use to convey your boundaries around sexual health? I always say, "Condoms are a nonnegotiable for me, and I think it's really hot when people prioritize their health, so I'd love to know when you were last tested or if you're planning on getting tested."
- If you have an STI, do you have a script you can use if you get nervous about disclosing that information?
- Do you have a gyno you like and trust for regular checkups, Pap smears, mammograms, and other health issues? If not, do you have a clinic or place where you can receive care?
- Have you talked with your gyno about big-picture issues like pregnancies, abortions, egg freezing, cervical pain, STIs, etc.? Know where your provider stands on these issues and make sure their care philosophies align with what you want and deserve.
- Do you have a plan of action should you suspect you have an STI, urinary tract infection (UT), or a medical emergency? If you don't have a gyno or can't get into one, what is your backup plan?
- Do you know when your last period was? On that note, do you have a way to track your periods? This won't be for everyone, but tracking has helped me become more in tune with my body. I realize women might not want to track their periods via an app or online, so I would suggest getting a paper calendar that is just for tracking your period.

These questions offer a basic start in terms of thinking about and crafting a plan for your sexual health. Try to answer all these questions if you can, but also, do what's right for you.

FWIW: The guys who balk at using condoms or conversations about sexual health are the guys who are generally less into making sure that pleasure is equitable. Having a conversation about sexual health is an *incredible* way to screen sexual partners.

A HINT OF DANGER

I never took the time to properly heal from my breakup with Chris; I just dove into dating. Because we'd ended amicably, remained friends, and I had no problems moving on, I thought I was fine.

Plus, I was busy. I'd sold my first television show, I was directing a bunch, and I'd recently started standup. I also looked great, not that it matters. But you know how some years you're in a flop era and other years you look back and think, *Damn, I looked good that year?* Well, this was one of those years.

I met my next boyfriend during a press trip for work. He was this nerdy-ass tech dude who never would have cheated on me in a million years, because he looked like a sad version of Waldo (sans striped shirt) but had the personality of Nathan Fielder, and I was the life of the party. Waldo, which is what I'll be calling him, would have said as much. When we started dating, I remember showing photos of him to my girlfriends and being met with their polite silence. "He's cute," Rhiannon said, in a tone that let me know she was choosing to be supportive.

Look, we've all fallen for an ugly guy once or twice, right? One rodent boyfriend?

I was burning out on "hot" guys who wanted to keep things casual or who only seemed to value me for superficial reasons, and Waldo was different: He saw me the way I wanted to be seen. He thought I was smart and funny, and he liked being around me with my clothes on. Waldo supported my creative endeavors, which was a breath of fresh air in a place like LA where so many people are competing.

So he wasn't the hottest guy in the world.

Who cares, I'm happy.

Like most females in horror movies, I thought I was fine—until I knew I wasn't.

WITCHES

I've never been stabbed, which is pretty impressive considering the mouth on me, but I imagine it feels like being cheated on. (Yup, second time!) That feeling when you're so blindsided by something that you can't even cry, because your whole body feels like you just jumped into ice water—where every cell feels like it's on fire and ready for war but is also simultaneously paralyzed by fear and it's unclear if you'll ever be able to breathe again, much less form a sentence. I'm honestly surprised I didn't shit my pants . . .

And let me tell you, being rejected by a guy you lowered your standards for is a niche sort of pain. Getting cheated on by Captain America is a lot less embarrassing than, say, getting cheated on by Shrek.

Waldo may have been less attractive than my previous boyfriends, but I convinced myself this meant he was safe. I'd traded good looks for security, which seemed like the mature thing to do at the ripe old age of twenty-eight. "He'd never leave me" was the hubris that came to bite me in the ass.

I discovered I was being cheated on via Instagram. God bless social media.

Yeah, this is one of those stories.

Something you need to know about loving an ugly (or unphotogenic) guy is that you'll find one or two great photos and you'll cherish them the same way WWII wives held on to photos of their husbands who were fighting overseas. In my case, it was a tagged pic on Instagram. It was a few years down on his grid, but it was the photo I'd show strangers when my boyfriend came up in conversation, and it was the photo I'd look at before I'd go to bed at night.

One fateful eve, I was doing my nightly scroll through Waldo's tagged pics when I was stopped cold in my tracks: Sitting at the top of his tagged photos for the whole world to see was a photo of *my* boyfriend in a hotel room with his arms around a hot brunette and thirteen hearts as the caption.

THIRTEEN HEARTS.

And that was the moment that *my* heart fell out of my asshole.

Even now I'm not sure what's more shocking: that Waldo was cheating on me or that I'd never even suspected it.

Waldo would probably tell you that we "weren't that serious," since this is how he tried to gaslight me after I called out his cheating during our breakup. And while I don't feel like I should have to defend myself, allow me to grace you with a couple of facts.

We'd been dating for eight months, which was long enough for me to be Waldo's emergency contact at the hospital after he had butt surgery for hemorrhoids. I brought him backstage as my plus one to a Fall Out Boy concert, and when he immediately and aggressively fell off Wiz Khalifa's PhunkeeDuck, proving to be the most uncoordinated dude I'd ever dated, I laughed instead of joining the witness protection program out of humiliation. It never occurred to me that the Apple TV, camera, and clothes he gave me for Christmas were guilt-fueled gifts because we regularly said, "I love you," and my dumbass thought we both meant it.

But this chapter isn't about him, it's about *her*. And once I got over the problematic number of hearts, I was immediately obsessed with figuring out who this seductress was.

So I did what anyone with Wi-Fi would do: I swan dove down the rabbit hole that was this girl's social media like I was Elle Woods guest starring in an episode of *True Detective*. Not to freak anyone out, but I should definitely be working for the government. All this to say that seven hours later, after the montage sequence in the procedural drama that was my life, I literally knew *everything* about this other girl, *this witch*.

Her name was Hope, which I found unbelievably ironic. She had long dark wavy hair and milky skin and a heart-shaped mouth that I wanted to punch right off her face. Much to my chagrin, she looked like Elvira—if Elvira lived in Brooklyn after graduating with a poetry degree from Bard and exclusively drank ceremonial matcha long before it was cool.

The fact that she was attractive ignited my insecurities. As if on cue, the demonic voice buried in the back of my mind sprang into action.

Uh-oh, she's pretty.

My inner demon had been hibernating for several years, lurking in the darkest corners of my psyche, resurfacing only at my lowest moments like a harbinger of doom.

Unfortunately, Hope wasn't just pretty; she was part of a coven of other cool witches and media "it" girls from New York. She wore wild vintage outfits, vaped with abandon, and regularly went viral on Twitter for her hot takes. She was everything I was not. I could feel my jealousy creeping in like a dense fog I would eventually get lost in.

As I sat there, staring at the digital footprint of the woman who had "ruined my life," the demonic voice said, *I wonder what kind of spell she cast on Waldo to make him betray you like this.* The statement summoned something dark inside me. You're not supposed to question the occult, just like you're not supposed to look into a witch's eyes, but here I was doing both. Looking back, this was the moment of conjuration, the moment that Hope's sorcery began to take over my mind, and it was all downhill from there.

Apparently, Waldo had met Hope on a flight home after visiting me, which is nauseatingly romantic, minus the part where I'm being cheated on. He sat down next to her, locked eyes, and the two fell in love. They'd been dating for four months—half of our relationship—and I was certain she must have drugged him with some sort of love potion; that was the only thing that made sense in my brain.

How else could he have replaced me so quickly and callously?

They hard-launched their relationship two weeks later, as if I'd never existed. I watched as Hope posted photos of them kissing in the park, laughing in bars, and snuggling on Sunday mornings. Things we used to do.

See! You are replaceable, taunted the voices in my head.

The ease with which they loved publicly propelled me deeper into my private investigations. I was consumed by how happy they were and determined to find some sort of crack in their facade—something, anything, to let me know that I had mattered.

Six weeks went by as I silently stalked. I told myself that I was in control and that I could stop at any time, but every day, I'd check Hope's social media, becoming more and more obsessed.

Valentine's Day rolled around, and I spent it maniacally refreshing my feed to keep tabs on Hope and Waldo's romantic night: cocktails, followed by dinner, followed by kissing against the backdrop of the New York skyline. It was like death by a hundred paper cuts; there wasn't one moment that particularly hurt, but the cumulative effect left me bleeding out. Any rational person would have looked at my behavior as an act of self-harm, digital cutting if you will, but as much as it hurt, I couldn't stop myself.

Time marched on, but to the rhythm of Hope's life on social media.

◆ ◆ ◆

Around mid-March, Hope tweeted, **Gonna be in the Bay April 2-9 get at me.**

The mere thought of her on my coast felt too close for comfort. My anxiety spiked.

Beneath it, Waldo had responded, **Catching flights and feelings.**

Based on nothing more than this Twitter exchange, I was positive that Hope was headed to meet Waldo's parents, something I had never done. Bitterness bubbled up inside of me like diarrhea after a night of heavy drinking. I didn't want to be with Waldo, but I couldn't stand to see Hope with him either.

As their excitement ramped up, so did my compulsion. I would unconsciously audit her socials, checking out the nooks and crannies of her online persona like I was a security guard shining a light down the same hallways for the hundredth time. I didn't even know what I was looking for at this point, but looking had become a habit.

I kept my proclivities a secret. There's a window of time where it's acceptable to talk shit about your ex or his new girlfriend, but anything after that and you seem deranged. And while I had the awareness to know it was time to stop talking about Hope, I was way too deranged to stop *thinking* about her.

She lived in my mind rent free for several months, because jealousy is a disease. I would zoom in on her photos to compare the size of our arms, our tits, or the whiteness of our teeth.

I would soothe myself by looking at her crooked nose or her pointy hat and her snarled fingernails and tell myself that I was prettier, as if this were a metric to be proud of. No sooner had I quelled that fear when a second would emerge:

If you're prettier, that means Hope has upstaged you somewhere else.

The not knowing was the worst part. I wondered if maybe she fucked better, if her personality was more palatable, or if she was just one of those "cool" girls that let everything slide. Without a definitive answer, the darkest parts of my mind were able to run free. Four months had passed, and somehow I found myself in a battle of good versus evil with a woman I'd never met. But her existence reminded me that I wasn't good enough to keep a dweeb from cheating on me. Her existence reinforced the idea that I was, once again, replaceable.

He left you for someone better, just like Jack did.

I was in hell, but my inner demon was *loving* it.

◆ ◆ ◆

Then, on a random afternoon in April, Hope posted about needing a sublet in Los Angeles, and I lost my damn mind.

She was moving to my city. Which meant that I could run into her. Which meant I *would* run into her. The thought of seeing her sent me into a tailspin.

I found myself having imaginary conversations, practicing what I was going to say when I inevitably saw her and Waldo. I woke up in cold sweats panicked about Hope weaseling her way into my friend group the same way she'd weaseled her way into my relationship. Every day I'd update myself on her life and count down the days until her arrival in Los Angeles, a city of thirty million people.

And somewhere between the 2,345th time checking her Instagram and the 657th time googling her, I realized why Waldo had cheated. I understood the gravitational pull of her sorcery—because I, too, was under Hope's spell. But the harder I resisted, the more it gnawed at me.

I wanted to quit her the way Waldo had quit our relationship—cold turkey—but something kept pulling me back. I was tethered to Hope like a deranged fan in a parasocial relationship. I wanted so badly to cut the cord, but morbid curiosity, unbridled jealousy, and my overwhelming desire to see her fail kept me from doing so.

The more I thought about her, the more it burned me up inside—which was exactly what I wanted to happen to her. I was like a puritan man, determined to watch the woman who had scorned me burned at the stake. Never mind that Waldo had willingly left me; in my mind, Hope had been the catalyst.

Everything came to a head on Cinco de Mayo. Research shows that, on average, it takes eleven weeks for most people to get over a breakup.[13] Yet here I was, five and a half months out and arguably more unwell than I'd ever been. I couldn't continue to live like this: I needed an exorcism.

So, I collected all my crystals, lit some uncrossing incense, and began a binding spell. It was time to fight the black magic that had cloaked me for the last five months with some sorcery of my own. I meditated, I journaled, I cried, and after several hours, the veil of wickedness lifted, and I could finally see the truth: Hope was not the problem—I was.

When Waldo cheated on me, I didn't miss him like I'd missed Jack. I was immediately turned off by his behavior and wanted nothing more to do with him. I had enough self-respect

---

13 Olivia Foster, "It Takes Just 11 Weeks to Get Over a Break-up (but Divorcees Need 18 Months to Move On)," Mail Online, January 19, 2015, https://www.dailymail.co.uk/femail/article-2916925/It-takes-just-11-weeks-break-divorcees-need-18-months-on.html.

to know that I deserved to be with someone who, at the bare minimum, was faithful. My experience with Jack made this part easy. Unfortunately, that was where my healing had ended.

Every one of us has a story we torture ourselves with. I'm talking about the voice in your head that goes, *He cheated on you just like they all do. You probably should have seen it coming.* Or, *Maybe if you hadn't been so needy, he wouldn't have left you.*

And it's not just in dating. For some of you, those voices might get louder when you're making new friends or showing up at work. These stories are a result of our fears and insecurities—and our brains trying to make sense of patterns in our lives. Some people refer to these as limiting beliefs. I like to collectively refer to them as my inner demon.

When my inner demon started whispering things like, *Maybe if you were just a little bit hotter, cooler, smarter, or more successful, Waldo wouldn't have looked twice at Hope*, I was afraid it was right.

What does Hope have that I don't?

The second I entertained this question, it was game over; the spell was cast.

I spent the next five and a half months unconsciously trying to prove to myself that I was worthy of being loved and that the demonic voices inside my head weren't right. The reason I had such trouble stopping my obsessing over Hope was that she was really an extension of my own ego and self-worth. I wasn't battling Hope; I was battling myself. I kept hoping that if I stuck around long enough I could see Waldo cheat on Hope the way he'd cheated on me and it would somehow prove that she wasn't special—Waldo was just *that* broken.

Let me be very clear about something: When people cheat like this, it's a flaw in them and not a reflection of the person who was cheated on. Intellectually, I knew this, but emotionally and spiritually, I was ready to blame anyone but Waldo.

As I sat in my empty living room, staring at the tear-stained pages of my journal, I realized Hope wasn't a witch; she was a girl I'd given an inordinate amount of power over me. I'd allowed my insecurities to build an idea of her in my mind. Hope wasn't a monster; I was just unhealed. I'd taken my self-loathing and blamed it on her.

I was scouring social media looking for clues to prove that *I* mattered—as if anything is real on social media. By its very nature, social media triggers us to be comparative. But it's an illusion, a sliver of truth that's been staged, filtered, and glamorized. Anyone who was following me during those five and a half months never would have known that my mental health was hanging on by a thread or that I was being plagued by a woman I'd never even met. The irony is classic. I was using social media to glean real insights into Hope and Waldo's relationship, but those images told me nothing of reality.

Faced with my own accountability, I realized Hope had done nothing wrong. Waldo had, but he was no longer my boyfriend, so I needed to stop dwelling and get my ass into therapy. In fact, as I sat with the last five months' worth of recon I'd done on Hope, I realized that I liked her. Had we encountered each other in the wild, pre-Waldo, we probably could have been friends. She was smart and funny, and she seemed to glide through the world immune to the opinions of others. Hating Hope was like holding on to a hot coal and expecting her to get burned, but it was only hurting me.

In a moment of clarity, I realized that Hope owed me nothing; the other woman never does. Even if Hope had known about me and had actively gone after Waldo, he was the one I'd been dating; he was the one who'd betrayed me.

But it was easier to hate her than to face the fact that another man I trusted had looked me in the eyes and lied when he said that he loved me. It was safer to believe that a witch came in and 'stole my man' rather than admit that maybe he wasn't that happy, maybe we weren't as solid as I thought—or worse, that once again I'd misjudged the character of someone I thought I intimately knew. Blaming her was simpler than admitting that I needed to look inward and address my inner demons. And quite frankly, society had spent years teaching me it was the other woman's fault anyway.

We were taught to fear witches.

It was instinctual for me to project the darkest parts of myself onto Hope. I'd grown up with movies that blamed women for men's bad behavior. I'd learned about the sirens who drowned sailors and the femme fatales who could manipulate men into leaking government secrets. I was taught that men couldn't be held responsible for their actions in the face of a seductress. Society has been pitting women against each other for as long as I can remember, so naturally I did the same.

Alone in my apartment, I felt embarrassed by my actions and ashamed of my jealousy. Hope and I were women both looking for a "happily ever after," and if hers happened to come at the expense of mine, then so be it. Waldo wasn't the guy I'd thought he was, but that shouldn't preclude Hope from her love story. Love is important, and I was reminded of how I truly do want everyone to experience it, even those who have hurt me. She and Waldo *seemed* perfect together, and I decided that should be celebrated. I reminded myself that my love story was coming, and for the first time, I felt at peace.

I wrote them both letters, then I burned them. I genuinely meant it when I said out loud to no one in my apartment, "I wish you well. Just release me. I want to move on."

I went to bed that night feeling lighter. Things were going to be different. And boy, were they.

The next afternoon, Hope followed me on Twitter, and I nearly crashed my car on the 101.

What the fuck is happening?

I'd barely asked the question when an unknown number called me on my cell phone.

"Hello?" I answered.

"You don't know me, but"—the voice on the other line could barely finish her sentence because she was crying so hard—"my name is Hope and I just found out about you."

She burst into painful sobs. And I sat there, stunned.

Is this really happening?

I did my best to calm her down. "Hey, it's okay. Whatever it is, it's fine. You're fine, please don't cry."

I wasn't even sure what she was going to say, but the anguish of her sobs dissolved any animosity I could have had toward this voice on the other end of the line.

"I'm so sorry," she choked out before breaking into full-blown wails.

I wanted to hug her. I wanted to reach through the phone and remind her that she was special—so special that she sent me into a five-month menty-B. Instead, I listened and offered words of support. I reminded her that Waldo was the one who'd betrayed me, she hadn't—and she had nothing to feel bad about. I genuinely meant it.

Eventually, Hope collected herself enough to tell me how she'd managed to get my cell phone number. Apparently, there was a *third* woman, and her arrival had led to Hope's discovery of me. When Waldo tried to gaslight her, Hope held his computer over their eighth-story balcony and told him she would drop it if he didn't come clean. Waldo opted not to lose his computer that day and instead lost his girlfriend.

We decided to get a drink and compare stories, because Hope was going to be in LA that weekend. What could have been an hour-long bitch session turned into a six-hour marathon date and the beginning of a beautiful friendship. I was right about one thing: Hope was funny and smart and started drinking matcha long before everyone else. I've got to hand it to Waldo: He had shit morals but *great* taste in women.

Years later, Hope and I are still good friends. She came into my life in one of the bleakest ways, but if I had the chance to do it all over again, I'd endure that heartache for Hope any day. And honestly, if you knew her, you probably would too.

Through Hope, I was given the rare opportunity of the other woman's perspective. But I had to come to terms with my own baggage first. Call it God, the universe, divine timing, or whatever, but I do believe that everything unfolded as it did so that I would grow from it. So that I could add to my final girl arsenal.

This will surprise no one, but Hope and Waldo's relationship wasn't as it seemed on social media. They weren't perfect. The same "quirks" that had annoyed me annoyed her, and in the end, Waldo cheated on her just like he'd cheated on me. Learning the truth about Hope and Waldo's relationship did eliminate the demented voices in my head (for the time being). The stories I'd made up in my mind were incomplete. She wasn't better; she simply had not learned the lessons I had learned about Waldo yet—until she did. Try to remember this the next time you find yourself playing the comparison game.

Like I said, I wouldn't opt for a heartbreak-free experience with Waldo, because the shitty experience taught me some valuable lessons. The other woman is not your enemy. You can't steal something that's free, just like you can't ruin a relationship that isn't broken. Hating the other woman is the patriarchy at work, and I refuse to play by those rules ever again. If my boyfriend leaves me for another woman who is actively trying to "steal" him from me, then so be it. But I'm done blaming the person that isn't my partner.

I often think about the Salem Witch Trials and how women have always been forced to be the scapegoats. Outside stressors like smallpox, famine, and attacks from Indigenous People who were defending against colonization threatened the God-fearing patriarchal structure of Salem because men were unable to protect against these things. Puritan values needed reinforcement, and that came at the expense of women's lives. Anyone could blame their afflictions on a witch—just like I had blamed Hope—and many Salem residents did.

For me, witches are synonymous with power, independence, and freedom. A witch is a woman who flies in the face of the patriarchy. To be confident and to love yourself in a world built for men is an act of rebellion. In the end, my experience with Hope made me realize that the fear and hate I possessed was misguided desire and longing. I needed to look inward and love the parts of myself that society made me doubt.

For I, too, am a witch—I was just struggling to find my power.

A FINAL GIRL'S GUIDE TO THE OTHER WOMAN

The rage and jealousy you feel toward the "other woman" is misplaced anger and hurt. You are mad at your partner who has deceived you and let you down, and that is normal. But don't blame the person you aren't in a relationship with (unless the other woman is a friend of yours and then, wow, they are both trash). The other woman owes you nothing.

Repeat after me:

You cannot wreck a home that was never built.
You can't steal something that goes freely.
If anyone takes my man, he was never actually my man.

And if you're worried about the tiny percent of women who know a man is taken and go for it anyway, take solace in this: You lose 'em how you get 'em. They will always get theirs but that's none of your business. And if you go from the side piece to the girlfriend, you've just created a job opening.

ZOMBIES

♦

I was butt-ass naked in Marcus's living room when I heard a loud banging on the back door. I froze, acutely aware of how vulnerable I was and terrified that we were about to be robbed. I looked at Marcus, and before I could say anything, he reassured me, "Rory, it's fine." This is the kind of shorthand that comes from knowing someone for more than half your life.

Marcus was my on-again-off-again boyfriend from high school, and at that moment, we were decidedly *on* and giving our relationship one last hurrah. After Waldo and some underwhelming situationships, Marcus was able to convince me to give "us" a final try. And honestly, I was ready to finally get it right with him and start the life I always thought we'd have.

Marcus and I had met at a very prestigious boarding art high school when we were fifteen. He was a former Abercrombie model with ice-blue eyes, turned art school weirdo covered in tattoos, which meant that he was conventionally attractive with a rebellious streak (i.e., extremely my type). He was also unbelievably talented. Technically, we didn't "date" in high school, because by the time we realized we liked each other, we were graduating and going our separate ways. A couple of years later, we reconnected in Los Angeles and began our tumultuous love story.

We had that intoxicating kind of young love that's hard to shake. No matter how many times we broke up, Marcus kept coming back, and I kept letting him. I thought he was my soulmate; he was really my zombie.

"It's probably someone who's lost," Marcus said.

This made sense. Marcus lived in one of two houses built on the same lot, and the back house was throwing a party. We'd been at the party earlier but had decided to call it a night.

As if on cue, I could hear someone trying to open the back door.

"*Marcusss*!" I hissed as I jumped off the couch.

"Wrong house!" Marcus called out, and they stopped trying to open the door.

I waited a beat before letting out the breath I was unconsciously holding. "Whew!" I said, before we both giggled.

Marcus held out his hand, motioning for me to come back and cuddle. I crawled into the nook under his arm. Even after all the terrible things he and I had been through, Marcus felt like home.

There was something poetic about being back with my high school sweetheart. Beyond our chemistry and our shared history, Marcus and I felt cosmically tied. Not to get all crystals and "woo woo," but we had a weird sixth sense about each other.

The first time it happened, I was probably twenty-two and I was driving home, when out of nowhere I was hit with an overwhelming sense of dread and urgency regarding Marcus. *Something is wrong*, I thought. I could feel it. I pulled my car over and called him only to learn that his mom had just been diagnosed with cancer. "How did you know?" he'd asked. I just did.

I could rattle off a list of similar stories that would have all of you thinking, *Holy shit, yeah, there's something special about you two,* but in the interest of brevity I won't. Instead, I'll say that it's hard to have a connection like this and not extrapolate it into something more.

As with most toxic relationships, we experienced periods where we didn't speak to each other. I'd decide that Marcus was unhealthy for me or we'd both need to cool off, and then something big would happen in one of our lives and the other would instinctively know to call. I'd never had this with anyone else, and at a certain point, I believed a cosmic force kept pulling Marcus and me back together. These were our "red string" moments, meaning that Marcus was my twin flame.

In East Asian folklore, certain lovers are fated to meet each other because they are connected by an invisible red string. Hence, the red string theory. The idea is that the string may tangle or stretch but it will never break. It represents the connection between two lovers who are meant to be together, even if they don't know it yet. They might drift apart or face obstacles (knots and tangles), but they will eventually make their way back to one another because they are forever tied. Marcus and I were forever tied, which meant that any of the drama we faced were the knots in our otherwise predetermined love story.

Plus, I had been primed for romantic disappointments. All the rom-coms I'd watched growing up had at least one moment where a character royally fucks up, causing the couple to break up until they realize they can't live without each other, then they get back together and the rest is history. These narratives had led me to understand that turmoil and strife were essential parts of an epic love story. So in my mind, that Marcus and I would also have our ups and downs made sense; it was par for the course.

Within less than a minute, the banging started again, but this time it was closer. Whoever it was, they were banging on the side door to the living room, which was about four feet from where we were sitting on the couch.

Bang! Bang! Bang!

I screamed and leaped to the other side of the room. Before I could process what was happening, a woman screamed at the top of her lungs, "FUUUCK YOUUUU, MARCUUUS!"

The fact that it was a woman's voice was both relieving and distressing. On the one hand, I felt better about not getting murdered; on the other, I'd seen this movie before.

Marcus was terrified of being alone, both metaphorically and literally, so he often found himself in situations with women that were, uh, messy. A "warm body complex" if you will. In the beginning, when Marcus lived in Chicago and I lived in Los Angeles, we had a mutual understanding that when we were together, we were *together* and when we were apart, we didn't ask questions. Naturally this led to some pretty fucked-up situations.

My close friends and family were not thrilled when I told them that Marcus and I were getting back together. They'd seen me shed too many tears over the years to be anything other than concerned about this reunion. We were a passionate couple, but Marcus and I had a hard time communicating. In our defense, we'd met when we were very young and never managed to break those early habits. I was allergic to vulnerability and felt more comfortable in screaming fights or cold-war standoffs. Marcus lives with bipolar disorder and had not been properly medicated early in our relationship, which meant he went through very dark phases, and I often became unintentional collateral damage. But that was years ago. We were older and wiser now. Marcus was medicated and in therapy, and vulnerability had become my superpower. I believed things would be different because we were *actual* adults committed to giving our relationship a real shot.

"I can hear you fuuucking her in thereee!" an angry woman screamed.

Okay, maybe *I* was the one committed to giving us a real shot.

"Marcusss, fuuuuuck youuuuu!"

Whoever she was, her rage emanated through the walls. She was circling the house banging on every window and door she could reach, with such force that I figured she'd make her way inside.

I looked at Marcus and cocked my head. "What is going on?"

"It's nothing. I promise."

"Enjoy him, you fucking sluuuuut!"

Marcus's eyes widened. Whoever she was, her timing was impeccable.

With the calm of a kindergarten teacher dealing with a midday meltdown, I asked, "Who is that, and why does she think I'm a slut?"

"Because she's crazy!" Marcus snapped. "Her name is Kelly-Anne, and we ended a while ago, so I don't even know why this is happening."

I also didn't know why this was happening, but I'd heard enough.

While Kelly-Anne was possibly "crazy," more likely Marcus had done something to trigger this level of a response. After all, this was not the first Kelly-Anne I'd encountered with Marcus.

However, at this moment, I felt closer to Kelly-Ann than to him. I could have easily written her off as out of control or nuts but that felt a lot like me calling her a witch. The dismissal of her feelings felt eerily familiar; the patriarchy pits women against each other. In my experience, most women want peace and security. I couldn't imagine a world in which Kelly-Anne woke up this morning and thought, "Today seems like a great day to embarrass myself over a man." It seemed far more likely that Marcus had left a loose thread, and now she was unraveling outside his house.

Either way, Kelly-Anne was irrelevant; this was about *me*. I was a thirty-year-old woman looking for a fresh start with an old flame, but all I was getting was déjà vu. This drama had been excusable—and maybe even exciting—when we were in our twenties, but it was cringe in our thirties.

The demonic voice in my brain tried to neg me: *Okay, but not everyone gets to have a perfect love story, Rory.*

I ignored it and calmy began to look for my clothes.

"Wait, what are you doing?" Marcus said. The panic rose in his voice as he watched me pick up my jeans.

I was sticking to my standards and telling that inner demon to fuck right off. I too wanted a partnership that gave me a sense of security and ease; instead I was stuck in a shitty episode of *Maury*. This was not what I wanted, and I was not going to let my inner demon convince me to settle.

Bang! Bang! Bang!

Kelly-Anne was still pissed.

"I fucking hate you, Marrrrcus! Rot in Helllll!"

I laughed. "She's kind of iconic, Marcus."

"I swear on my life, Rory, I am not dating her."

"Oh, I believe you." And *I did*. I felt confident that Marcus wanted to make things work between us; I just didn't think it was possible. And for the first time, I was okay with that.

"Then why are you leaving? Let's talk about this."

I was leaving because of all the other times I'd stayed. This wasn't about Kelly-Anne; it wasn't even about Marcus. This was about the reality of our relationship versus the story I'd been telling myself for years. Like that moment in the club when the lights come on and you realize you should have left fifteen minutes earlier, I was standing in Marcus's living room realizing I'd never want this relationship for any of my best friends.

Marcus wasn't safe; he was familiar. And I was finally starting to see the difference. I found comfort with Marcus because we'd been repeating the same patterns since we were teenagers, but that didn't make him safe; it made him predictable.

I could be the worst version of myself, and I knew that Marcus would love me anyway. I'd ping-ponged between him and my other relationships for years because Marcus always wanted me back, and on some level, being desired felt great. I wasn't looking at the hundred times we'd broken up as evidence that we shouldn't be together; I was looking at the hundred times we got back together as a testament of our undying love. But Marcus wasn't my prince charming; he was a zombie that kept rising back from the dead to reenter my life with the same old baggage. And while that might have been fine when we were younger, now it felt like trying to reheat a gourmet meal for the hundredth time—it was getting gross.

Suddenly, the banging stopped.

"Rory, here!" Marcus held out his phone. "Look through my phone—see for yourself. We haven't talked in weeks."

If I'd wanted to litigate the moment, I would have focused on "weeks," but I didn't want to. I didn't want to fight, and I didn't have the words to express a decade and a half of disappointment, in not only Marcus but also in myself.

Why am I in a relationship I wouldn't want my friends to settle for??

Much like in the actual horror rom-com *Warm Bodies*, I felt like if I kept giving Marcus another shot, eventually we would figure it out because, underneath all his chaos, I saw an imperfect person who wanted to be better. Zombies aren't inherently bad. They're humans who were bitten by other zombies.

Marcus was a deeply complicated person with a lot of feelings, insecurities, and family trauma, but he never hid these things from me. He was always honest, and given my history, that counted for a lot. So even after he'd turned into a zombie, I could still see the beautiful human trapped inside the rotting flesh. Even with Kelly-Anne trying to break down his door, I knew Marcus wished for something different. He too wanted peace but didn't know how to get there. Maybe I was trying to save him, or maybe I just identified with his broken parts; either way, I thought my love could help make him whole—and vice versa. I kept showing up for Marcus in the ways I wanted someone to show up for me, but after a decade, I was done.

At thirty, I didn't want to make excuses for bad behavior anymore. I was trying to prove the demonic voices in my head wrong. I desperately wanted to believe that I was worthy of the fairy-tale love that I'd been dreaming of, but I was never going to get it if I settled. Somehow over the last few years our red-string love story had lost its luster. A zombie is a zombie for a reason: They're meant to stay in the past. So I grabbed my purse, hugged Marcus, and left. Thankfully, Kelly-Anne was not waiting outside.

Leaving wasn't dramatic or painful like any of our previous breakups had been. It was easy. Once I saw our relationship for what it was—instead of what it could have been—I didn't want it.

We talked a week later to officially lay our relationship to rest, and it's been dead ever since.

My story with Marcus might be niche, but I do think most people have a relationship they've overly romanticized or a friendship they're holding on to because of the past. I'm not here to tell you what to do, but I am here to point out *my* patterns. Maybe my words will inspire you to do the same.

Marcus meant different things to me at different points in my life: a lover, a bandage, a source of validation, and a place to project my romantic desires. Growing up and learning from past relationships taught me to realize that I wanted—and *deserved*—more. I was so caught up in the lore of us that I'd failed to see the reality of us. Then again, spotting red flags when you're wearing rose-colored glasses is hard.

Few relationships are meant to come back from the dead. Obviously it happens, but those are the exceptions—not the rule.

Most breakups happen for good reasons, and unless meaningful change occurs, getting back together probably won't work. Remember, undying love is a narrative Hollywood created because it's fun to watch, but it's a lot less fun to live. Let them go!

A FINAL GIRL'S GUIDE TO KILLING ZOMBIES

Before you get back with an ex, ask yourself these questions:

- Why did you break up? Have those issues been addressed and changed, or are you getting back together because you miss and love each other? Unless you and your ex have both addressed the issues that caused you to break up the first time, you are likely to break up again. Love is not always enough.
- Is this relationship safe or is it familiar? Are you repeating a familiar dynamic or pattern by getting back with this person? "Toxic" feels safe when it's familiar, but feeling safe doesn't reduce the toxicity.
- Would your love story make for an epic movie? Spoiler, that is probably a bad sign.
- Do you find yourself saying things like, "When it's good it's incredible" or justifying the relationship based on how great it once was or could be? In my humble opinion, you should judge a relationship by how bad the bad times are. Don't let the good times blind you.
- Is the short-term relief of getting back together going to be worth the long-term pain of wasting another six weeks, months, or years?
- Are you confusing forgiveness with forgetting? Holding on to anger and resentment only hurts you. Resentment is like holding on to a hot coal and hoping

that the other person gets burned—but they don't even know you're thinking about them. Forgiveness *is* the goal. Just don't forget. And please don't repeat!
- Are you getting back with your ex because it feels easier than starting over? Are you letting limiting beliefs or your inner demon gaslight you into thinking this is the best you can do?

Remember, if you do not believe you can make it to the end of the movie, you will never survive the horror. The first rule of being a final girl is trusting that you will find your happy ending.

DEMONIC CLOWNS

After Marcus, I reentered the dating scene with clarity and confidence. I wanted a healthy, healing type of love, and I wasn't going to compromise for anything less. No one tells you how satisfying it is to set a standard for yourself and hold firm to those boundaries, so let me be the one to say it: That is self-love.

Walking away from situations—and people—that don't align with what you truly want is a self-love grand gesture. It's the equivalent of standing outside of your bedroom window with a boombox saying, "You complete me!" I realize that metaphor combines *Say Anything* with *Jerry Maguire*, but you get the picture. These are the moments when you show yourself that you have your own back. Knowing your own worth and not being afraid to stand on business builds self-trust, and nothing quiets those little demonic voices in your mind like self-love and self-trust.

So yeah, I was riding high. I'd just evaded a zombie, and I thought, *Hey, I might be figuring out this dating stuff after all!*

As if the game of love was an *actual* game where defeating monsters would give me extra lives or gold coins, I half expected Prince Charming to pop out from whatever office he was hiding in and sweep me off my feet. In my mind, the universe was about to reward me. Maybe this is millennial brain rot, but I genuinely thought, *Okay, zombie defeated, lesson unlocked. Now I will be rewarded with my person.* He had to be right around the corner, and thus, I was excited to hit "the streets" and find him.

If you've seen even one horror movie, then you know that every final girl gets in a few wins before facing her toughest battles, so this celebration was premature on my part.

I was late to dating apps, which were reaching a fever pitch at this time, but with my renewed excitement for dating, I downloaded all of them. At first, I had a blast. I was introduced to hidden dive bars in new neighborhoods, bands I'd fall in love with, invite-only dinner series, and men from all walks of life. One guy grew up in a crime family. He'd robbed people at the age of seven, and his stories made for a fascinating first (and only) date. Another was a private detective with a full-on alias for his job. As I listened to wild stories and went on fabulous dates, my world expanded like a balloon. Somehow a year flew by, and then one day the balloon popped.

The constant newness of dating created a loneliness that crept up on me like a seven-year-old burglar: I never saw it coming. You know what wasn't right around the corner? My person. You know what was? Demonic clowns. These men were so unserious!

The proliferation of dating apps, the expectations around casual sex, and the rise of social media made gameplaying easy, giving the fuckboys their time to shine—and shine they did. I found myself wandering through a circus full of clowns who never seemed to drop the act. I met men who told me they wanted a relationship—and many who told me they wanted a relationship *with me*—but their actions never seemed to match their words. Instead they hid behind carefully curated personas, well-crafted one-liners, and promises that went unfulfilled.

After a year of dates that went nowhere, relationships that went undefined, and lots of micro-rejections, my inner demon awoke from its slumber like a bear reemerging after winter.

You're single because you can't play it cool.
You're single because you're not sparkly enough for LA.
You're single because . . . because . . . because . . .

I should have stopped dating and focused on where those voices were coming from, but I didn't have the tools to excavate those parts of myself yet. Instead of running toward the voices, I tried to outrun them by finding someone else. I'd soothe the sting of another failed situationship by swiping until I matched with an exciting new prospect. The little hurts piled up, but the stack only made me more determined to find someone who would love me.

I saw a quote that said: "You can't put a crown on a clown and expect a king." But that was what I was doing. I kept trying to turn jesters into white knights, and slowly but surely, the gains I'd made walking away from Marcus started to fade. A year on "the streets" had left me broken and beaten down, and I found myself willing to compromise on my standards.

Don't roll your eyes at me. I'm being honest! Trust me, I wish I'd known then what I know now, but I didn't. I thought that if I pushed through the rejections and just kept going, my love life would eventually work itself out. I did not realize that if you allow a clown into your life, your bed, or your heart, you will ultimately end up the joke. I was searching for love at the circus, but it was turning *me* into the fool.

I was a year older post-Marcus, not much wiser, and a lot less confident. The demonic voices inside my head kept telling me that I was unlovable, and with every day that passed, I became closer to believing them.

You might be thinking, *Again?* And to that I would say, unfortunately, yes. Growth isn't linear and neither is healing. You can't check off life lessons like errands on a to-do list, because oftentimes you'll need to learn those lessons more than once. Or, in my case, four million times.

I've always wondered why the characters in horror movies don't bail the second things turn spooky. Why is it that the final girl continues to walk into the dark basement even after she realizes it's haunted? As an audience member, I want to shake her. I want to tell her to run, to leave the house or call the cops, anything but to try to solve it on her own. And yet that is what she does. It's infuriating to witness—shout out to the friends who support us through those ups and downs— but remember that it's also a part of every final girl's journey. Including mine.

ACT II: THE CALL IS COMING FROM INSIDE THE HOUSE

MONSTERS

———◆———

I was two Xanax and one mixed drink deep by the time I made it to hell, aka the back of the line for Halloween Horror Nights. Every October, Universal Studios in Los Angeles turns their amusement park into a fright fest. They spend months building haunted houses that they fill with the most terrifying characters from popular horror franchises. The festival's slogan is "It's never too soon to start panicking," and boy, was I on top of it. From the moment I'd agreed to go, I regretted it. Because I *hate* being scared. But I was also in a season of life where I hated being single, and on this night, my hate for being single trumped my hate for being scared.

So I dragged my ass to the one place I swore I'd never go for a boy.

Chad and I had been dating for a month, and he looked forward to this night all year long. Honestly? *Red flag.*

Unfortunately, I was back in my "color-blind" phase of dating, so that flag blew by me like a couple of lines in front of John Mulaney circa 2020. Chad was a five-foot-ten preppy brunette with a cute rescue dog and a job writing for your favorite *Late Night* hosts. Otherwise, he was unimpressive. He was the kind of guy who fails up, toes the status quo, and is just cute enough to slay on dating apps in the Midwest. He wasn't remarkable in any way, but I figured that meant he wouldn't be remarkably bad either, and *that* was good enough for me.

I was dating him because he'd asked me out and I was sick of the demonic clowns I kept meeting on the dating-app circus. Because we had mutual friends and we'd met in real life, Chad felt like a safe place to land and a nice palate cleanser before whomever my main course would be. I never saw a future with Chad, so consequently, I let a lot slide. This is why I found myself alone waiting to enter a park that would reenact my past traumas and current fears for the cool price of $200.

When Chad had originally asked me to go, my immediate thought was, *Fuuuuuck no*. My friends still tease me about the time I once ran from my own shadow because I genuinely thought someone was following me. Instead, I said, "I'm pretty sure horror theme parks were not invented for women with PTSD."

Chad didn't follow.

"Like, I'm already in fight-or-flight mode just walking to my car."

He stared at me blankly.

"As a woman in the world, I've been attacked more times than Brady's won Super Bowls, and the thought of recreating this for fun seems insane to me."

For someone with such an impressive Twitter following, Chad wasn't especially bright. But he was a good kisser. So when he reassured me that the theme park wasn't *that* bad, brushed his lips against mine, and promised to hold my hand *the entire time*, I chose to believe him.

And that's on me. I should have known better.

So there I was, moments from the entrance, manically checking my phone for a text back from a guy who wasn't holding my hand—because he was already inside the park with his friends.

I'd given him regular updates:

in car

ten away

just got out of my Uber

To which he finally responded:

Ok when you get in, come to Springfield

This meant nothing to me at the moment, but looking back, it was the first of many omens.

I held out my phone for the weary attendant to scan, but instead of waving me through, she politely said, "I'm sorry, but this ticket has already been used."

They say God sends you signs, and I'm pretty sure this was her way of saying, *Bitch, turn around now, this is not going to end well!* But like most blonds in horror movies, I decided to ignore all common sense and keep walking down the dark alley of this night.

I stepped aside and called Chad, which he let go to voicemail. *Fantastic.*

I texted him:

I can't get in. Mike has to bring the paper ticket.

To which he *immediately* responded that they were about to get on a ride. He asked if I used Shane's barcode, which was **"like the third one down."** I clicked back to the PDF he'd sent and scrolled. Instead of one ticket, I had all of them.

lol, I'm so dumb

I still regret sending that text. I'd been sent a PDF that contained one ticket per page and was told:

Here yo ticket.

The instructions were not to scan the third ticket or that he'd sent me multiple tickets.

How exactly did he think I was going to know which ticket to use? And why was I so quick to apologize for his inconsideration?

Unlike the line, with its fluorescent stadium lights, the park was dark—so dark that a solid three minutes went by before I realized I was holding my map upside down. I was already lost, but I forced myself to blend in. In addition to featuring haunted houses, the park was also filled with unemployed actors dressed as creepy horror characters who took out their frustrations on unsuspecting passersby in areas called "scare zones." Every year, video footage of some girl losing her mind as she gets chased by a zombie goes viral, and I was hell-bent on that not being me. I'd been told that they target those who look excitable, so I resolved myself to be the ultimate Cool Girl™. After all, I'd had a lifetime of training.

I didn't start out this way: In the third grade, Justin Miranda told me he wanted to walk me like a dog, and I ran straight to the principal's office. Decades later, I would laugh off sexual innuendos from my male colleagues and pretend not to notice when my boyfriend followed random girls on Instagram. I'd been taught that calling out that kind of behavior made a woman "crazy," the worst C-word of all. Naturally, I adapted. I learned to take rejection without flinching—the same way I learned to shoot whiskey without wincing.

After twenty minutes of searching, I texted Chad:

What's Springfield near on the map?

I thrusted my cold, clammy hands into the pockets of my leather jacket. I tried to look bored as I sped up or slowed down to shroud myself with the groups of people passing me by.

Text me back, text me back, text me back.

I repeated this in my brain like a prayer, trying to manifest a response.

While it was too soon for labels like *boyfriend* and *girlfriend*, Chad and I had agreed that we were exclusive, yet here I was trying to Jedi mind-move my date into giving a shit—the same way I'd spent years of my life silently willing attention from men that I was interested in.

This sucks.

Out of nowhere, a cursed rag doll lurched from the shadows and ripped its chainsaw at a group of teens next to me. They screamed and ran as more demented *Hell's Harvest* characters chased after them.

I was officially in over my head, all because a medium-ugly, mediocre man had convinced me to "live a little."

So I did what many brave people have done before when regretting the choices they've made: I bought a beer the size of my forearm.

Ok we're out. Did you get in or not? I'm trying to call.

I texted Chad back as the bartender ran my credit card and told him I was getting a beer by the *Water World* ride. He told me to hurry because they were going to the lower level. Even over text, I wasn't liking his tone. The bartender handed me my beer, which I grasped with two hands. I didn't know where the lower level was, but Chad had insisted the park was small. Universal Studios is small in comparison to say, the city of Los Angeles, but it's four hundred fucking acres. That's more than ninety Grand Central Stations.

My phone rang. I tried to palm my beer like a basketball so I could answer with the other hand.

"Hey!" I chirped.

Chad was already barking at me. "I can't believe you're making everyone wait while you get beer. We're literally waiting on you."

"Chad, I don't know where I am!"

I explained that the ride wasn't on the map and that no one knew where it was, but he could find *me* by *Water World*.

"I don't know where the *Water World* ride is, Rory."

He seemed to be unintentionally validating my point.

"Walk to the center of the park, look for the fire. We're near that."

His behavior was starting to feel like he'd taken the horror theme to heart, and I was not loving it. There I was, standing at the precipice of all my fears, alone, getting yelled at by my non-boyfriend. Great, another monster I'd have to deal with: my situationship.

I had to make it through another "scare zone" by myself, but I was so focused on hustling that I barely blinked when a bunch of creepy Frankensteins surrounded me. I stopped and looked them dead in the eyes as if to say, *I am having a night. Try me bitch*, and they swiftly moved on to another group.

Noice.

I'd managed to conquer my fear of the roaming ghouls, and just in time. Standing under a metal arch that rhythmically shot out flames was Chad and four friends I did not know.

I did my best to seem easy-breezy and "chill." No one was friendly, but they were comedy writers, so that was to be expected. The great myths about professionally funny people are that they are, one, funny in real life, and two, simply fun to be around. We only had time for one haunted house before the comedy kids had to leave, and I'll give you one guess as to where we went next . . .

Fucking *Water World*. That's right. We walked *back* to where I had *just* been. At this point, I wasn't having fun, which had very little to do with the park. I gulped down my beer and tried to hide my growing panic as we cruised through the express line. I gave out an unsolicited disclaimer to the group.

"Sorry in advance if I lose my shit."

"You'll be fine," Chad's pal said. "It's really not that bad."

I chuckled nervously, and I swear I saw Chad roll his eyes.

I went in last so as not to disrupt the group, which was Chad's idea—*of course*. The minute we stepped into the entrance, smoke billowed out from every angle, making it impossible to see. I'd barely blinked before everyone took off and I found myself completely alone. Before me, a door-lined hallway seemed to go on forever. I took a deep breath and braced myself for the worst. I peered down the dark corridor, paralyzed by the paradox of choices. Which door should I open? What would be on the other side? And what if I opened the wrong one? As I stood there frozen, two teen girls whizzed past me, squealing with glee. It was at that moment I realized I was living in a metaphor for my love life as a whole.

I walked into new relationships the way most people walked into haunted houses: eager, excited, and a little apprehensive about what they might encounter. Not knowing what's around the next corner can be thrilling, but most of the time, dating results in a series of unexpected scares, cortisol spikes, and a cocktail of emotions. Like most singles, I was fumbling in the dark trying to find the exit—*and* my happily ever after.

I reached for the handle of a nearby door, but before I could grab it, the door swung open and a bloody man lunged at me with a knife. I all but levitated across the hall into a corresponding room, just like I'd jumped into my relationship with Chad. I was running away from the pain that a year of demonic clowns had inflicted. And in the same way I felt silly being scared by an actor holding a plastic knife, I also felt embarrassed to admit that guys I'd only been on a handful of dates with had hurt me so badly. But both were true.

Long plastic sheets splattered with blood concealed my view of what appeared to be a makeshift morgue. As I bravely tried to find my bearings, I was surprised by the intensity of my emotions. I knew better! I understood that someone or something was going to jump out at me, and I'd been mentally preparing for this all day, yet the bloody man still caught me off guard.

In the eerie blue light of the fake hospital room, my eyes darted around trying to spot the next monster before it made its move. My single life had been rife with monsters too. Sure, I'd known that the dating pool was full of cheaters, fuckboys, and flat-out abusers, but that knowledge hadn't stopped me from walking into their traps. It's hard to fully participate with your guard up, just like it's impossible to walk through a haunted house with a shield obscuring your view.

I maneuvered around the bloody gurney in the center of the room, waiting for a mad scientist or an evil nurse to pounce. I steeled myself, determined not to get got. As if on cue, what I swore was a mannequin vaulted up from the metal bed, prompting my soul to leave my body then and there. I screamed so loudly, I'm pretty sure people in Vegas heard me. Being savvy to the horrors of dating hadn't prevented heartache, just like knowing I was about to be scared didn't stop me from screaming. No matter how much my head knows the facts, I'm still bummed out when my heart skips a beat.

I watched as the mannequin lay back on the gurney, resuming his position, presumably waiting for his next victim, and I hesitated. I thought about staying in this room, because at least I knew what I was dealing with. They say the devil you know is better than the one you don't, but I forced myself to walk back into the dingy hallway.

My eyes adjusted to the darkness, and my heart beat to the rhythm of the music in shower scene from *Psycho*. I inched forward. I was petrified, but I kept going. I tried to tell myself that I was brave, that it takes courage to keep walking down the same dark corridors that you've been scared in before, knowing that at any moment the bloody man with the knife might jump out again but having faith that this relationship will be different. *This time* you'll find love.

As I neared the end of the hall, a ghost dropped down from the ceiling, and its fabric grazed the top of my head. I ducked before blindly ripping around a corner.

I stumbled into what looked like the front yard of an A-frame house decorated for Halloween. I'd barely noticed the old man with a shotgun standing in the doorway when a maniacal pumpkin-like creature catapulted itself across my path. I recognized the orange and burlap figure as Sam, the demon from the *Trick or Treat* franchise. It's a movie about a suburb in Ohio that has a set of rules to protect the town from the evil that returns every Halloween. Break the rules and you die—pretty simple. I sidestepped grotesque pumpkins in a hazy cemetery, thinking about how having a set of dating rules that I could follow would be nice.

I wish someone would tell me how to find the right person or how to fall in love, but the dating etiquette of our parents' generation is long gone. Today's relationship books are largely still based on the patriarchal narrative of trapping a man or the conventional wisdom of withholding sex as a tactic. These narratives seem wildly outdated in a world where people are exchanging nudes with strangers on apps before they ever exchange last names. In fact, one could argue that our collective unattainable expectations were created by a mashup of dating-book authors, romantic-comedy writers, and the advice of people who got married before divorce was normalized.

I'd made it to the other side of the room, where I was directed toward a dark pathway lined with slatted wood walls. Suddenly, a dirty hand reached through one of the slats, grabbing at me, and I recoiled for the hundredth time.

When will it end? I thought.

I took a deep breath and trudged forward. The path split: I could go right or left.

I turned right, only to come nose to nose with a possessed bunny screaming in my face. As I let out a blood-curdling shriek, I thought about all the terrifying shit I'd already been dealt: werewolves, witches, zombies—the list went on. I was ready to escape this maze, but I had no idea where I was in relation to the exit.

I wondered where I was in the haunted house of my love life. I hoped I was near the end, but a sinking feeling said I was probably somewhere in the heart of the horror, another half of a haunted house to go. That thought alone was more spine-chilling than anything in the park. I wanted to curl up into a ball, but instead, I kept walking, knowing that the only way out was *through*.

I doubled back with a renewed sense of urgency.

I am going to get out of here.

I strode into the next room and immediately recognized it as the Freeling family's house from *Poltergeist*. Carole Anne's little blond head stared into the snowy television, reminding me of my younger self. "She'd be horrified," I said. Young Rory assumed I'd be happily married with a kid by now, but instead, here I was, criminally single. I stopped to take in the macabre details of their house, and I couldn't help but appreciate the set designer's attention to detail.

If my romantic life was, in fact, a haunted house, what had I walked into when I met Chad?

Everyone has skeletons in their closet, but not everyone is scared by them. When I'd met Chad, I was focused on fleeing the demonic clowns of the dating scene, so I ignored a lot of the haunting things about him. For instance, we'd met several times over the last year, but he always reintroduced himself, making clear he had no recollection of who I was. Despite his aloof persona, once we were dating, Chad quickly admitted that he'd wanted to ask me out for a full year, which confused me. I assumed he had been pretending not to know who I was to seem cool, but eventually I realized that Chad had been drunk.

I hadn't realized he was an alcoholic when we'd started dating, because Chad was an expert at hiding it. I connected the dots when he housed a full bottle of whiskey without catching a buzz. I flashed back to all the times Chad had gone MIA, the underwhelming impression he'd made on my friends, his financial situation, and his poor, untrained dog, and everything made a lot more sense. I was dating a functioning alcoholic.

He *seemed* like an eligible bachelor and a comedy darling, but Chad was a mess. He was broke, secretive, easy to anger, and he lived in a shithole apartment where his dog frequently pooped on the floor.

Dating Chad was like walking into a room with crown molding and decorative wallpaper and finding out that the drywall was covered in black mold. I wasn't in any immediate danger, but if I stayed too long, I'd probably get sick.

I walked out of the Freeling's kitchen into an adjoining room where I was promptly greeted by a murderous clown. I jumped back, but I didn't scream. I wouldn't say I was enjoying the experience, but I hated it less. I'd gotten used to the rhythm of the horror and had become acclimated to the steady stream of terror being thrown my way. My romantic life was no different. I'd also gotten used to clowns and bad behavior, and as a result, my threshold for bullshit had grown.

In comparison to what I'd been through, Chad didn't seem so bad. Obviously, there were things I didn't like, but they seemed safer than whatever fresh hell might be around the corner.

In my immediate case, it was another corridor. Except this time, I took one step in, the lights immediately cut out, and I was left in total darkness. I could hear the sounds of distant screams mixed with muffled footsteps, and even though only a few seconds had passed, I thought about giving up, calling out for an attendant and asking them to escort me out. Just then the lights strobed, and through the flashing haze, I saw the familiar green hue of an exit sign in the distance.

Fuck it. I thought, as I started sprinting.

I was so focused on the neon-green letters that I didn't think twice as I passed a row of coffins, and I barely even noticed the skeletons swiping at me as I cruised toward the door. Maybe this was what marriage was like, a mad dash into the comfort of the known.

Finally, I reached the threshold and sprang into the October night. No sooner had I taken my first breath of fresh air when Chad publicly chastised me for being slow.

"For someone who hates being scared, you sure took your sweet time in there."

His friends chuckled, and I flashed a half-hearted smile. I felt like the virgin in every horror movie, the one the frat boy fucks then promptly fucks over in a bid to save himself. My date had lured me here under the false pretense of being my guardian for the night, but apparently not if it inconvenienced his friends.

We lost three out of the four comedy kids, so it was just me, Chad, and Chad's boyfriend. To be fair, the guy was pleasant, I just quickly realized I was third-wheeling on *their* date. The boys decided we were going to the lower level of the park and took off for the escalators. I trailed behind.

We toured four more houses that night, and I genuinely hated all of them, but I was proud of my accomplishment.

I'd survived.

I walked out of the last house, relieved that it was over but feeling heavier than ever. The night had been illuminating in ways I never saw coming. I'd gone to Halloween Horror Nights expecting to be scared by the creatures in the park, but I left feeling like my date was the ultimate monster. Yet the most unnerving part of the night was not his behavior but how much of a consenting participant I was.

Sometimes the scariest thing is not the monsters we encounter but how we react to those monsters and what that reveals about ourselves. I was letting my fear of being alone keep me from leaving Chad. The demonic voices in my head had been telling me to settle for what I had because it might be the best that I could do, and I had started to believe them. I was tired and very ready to exit the proverbial haunted house of my love life, but unlike with Halloween Horror Nights, I couldn't flag an attendant to escort me out. I was on my own. So unlike my time in the park, I decided to stay put. At least until I could catch my breath and regroup.

I hadn't told my friends about Chad's alcoholism, and I knew I wasn't going to tell them about this night. My silence was an act of self-preservation, but it was also an avoidance of shame. You don't want everyone to know how terrible or broken your significant other is, because it ultimately reflects poorly on you. What kind of person puts up with mistreatment? How pathetic do you have to be to put the bare minimum on a pedestal? I didn't want to think about these questions, because I knew the answers would require some serious introspection, and it would be too painful.

There's comfort in having a partner. Even if that person kind of sucks, it still feels good to be chosen and to not be alone. Plus, as long as I could focus on my relationship, I wouldn't have to deal with the demonic voices in my mind. Chad's behavior seemed infinitely safer than dealing with my own baggage.

The boys were done, so it was finally time to leave the park. *Halle-fucking-lujah.*

In order to do so, we had to cross through another "scare zone." This one was in a claustrophobic tunnel, but I remained unfazed. Coincidentally, so was Chad. You'd have thought he'd be proud, or at the very least relieved, that I wasn't death-gripping his hand, but he was far too wrapped up in a conversation with his boyfriend to notice me. So I gave myself a mental pat on the back.

You can be your own cheerleader.

If only I had realized this sooner!

I'd wanted to be loved so badly that I was willing to accept it from anyone and in microscopic doses. I didn't need another boyfriend; what I needed was more self-love. If I had cherished myself more than I'd feared being alone, I never would have settled for the bullshit Chad put me through. Unfortunately I'd not yet realized that it would be hard to find the kind of adoration I sought in a lover without first feeling it for myself.

I stopped a third of the way through the tunnel to take a photo. I wanted to be able to prove that I'd been here, and my adrenaline had finally normalized enough to where my hands had stopped shaking. I whipped out my phone and fired off a few selfies with neon mutants in the background. When I pocketed my phone, Chad and his boyfriend were nowhere to be found. I spun around, looking for them, but they were gone.

Shit.

I jogged to the end of the tunnel, expecting to see them, but I saw more couples, teens, and a few parents chaperoning their kids.

I hiked up to the parking lot and found them halfway up the hill. Chad scolding me for holding them up. Enough was enough. His general disregard for me as a friend, much less as a woman he was seeing, was terrifying. I needed to break up with Chad, and if I had any self-respect, I'd do it tonight.

We broke up ten days later. And no, *he* dumped *me*. That's how much I dreaded the thought of being single.

I was sick with a fever when he called me, but I do remember him saying, "I just feel like you really want a boyfriend, not that you want *me* as a boyfriend." I bristled at the accusation, though I knew he was correct. Even in his booze-soaked haze, Chad had managed to read me.

But I was right about one thing: I was not near the end of my romantic haunted house. The party was just getting started, and I had a lot more frights headed my way.

A FINAL GIRL'S GUIDE TO NOT SETTLING

What if I told you that you only had three more months to be single? How would you spend those last three months? Would you enjoy the journey more? Would you take things less personally? Would you take a few more risks if you knew that love was coming and you were going to be okay?

Because at some point you *will* go on your last first date, you *will* kiss your last stranger, and you *will* exit this phase of your life—assuming that partnership is something you want. I know it can feel like the dating phase never ends, but it does. And one day you will miss it. That probably sounds crazy, but ask your married friends; they'll tell you they love their partners but sometimes they miss being single.

So, take a second to write out all the best parts about being single right now. I'll start:

- I don't have to share my bed with anyone, and I can sprawl out or get up to pee two-hundred times without bothering anyone else.
- The dirty dishes in the sink are mine.
- Possibility! I am open and able to go on adventures at any moment.
- I get to live my life however I want, and I don't have to compromise on anything.
- My house is a bachelorette pad, and it's decorated *exactly* as I like it.
- I can be my worst self without any judgment—think rotting in bed with dirty hair and eating takeout all day if I want to!
- I can come home at 3 a.m. and I don't have to give anyone the heads up.
- I get to kiss whomever I want.

You get the idea.

When you are feeling sad or frustrated, your list will remind you of all the freedoms and privileges this phase of your life offers. (This works for any stage of your life, FYI).

While we're making lists, I also want you to think about your standards. What are you looking for in a relationship? I am not talking about a list of things like height and hair color or how much money a person makes. I am talking about a list of values, traits, and feelings. Write it out so you can refer to it while you're getting to know someone. Personally, my list of things I need looks something like this:

- Someone who is ambitious but not at the expense of others
- Someone who is curious, kind, and considerate
- Someone I feel safe with (both together and apart)
- Someone who values my opinions
- Someone who leaves me feeling energized, not depleted
- Someone who makes me feel attractive
- Someone who makes me feel seen and appreciated
- Someone who helps me co-regulate a calm nervous system

And so forth. Periodically reference this list to make sure the person you're with aligns with your standards. For example, if you feel safe and secure when you are with someone but your fight-or-flight mode kicks in every time you're not together, well, that's a red flag that deserves to be examined. Similarly, if you know you want to feel appreciated but the person you're dating never says thank you or never gives you compliments, then ask yourself if this is something you are willing to compromise on. Take note of how many times you find yourself compromising.

Finally, I would challenge you to think about the ways in which you feel like your life is lacking. Outside of romantic love, what are you missing? Where do you feel like you could improve? There's an adage that says you should write down everything you want in a partner and then become that list—because you need to embody what it is that you are looking for. I agree with this advice to a degree. I don't believe you have to be exactly what you want in order to get what you want, nor do I believe you have to be perfect or your "best self" to find love, *but* I do think these factors help prevent settling.

If you are happy with yourself and your life—you have a great group of friends, work is stable, you're healthy, busy, and relish the nights you get to spend alone—you'll be less likely to swap that for a lukewarm date with a mediocre man. You certainly won't trade your fun night with friends for a night with a guy who ignores you at Halloween Horror Nights! Do you think I would have put up with Chad and his bullshit if I'd been self-fulfilled? No! So learn from my mistakes.

Let's use pizza as an example. (Because everyone loves pizza!)

You're hungry and you want a pizza, so you call your go-to spot and they tell you they can only give you half a pizza. You'll still have to pay full price, but you're only going to get half the pizza. What would you do? You'd probably hang up and call another pizza place—because that's crazy and you have options.

Now, imagine you're *starving*. So you call the place that you know is the fastest. They tell you the same thing: You must pay full price, but you'll only get half the pie. You might take the deal, especially if the other pizzerias are far away and you're worried about how long it will take them to deliver. Or maybe you're worried about trying a new place that could have awful pies. Dating is no different. Don't date hungry; go into it full.

TL;DR: Learn to be happy on your own; when you are, others will have a hard time convincing you to settle for less.

VAMPIRES

◆───────

When my friend Bonnie asked if she could set me up with one of her guy friends, I jumped at the opportunity. After Chad and the clowns, a friend-vetted man was a welcomed reprieve from the hell of endless swipes. I said yes and she text-connected me with a New York number. Three hours later, I was meeting up with a man named Dean for an impromptu dinner.

A quick google search let me know that Dean Winchester-Bass IV was a native New Yorker with pale freckled skin, auburn hair, and signature thick rimmed glasses. His social media was littered with photos of him and various celebrities at Lakers Games, restaurant openings, and award shows. He seemed to have a vibrant social life, and from what I could tell, Dean owned part of a clothing brand, several restaurants, and a media company, so his work life was also thriving. When he pulled up in a G Wagon, I was not surprised. I expected him to be a little douchey. I did *not* expect him to sweep me off my feet.

Ten hours later, Dean and I were watching the sun rise from his rooftop deck. We'd spent the whole night marathon-talking about everything from our hopes and dreams to our childhoods and how we'd theoretically handle raising kids someday.

"I can't believe it took this long for us to meet," Dean said.

In talking, we realized how often our paths had overlapped and that we'd matched on Raya two months prior. Turns out Dean was just as exhausted with dating in LA and eager to find the person he could start building a life with. Based on our chemistry and how effortlessly our conversation flowed, I decided Dean might be the needle in the haystack I'd been searching for.

We sat in comfortable silence, watching the Los Angeles skyline slowly fade from blue to orange. Then Dean very seriously said, "Rory, I need to tell you something." He turned to face me, and I could see that something was wrong. "I like you and I feel like I have to be honest with you."

My heart sank. "Okay?" I said, as I braced myself for the worst. "I've dated some pretty terrible women, and I've been cheated on *a lot*. So it's really hard for me to trust." Dean looked embarrassed as he admitted this.

I felt relieved. "Dean, *I've* been cheated on a lot too. My last serious ex literally had a secret girlfriend."

Dean looked shocked. "How? How could anyone cheat on you?"

My cheeks blushed. "I don't know—the same way they cheated on you?"

He grabbed my hand before turning back toward the sunrise. "I can already tell you're one of the most amazing women I've ever met."

I looked back out at the horizon, grateful Bonnie had set us up.

We spent the next hour cooking breakfast and swapping cheating stories before Dean dropped another bomb.

"Are you seeing anyone else right now?" he asked in between bites of eggs.

"No, but I'm on the apps," I said.

"I'm not seeing anyone either."

I tried to conceal my excitement by coolly asking, "Why do you ask?"

"Because I'm really attracted to you, but I can't do casual sex."

"Because of the cheating?" I asked.

"Yes, partially because of that but also"—Dean paused for a second—"because I was molested as a child, and as a result, I can only have sex in an exclusive monogamous relationship, and I'm bringing this up because I obviously like you and I can see a future with us but I have to take things slow and I wanted to be upfront about it."

"Oh my god," I said. "I'm so sorry, Dean."

"It's pretty fucked up, but I've been in therapy for years now." His voice trailed off.

I had so many questions, but I didn't want to pry, so I just nodded.

"I really want to kiss you, but I also don't want to give you the wrong impression, because like I said, I can't have sex unless it's monogamous, and we just met and I need to take things slow."

"Look, I like you too, and I'm happy to go slow, and we can just figure it out as we go along."

Dean smiled, "Okay," he said, as if we had come to a formal agreement. "We're going to give this a try, and in the meantime, we can both date other people, but we need to be radically honest about it with each other."

"Deal," I said, knowing full well that I had zero interest in dating anyone else at that moment.

Dean walked over to where I was sitting, cupped my face with both hands, and gently pulled me toward him. He kissed me in the middle of his kitchen, and I felt like the luckiest girl in the world. When he finally pulled away, Dean shook his head in amazement.

"What?" I said.

"You're the first person I've kissed since my ex, and it's been a long time."

I wasn't used to this level of candor from a man, much less one I'd just met.

"I forgot how nice it feels to like someone," he said.

Dean's transparency made me feel weirdly safe, like he would tell me anything. I kissed him again. "There, now I'm the first and second person you've kissed."

Dean smiled and my heart skipped a beat.

One sunrise, twelve hours, and several kisses later, Dean dropped me off at my apartment. I skipped up the two flights of stairs to my unit, and just as I was unlocking my door, my phone buzzed with an incoming text. It was Dean.

I already miss talking to you.

I already missed talking to him too. We texted for another hour before I finally fell asleep at 10 a.m.

I woke up a couple of hours later to several missed texts from Dean. He wanted to know what I was doing, if he could read my work, and if he could send me some articles on child molestation that might help me understand what he'd been through. I said yes, and he sent me a flurry of articles and podcasts to listen to. I spent the rest of the day feeling sick to my stomach as I read and listened to horrific stories. I felt grateful for Dean's vulnerability but heavy knowing that he'd been through something so traumatic.

That evening, Dean texted me.

I know it's last minute and that I'm probably supposed to be playing it cool, but I don't want to play games with you. I want you to come with me to this art opening tonight, so can I pick you up in an hour?

I bolted from the couch and immediately started to get ready.

As we walked around looking at art, Dean kept his hand on the small of my back. He had this ability to make me feel like I was the only person in the room, despite the busy opening. We'd only known each other for twenty-four hours, but I already felt like we'd been together for weeks.

We walked outside to the courtyard where the gallery had a small bar and a live jazz band. Dean went to grab us drinks, and I quickly texted my girls.

Having the best time, he might actually be perfect!

Then, I placed my phone face down and watched Dean make his way back to our table.

We were about halfway through our drinks when Dean finally blurted out, "Can you flip your phone over? It's one of my triggers. My ex always kept her phone face down because she was hiding things, and I feel like if we're going to be dating, we should be able to keep our phones face up."

I wasn't used to a man revealing his insecurities, so this admission felt like intimacy. It should have felt like a warning.

I flipped my phone face up before apologizing. "I'm sorry. I didn't want to be rude!"

After the opening, we went back to Dean's place. We were sitting on the couch when he turned to me and said, "Are you dating anyone else?" I laughed, but Dean was serious. "I know we're not exclusive and we're allowed to date other people, but we promised to be honest with each other and I'm not seeing anyone else."

I was stunned. "Dean, *when* could I have met someone else? I've been with you for the last twenty-four hours!"

"I know, but I just think it's a good habit for us to check in and be honest with each other."

I crawled over to where Dean was sitting and kissed him. "I'm not seeing anyone else."

From that day forward, Dean would ask if I was seeing anyone else every single time we saw each other. It became our ritual. It felt reassuring to know that even though we were trying to take things slow and we were allowed to date other people, neither one of us was—or wanted to. I had no idea this was part of a sinister power play Dean got off on.

I thought Dean was a friend-vetted knight in shining armor, so I missed the warning signs telling me he was a vampire. His vulnerability disarmed me. I saw a man who was hurt in the same ways I'd been hurt, and I felt like I could be the person who finally showed him how pure a relationship could be. Through my love and loyalty, I hoped I could heal Dean the way I wished someone would have healed me. Women had let him down in the past; I wanted to show him that love could be good and safe and consistent.

That night, Dean and I fell asleep holding hands, and for the next thirty days, we were inseparable. If we weren't together, we were texting each other. It was full-*on*, and my inner demon fully disappeared. My life and brain had no room for those demonic voices, because Dean was consuming all my time. And even though I was a little overwhelmed at times, I was also excited. I'd finally found someone whose love burned brighter than mine.

Here's the thing about vampires though: They're known for being suave and sexy, and they entice their victims with a mixture of charm and intrigue. I thought I'd met a man who finally saw the best parts of me and couldn't help but fall in love; I didn't realize that man was love bombing me. Dean roped me in with a steady stream of attention. If we weren't physically together, he was sending me funny memes, playlists, or articles he was reading, and as a result, he was always top of mind and at the top of my text messages.

Until the energy shifted.

To an outsider, we probably shifted into what would be considered "normal," but when you go from a hundred miles an hour to twenty-five, it feels like slamming on the breaks. Without any warning, Dean stopped love bombing me. He stopped initiating plans, stopped texting 24/7, and started taking longer to respond. He seemed to have lost interest overnight, and I noticed the difference *immediately*. And so did the demonic voices in my head.

Count your days, Rory.
See, we knew it was too good to be true!
You probably fucked it up again.
Looks like he finally realized he could do better.

Fear-based thoughts ripped through my mind like a tornado ripping through Kansas. You could've called me *Twister* 'cause I was spiraling. I tried to tell myself to stay calm and that things would go back to normal.

A week later and it was a totally unfamiliar relationship. I mentally retraced every step of the last few weeks, looking for anything that could help me figure out why Dean was suddenly retreating.

What'd I miss?

My constant rumination ignited a panic inside me that I was never able to shake. I was so distracted by the shift in our dynamic that I never felt Dean's fangs sinking into the side of my neck. I was too busy worrying if "we were okay" to notice that I'd been bitten by a vampire.

Finally, I just asked. "Is everything okay? You seem a little distant."

Dean reacted like I was crazy. "Distant? I saw you three nights ago, Ror." He had a point, but I was also used to spending *every* night at his house.

"No, I know. I just feel like there's been a shift. I don't hear from you as much, and I want to make sure we're okay."

"I have to work, Rory. I can't just text you all day every day. I mean I'd love to, but that won't pay the bills."

I was confused. We'd been texting all day, every day for the last month, so why was it a problem *now*?

I didn't get to ask this, because Dean quickly flipped the conversation back on me. "Is there something that *you* need to tell *me*? Because if I'm not enough for you, please let me know now so I can protect my heart."

"What?!" I responded, "No! That's not at all what I'm saying."

"Well, are you seeing anyone else right now?" Dean asked with suspicion in his voice.

"No! Are you?"

"Of course I'm not, Rory, but I also thought that we were good. I'm not the one who's unhappy."

I could feel my heart pumping and my palms sweating. I just wanted us to go back to how things were, so I blurted out, "I'm sorry—we're good. I just miss you."

Dean pulled me closer. "Aww, well that's cute." He kissed me on the forehead, transporting me back to the euphoria I'd felt after our first kiss. I promised myself then and there that I was going to do everything I could to get us back to how things were in the beginning.

So when Dean started taking hours to respond to my texts, I told myself not to freak out.

Play it cool, Rory. Don't drive him away.

But playing it cool consumed all my mental energy. I quickly found myself walking on eggshells and celebrating the bare minimum—anything to maintain the status quo. Gone were the days of memes and playlists. Instead, an entire day could go by before Dean would return my text, and I would say nothing. But on the inside I was a mess.

The demonic voices set up shop in the forefront of my mind, and their torment was relentless.

He probably realized you're not as special as he thought you were.

You have been looking a little less attractive lately.

He knows you're not on his level.

You should probably hit the gym.

Maybe if you weren't so demanding, guys wouldn't leave you.

The constant negging was exhausting, but so was the fear of losing Dean. And just when I felt like I couldn't do it anymore, Dean would do a 180 and remind me of the romantic man I'd first met. He'd dazzle me with a thoughtful date or a flurry of texts, and I would remember everything I loved about him. I was in a state of constant whiplash, dating both Dr. Jekyll and Mr. Hyde.

A few weeks later, I was at Dean's place to watch a movie, and I accidentally put my phone face down. I was used to turning my phone over when I was at dinner or with friends and I had to make a conscious effort to break this habit with Dean. When he saw my phone, Dean lost it.

I tried to explain that I'd set it face down on accident, but Dean was already grilling me about who I was texting and what I was hiding.

"I swear on my life, it was an accident, Dean!" I held up my phone to prove that I didn't have any notifications.

"Who are you texting?"

"No one!"

"You told me you weren't seeing anyone else, Rory, and I trusted you."

"I swear on my life, I'm not dating or even talking to anyone else. In fact, I'll delete my apps right now if you want."

"No! I'm not having you hang that over my head."

"Here, check the texts." I handed him my phone. "I promise I put it down on accident."

Dean reached for my phone but stopped himself before taking it from me.

He started to crumble. "I'm sorry, Rory. I trust you."

As cortisol pumped through my veins, Dean continued to backtrack. "I'm just so messed up from the girls before you, but it's not right for me to take it out on you." He pulled me closer, and for a moment I thought everything was going to be okay.

Dean was extra loving for the rest of the night.

A couple days later, Dean had gone back to ignoring me and I had gone back to spinning out. In my quest to make sense of what was happening, I tracked Dean's behavior on social media, which only added to my anxieties. I walked around feeling nauseous, terrified that Dean was looking for someone else. On one fateful afternoon, I remembered we had matched on Raya. I opened the app, and my heart sank: Dean had updated his profile. I was beside myself.

I took the next few days to build up the courage to ask him.

The next time we were hanging out, Dean inevitably asked me if I was seeing anyone, and I said, "No, but I did notice you updated your Raya." I tried to sound playful and nonconfrontational, but Dean wasn't having it.

"Oh so you're allowed to be on the apps but *I'm* not?"

"That's not what I meant."

"Well, it seems like a weird double standard."

I took a deep breath. "I just don't know why you'd update your profile unless you were actively trying to meet someone else."

Dean cocked his head. "What are you insinuating?"

"Nothing," I said. "It just feels like you might be seeing other people, or that you want to."

Dean's eyes widened. "I was molested!" he screeched. "How dare you insinuate something like that when you know that I can only do monogamy!"

I wanted to respond, but I was frozen.

Shame and regret filled me to the point of tears. "I'm sorry," I said. I didn't understand why Dean was still using Raya, but I felt bad for questioning his trauma. He continued to yell at me about being molested as a child, and I continued to apologize.

Moving forward, Dean would update his Raya photos every couple of days, but I never mentioned it. I didn't understand why he was doing this, but I trusted he wasn't able to be with more than one person at a time. After all, this was why we had not had sex yet.

The longer we dated, the deeper Dean sank his fangs into my psyche and the more he sucked out of me. I was getting smaller and more insecure by the day. I'd already lost my backbone, and I was starting to lose my sense of reality. My instincts told me Dean was seeing other people, but Dean made me doubt myself. The cumulative effect was eroding my self-trust. I no longer knew what to believe, and the demonic voices in my head were having a field day.

I lived in a constant state of fight or flight until Dean decided it was time to take things to the next level.

One day he said he was ready to have sex. Obviously this was a big deal because of his story, and the reassurance that we were going to be exclusive calmed my nerves. I looked back at all the times I'd panicked and told myself I really needed to chill out and work on my "issues," as if having sex somehow proved that Dean loved me, and that my instincts were nothing more than insecurities. I was prepared for sex to change our relationship; I just didn't realize it would change it for the worse.

A week later, Bonnie called me with "some bad news." Minutes later, I was staring at time-stamped text messages between Dean and a girl named Haley. He was asking her out on a date, and according to Bonnie, they'd been flirting for a while now. Based on the time stamps, the texts had been sent from my bedroom, approximately twenty minutes before Dean and I'd had sex. I had literally been sitting next to him, on my bed, when he'd asked Haley out on a date, and he proceeded to have unprotected "monogamous" sex with me immediately after.

I felt myself getting dizzy.

How is this real?

I headed to his house, determined to get answers, but somehow, I spent most of the night apologizing. Dean redirected the conversation to be about my disrespectful tone, my "insane" lack of trust, my poor communication skills, and my immaturity. "I just don't think you're ready for a *real* relationship, Rory," and, "If I'm too broken, and this is too much for you, then go ahead and bail" were some of the choice accusations he used against me—a master class in gaslighting and manipulation.

Eventually we made up around 3 a.m.

I left Dean's house under the impression that "we" were going to work on "our" issues, but I never heard from him again. He waited until he had regained the higher ground, until he'd gotten me back to a place where *I* wanted to make things work, and then he cut me off cold turkey. Textbook narcissist.

In the days after, I was confused and hurt by his disappearance. *I thought we were going to work on things?*

I still couldn't see that Dean was a vampire, because hope and delusion clouded my vision. I was eager for love, and Dean was thirsty for blood. So, like any other vampire, once he'd sucked me dry, Dean cast me aside and moved on to his next victim. One week later, he was posting photos of another blond to his Instagram stories.

This triggered an overwhelming feeling of unworthiness in me. After Jack left me, I had a deep-seated fear that I was replaceable, and here I was, *yet again*, being replaced.

The aftermath of our breakup was ugly. My mental health was at the lowest it had ever been, which, in the context of this book, tells you a lot. Dean had weaponized my empathy and used it to strip me of my self-worth in a matter of months. As a result, insane thoughts flooded my mind 24/7.

Maybe if you didn't have such trust issues, guys wouldn't leave you.

Maybe you're just bad in bed and that's why Dean ghosted.
You're going to die alone!

The worst part was the self-doubt. Dean's constant gaslighting left me feeling unsure of the facts and questioning my own memories.

What if he wasn't asking Haley out?
Maybe you missed the context of those messages?
Were you too hard on him?

I was consumed with self-blame and self-loathing. Even in the aftermath, I felt like I was the one at fault. The way I saw it, Dean was a catch and *I* had fumbled the bag. I immediately got into therapy and started going twice a week. My therapist did her best to help put me back together, but it would take more than therapy.

◆ ◆ ◆

FOUR MONTHS LATER...

I decided it was time to get my things from Dean's house. I'd been in therapy long enough to know that Dean was unhealthy—and unhealthy for me—but not long enough that I didn't care about his approval. The memories of his love bombing still held me hostage, and I fantasized about him begging for us to get back together. On an intellectual level, I knew this was pathetic, but it didn't stop my ego from dreaming about it. Once you're bitten by a vampire, it's very hard to return to your mortal self. So, imagine my shock when Dean apologized.

For thirty minutes, Dean told me everything I wanted to hear—namely that I was the only woman he wanted to be with. He kissed me, and for a moment, I thought I would cave, but when he started to take off my shirt, I heard my therapist's voice in my head. I told Dean that if he wanted another chance, we needed to start over as friends and rebuild trust from there. He agreed, but when I made a few attempts to set up platonic hangs, Dean was never free.

He was rejecting me all over again, but this time I'd built a backbone. This time I refused to fall back into the warm embrace of codependency and love bombing, and every day that passed and I held firm to my boundaries, I grew a little stronger. I'd love to tell you that eventually I healed and that Dean became a distant memory, but that's not what happened. It wasn't until I learned the truth, that I finally felt Dean's fangs leave my body.

I was on set for a friend's movie when I hit it off with one of the makeup artists. We got to talking about terrible exes, and she mentioned Dean.

"Let's just say, I could've bought a car with the therapy bills I've spent on that man," I quipped.

She laughed. "Tell me about it. We broke up six months ago, and I *still* shudder at the thought of dating." She must have seen the color drain from my face because she asked me if I was okay.

"I was with him six months ago," I said. Then I watched as the color drained from her face.

Turns out, Dean had been having unprotected sex with this makeup artist for half of our "relationship". In fact, when we pulled out our phones to compare timelines, some days we would miss each other by less than an hour. Everything I knew about Dean had been a lie.

I would come to meet tens of women with their own stories of manipulation, abuse, and assault from Dean. I would learn that he was, in fact, not molested and that the stories Dean told me about all the cheating *were* true—except that he was the perpetrator, not the victim.

It's no accident that vampires can't be in the sun—evil grows in the dark. And just like light reveals what cannot be seen at night, once I knew the truth about Dean, I could finally see him for what he was: a vampire. He was a narcissistic predator, and I had been his prey. Remember our ritual, where we would ask each other about seeing other people? Dean had been lying to my face for months.

He hadn't made me wait to have sex because of his fragility; he'd made me wait because it was a game to him. He got off on being a puppet master. Every rule he established with me—like keeping my phone face up—was a string he could pull. Dean was never trying to create an honest relationship; he was training me—to control me. And it worked.

My body had been trying to warn me. My anxiety and the constant state of fight or flight that I found myself in was my nervous system's way of telling me that Dean wasn't safe. Unfortunately my mind was so convinced that he *was* safe that I learned to ignore my intuition. I learned to stop trusting myself. And the loss of self-trust erodes your confidence.

Dean systematically broke me down by weaponizing my empathy and my history with cheating. His constant gaslighting had me believing that my instincts were old insecurities and baggage that I needed to address. I was accurately picking up on his lies and manipulations and it was creating turmoil for my nervous system, but Dean was able to convince me that *I* was the problem. It never occurred to me that he might be lying about being molested.

Why would someone lie about this?

Instead, I thought that I was the broken one and I needed to be fixed. I went from being an easygoing, confident woman with self-respect to an unregulated mess, desperate for crumbs; but that's what vampire's do: They drain the life out of you. Unlike what we see in film and TV, romantic vampires don't drink blood or rise from the dead; instead they feed off your empathy and bleed you of your self-worth. They're emotional terrorists, also known as psychological abusers, pathological lovers, or narcissists.

The havoc that an emotionally abusive relationship wreaks on your life is hard to explain to people who haven't experienced it. Because I don't have physical scars, it's easier to dismiss the negative impact Dean had on my life, but my mental health was in shreds. Even now, years later, I'll find myself questioning if the butterflies in my stomach are my instincts or my insecurities.

If I'm being honest, I didn't want to share this story. It's humiliating. I should have been able to see Dean for the monster he was—because I was smart and savvy and not the type of person who falls prey to manipulations. I was raised to be the kind of woman who was strong enough to walk away when mistreated, rather than doubling down on being a more palatable version of myself. So what happened?

I think the trauma of dating finally caught up with me. Years of rejections, micro-hurts, and betrayals chipped away at my once solid foundation. Or maybe Dean was just *that* good at getting what he wanted. He was a narcissist who had perfected his tactics. Either way, it's hard to admit that I was once the type of person who fell for Dean Winchester-Bass IV.

But here's the thing—no one starts off thinking they're dating a vampire; you start off thinking you've met the one. Like the frog in boiling water, you don't notice the temperature of the water slowly increasing until it's too late. One second you're chilling on a lily pad, then you decide to take a refreshing dip and before you know it you're being boiled alive. That's what happened to me.

Ultimately, I decided to share my story because shame is a prison. While I'm embarrassed to admit how small I felt and how quickly I betrayed myself for a man, I refuse to let that be the reason I stay silent. If you've been through this level of trauma, I want you to know that you're not alone. At the height of professional success, when my life felt better than ever, a pathological partner brought me to my knees—because *it can happen to anyone.*

I'm also sharing this for the readers who haven't experienced this kind of relationship. I could have just listed the warning signs of narcissism and emotional abuse, but it's another thing to see those red flags in context. If you're like me, it's easier to remember lessons when they are attached to stories. Now that you know what happened with Dean, I want to share some of the pitfalls I wish I'd known sooner.

A FINAL GIRL'S GUIDE TO VAMPIRES

LOVE BOMBING

Dean and I jumped in with both feet, and it went from zero to one hundred almost instantly. My friends, this is not normal. You know what else isn't normal? Trauma-dumping on strangers. Oversharing on the first date might feel like radical honesty or vulnerability—and sometimes it is—but oftentimes it's trauma-bonding. Relationships should be able to withstand space. If the person you are with needs to be connected nonstop, that's a red flag.

We all want to believe that someone could meet you and be hopelessly in love. We all want to believe that someone can see us for who we *really* are and fall deeply in love. (And I do believe that happens!) However, trust is not something that can be built overnight, and love is built on trust. In other words, love takes time. If you feel like someone is "too good to be true," they honestly might be. Mirroring is a common tactic narcissists use that can make you feel like this person was meant for you. You think you're falling in love with your soulmate, but really you are falling in love with the best parts of yourself mirrored back to you.

Remember, intensity does not equal depth. Would you give a new friend the keys to your home after two weeks? Then maybe don't give someone the keys to your heart that fast either.

Love bombing is a key part of the cycle of abuse; it's a way to establish connection and trust in a short period. This trust becomes the foundation of coercive control.

Other things to be wary of:
- Do they overwhelm you with compliments?
- Do they monopolize your time?
- Does the intensity feel unlike anything else you've experienced?
- Do they constantly stay top of mind by giving you homework or things to do that make you think about them (e.g., listening to playlists or reading books they've recommended)?
- Do they make declarative statements about being "soulmates" or that you guys are "meant to be"?
- Do they dislike boundaries?

These are all warning signs.

DEVALUING

At some point, you'll experience an energy shift. It might start slow. It might be abrupt. But once the pathological partner feels like they've established control, they will start the manipulation process. This can happen weeks or months into a relationship, depending on how fast the victim falls for the love bombing.

My first indications of devaluing were the abrupt shift in communication and the sudden lack of effort on Dean's part. If I had known better, I would have jumped ship, but I didn't. As these behaviors intensified, I experienced gaslighting, lying, jealousy and control.

"The shift" can look different for everyone. Some examples of narcissistic behavior include withholding (aka pulling back), criticism, controlling, gaslighting, stonewalling, lashing out, or passive aggression. Your partner might pick apart your appearance under the guise of "wanting to help you," or they may tell you that you need to be a certain way for them to be attracted to you. They might give you the silent treatment (aka stonewalling) to punish and retrain you to act according to their liking, or they may decide that you can no longer talk to certain people, wear certain clothes, or do certain things because your behavior makes them uncomfortable. They might demand the passwords to your devices or that you share locations. All these actions will feel at odds with the love you were used to receiving. Many of these actions are often framed as something that's "best for you" or because they care about you.

The result of these actions will leave the narcissist's partner feeling anxious, isolated, and confused. Suddenly you'll need to follow a whole new set of rules to avoid conflicts and keep your partner satisfied. Keeping the peace becomes a full-time job that's hard on one's nervous system.

If you catch your narcissistic partner in a lie or bring up a grievance, they will rarely apologize and almost never take accountability. Instead they will try to flip the blame to you or gaslight you into thinking you're crazy. For example, I went to confront Dean about his messages to Haley, and he turned the conversation into an attack on my tone. He also positioned me as the person who wasn't strong enough to handle someone like him and that I could quit if I wanted to, but at no point did he address his own actions. For months he used the cover of "molestation" to gaslight me when my instincts were telling me that something was wrong.

DARVO is an acronym for deny, attack, reverse, victim, and offender. Many narcissists use this defense pattern when someone calls them out on their manipulations. When I tried to ask Dean about his Raya profile, he denied any wrongdoing, attacked me for being on the app, and then made me the villain for even assuming that something shady was happening. I was left apologizing, despite the fact that I never even got an explanation as to why Dean was active on Raya.

This process makes a sane person feel crazy. It starts to erode your sense of what is real, and this is why many people refer to this stage as the "devaluing phase."

Ironically, the person who often saves you from this feeling of anguish is the same person who inflicted it in the first place: the narcissist. Just when they feel like you might be pulling away, they revert to love bombing and hook you right back in. The cycle repeats.

DISCARDING

The last step in the narcissistic cycle is discarding. Narcissists use people, and when they are done, they get rid of those people like trash. It's swift and cold and damaging to the person being discarded. Whether you've been in a two-week relationship or a twenty-year marriage, once the narcissist is done with you, they emotionally detach.

This rejection can be traumatic for the victim because narcissists make you dependent on them; losing them can feel like a loss of self. The narcissist's callousness can make you believe the relationship meant nothing, further perpetuating the idea that you never really mattered.

When Dean left me and immediately moved on, I internalized it as a reflection of my worth and it made the "breakup" even harder. I had become too hard to control and/or Dean had moved on to someone else who would fuel his ego, and once he made up his mind, I was nothing more than a footnote in his biography.

As much as this experience might hurt in the short run, the discarding is a blessing giving you the opportunity to get out and to heal.

POWER IMBALANCE

Emotionally abusive relationships have a power dynamic. It can take many shapes—such as a parent abusing a child or a boss abusing an employee—or it might be a relationship where one person is physically or financially dependent on the other. Regardless of whether a relationship starts out with the power dynamic, the longer someone stays in an emotionally abusive relationship, the greater the power imbalance becomes. The person who is desperate for love does not hold the power, and the longer you endure a narcissist's manipulations, the more you will depend on their love as a reprieve.

Dean seemed like this very successful, well-connected man in Los Angeles. He appeared powerful and would often tell stories where he got revenge against people who had wronged him. I was afraid to anger him out of fear of retaliation, and fear that he could have me blacklisted in the entertainment industry. In my case, the power imbalance was imagined; I thought Dean was powerful, and I was afraid of potential consequences. I also cared about him, and whenever you love someone more than they love you, there's a power imbalance. Time would eventually show me that Dean was not nearly as beloved by the industry as he had led me to believe.

I'd like to reiterate, I am not an expert on this topic; I'm a survivor who wants to share what I learned. For those of you who might be thinking, *I think I'm in an abusive relationship. What do I do?* I would encourage you to seek out credentialed therapists or people who specialize in psychological abuse, trauma bonds, narcissism, or pathological relationships.

It's never too late to leave.

The goal is to put distance between you and your abuser so you can begin to reclaim your sense of self. A narcissist gets off on your reaction, so staying calm is one of your greatest assets. You can try a technique called "gray rocking," where you make your responses unrewarding, which in turn makes you an undesirable target so that the narcissist moves on—think short unemotional answers with the goal of disengaging. If this resonates with you, I again encourage you to dive deeper into these topics, as my advice is general and broad, and everyone's situations are different.

TL;DR:
-Abusers are good at this.
-The traits that make you a good person also make you a target.
-Trust your gut the first time and bail.
-Trust the opinions of your close friends/inner circle, as they only want the best for you.
-Boundaries are your best friend.
-Abusive relationships can happen to anyone, including you, so do your best not to judge.
-In the same way that vampires can smell out victims, narcissists are also great at sniffing out empaths. If you've found yourself on the wrong end of a narcissist, keep your self-compassion high! Resist self-blame!
-As long as there have been vampires, there have been vampire slayers—and you can absolutely be a slayer.

FLYING MONKEYS

I would be remiss not to at least mention flying monkeys.

When Dean and I broke up, Bonnie texted me.

He's so awful. I think he's showing his true colors. He's a bad sick guy. I'm very surprised.

And.

I think Dean is a bad guy that doesn't have feelings for anyone but himself. There's probably ten Haleys. I think he's a bad guy.

You might think that with texts like this, Bonnie had taken a step back from Dean, but you'd be wrong. Instead she doubled down. She went to work at one of his clothing companies, continued to supply him with women, and often posted about him on social media, talking about what a great guy he was. Bonnie was a flying monkey, so in hindsight all of this makes sense, but at the time, her behavior was confusing and hurtful.

Madeline Albright once said, "There is a special place in hell for women who don't help other women," and if that's true, then female flying monkeys belong in hell's basement. The term "flying monkey" originates from the *Wizard of Oz* and refers to the winged monkeys under the spell of the Wicked Witch of the West. These monkeys did her bidding in the same way that narcissists and abusers have people who help them do theirs. A famous example would be Ghislaine Maxwell helping Jeffery Epstein, and a way less extreme (and personal) example would be Bonnie helping Dean.

Identifying a flying monkey is hard if you don't know that you're interacting with a pathological person, so give yourself grace if you only realize it after the fact. However, if you've identified a narcissist in your life, then look for their flying monkeys. Once you believe you've encountered one, your best bet is to cut them out of your life, distance yourself as much as possible, and be extremely careful about what you say or share. Do not try to figure them out or reason with them; focus on extricating yourself and healing. Remember that whatever you say to a flying monkey can and will be used against you by the narcissist. Less is best!

Flying monkeys can be divided into two categories: benevolent and malevolent. Benevolent flying monkeys only see the sparkly love-bombing version of the narcissist and are unwittingly manipulated into believing the narcissist and their lies. Generally, these are people pleasers with poor boundaries who often view themselves as peacemakers, rescuers, or saviors. They derive validation from helping the narcissist in times of need, and although benevolent flying monkeys can still inflict harm, their actions are largely unintentional or uninformed.

On the opposite end of the spectrum, a malevolent flying money is someone who derives pleasure in hurting people. This is because they also fall somewhere on the narcissism spectrum. Think of malevolent flying monkeys as the gatekeepers to capital N narcissists. They know about the manipulation that's occurring, and they're willing enablers or participants because it benefits them in some way. Malevolent flying monkeys attain a sense of power and belonging in their roles as foot soldiers.

Ultimately they know what they are doing, but they've found a way to justify their behavior.

It's important to note that flying monkeys aren't limited to messing with your romantic relationship dynamics, nor are they inherently female.

I'll never really know why Bonnie did what she did, but I imagine she loved being the token woman in Dean's life. Dean whipped through girlfriends the way your ADHD friend rips through music when controlling the aux. Bonnie got to be the constant female in Dean's life, and that probably felt great. Again, this is just my best guess.

What I can definitively say is there's a niche type of horror that comes from realizing your friend (flying monkey or otherwise) has betrayed you because of a man. I thought I was a good judge of character, especially when it came to friends, but the one-two punch of Bonnie and Dean really knocked me off my equilibrium. After the fallout, I had trouble trusting not just other people but also myself. This betrayal added to my self-doubt and kept me second-guessing my own instincts.

The only silver lining in realizing Bonnie was a flying monkey was that I removed her from my life. Not everyone will be in a position to extricate themselves from toxic people, but if you can, it is so, so worth it. Cultivating a safe group of girlfriends has been one of the greatest accomplishments of my life and one of my best assets as a final girl. You might not always be able to protect yourself from a vampire or a flying monkey, but at least you can control how you recover from their mistreatment.

Speaking of recovery . . .

DARK NIGHT OF THE SOUL

In most movies, about two-thirds of the way through, the lead character inevitably hits rock bottom and loses everything. This is the moment when, despite her main-character status, the audience thinks the final girl might not survive after all. Screenwriters know it as "The Dark Night of the Soul," which according to Blake Synder, comes right after the "All Is Lost" moment.[14]

And it's not just in movies. Every one of us will have a dark night of the soul montage in the movie of our lives (and some of us more than once). These are the points when you're at your lowest, when you're forced to dig deep, reinvent yourself, and rise like a phoenix. The aftermath of Dean was my dark night of the soul.

On the romantic front, I was crashing out. I tried to revert to my old ways: nursing my wounds for fifteen minutes, slapping on a couple of Band-Aids, and diving back into the dating pool. Except this time, I was traumatized.

I wanted to trust the men I was dating, but I didn't. I couldn't. I was too scared of repeating the mistakes I'd made with Dean, so I became hypervigilant. I monitored my dates' so-

---

14   Blake Snyder, Save the Cat!: The Last Book on Screenwriting You'll Ever Need (Michael Wiese Productions, 2005).

cial media habits, freaked out if they didn't text back fast enough, and routinely checked their apartments for other signs of female life. Searching for long hairs that don't belong to you or checking bathroom trash cans for extra condom wrappers isn't normal. The little demon in my mind was working overtime!

I craved intimacy, but the demonic voices had me convinced that rejection was always right around the corner and that every guy I met was a liar. I was so anxiously attached that even when I met great guys, the relationship would end because I needed a level of reassurance that wasn't healthy or sustainable in the early stages of dating.

Curtis, a sweet video game designer I dated, once waited in the rain so he could walk me from my Uber to the restaurant under his umbrella. But no matter how great he was, I couldn't trust it. The voices in my head would taunt me.

Give it time. He's probably good at hiding his true colors. Remember, you're a bad judge of character!

We were together for about two or three months when I called to ask him why he'd followed a pretty redhead on Instagram. I think back on that phone call and cringe. It had to be hard to date me; I was with myself all the time and, boy, was it draining.

I've often thought about the ripple effect of Dean's actions and how the men I dated after had to pay for his sins. If you don't heal your wounds, you'll end up bleeding on people who didn't cut you. At this point I was bleeding all over the place, and I needed medical intervention. Unfortunately my love life wasn't the only facet of my existence that required medical attention.

My physical health was starting to nosedive. Being in fight or flight for days on end had taken a toll on my body. Suddenly I was sleeping fourteen hours a night and still waking up tired. I was suffering from migraine attacks, acne, random bouts of nausea, and debilitating fatigue. I went to multiple doctors, but no one seemed to know what was wrong with me, and as time went on, my symptoms got worse. My labs said I was the picture of perfect health, but I knew better. *Something was wrong.*

Doctors told me I was probably depressed, but I wasn't unhappy. Sure, I had romantic insecurities and inner-demon issues, but outside of my love life, I was thriving. I was making new friends, walking red carpets, and traveling. Aside from my health, I was genuinely thrilled about the direction of my life, so depression didn't make sense.

Without answers, my health got worse. I would walk into rooms and not remember why I was there. I would look at photos of my friends but couldn't remember their names. My brain fog was so bad, I could hardly write more than a few sentences. I had to miss birthdays and turn down work opportunities because I physically couldn't handle being a person for more than a couple hours at a time.

I wasn't even thirty-five and I felt like I was staring down the barrel of a gun. I could feel my life slipping away.

For inquiring minds, I was first misdiagnosed with Lyme disease and then re-diagnosed with myalgic encephalomyelitis/chronic fatigue syndrome (ME/CFS)—which has a 5% chance of a full recovery.[15] The hellish journey of reclaiming my health is a book in itself, but all you need to know is that slowly but surely I got better—not overnight, but gradually, one day at a time.

There, in the trenches of my lowest hours, I really learned what I was made of. Clawing myself out of rock bottom reminded me that I'm a resilient badass who can overcome the impossible if I set my mind to it. Through this process, I was forced to reconnect with my body, which helped me tap back into my intuition. I knew something was off, and I was right—and by

---

15   Luis Nacul et al., "How Myalgic Encephalomyelitis/Chronic Fatigue Syndrome (ME/CFS) Progresses: The Natural History of ME/CFS," *Frontiers in Neurology* 11 (August 11, 2020), https://doi.org/10.3389/fneur.2020.00826.

showing up for myself day after day, I built back my self-trust. And eventually, I evolved into my next iteration.

That's the thing about the dark night of the soul: It's a catalyst for growth. Ask any writer and they will tell you that your main character needs to bottom out so she can learn the lessons that will prepare her and propel her into Act 3.

And so did I.

SPELLS

♦

I think you've lost the plot.

This was the thought that ran through my mind as I surveyed pages of text messages between me and the man I was newly dating. The energy had recently shifted, which prompted me to do a forensic audit of our communication patterns to try and figure out if my anxiety was a result of my intuition or old baggage resurfacing.

Like clockwork, the demonic voice shot to the front of my brain where it could not be ignored:

Here we go again, bitch. Another man you've driven away.

I'd taken a break from dating, so I hadn't spiraled in a while, but old habits die hard. After all, I was the Simone Biles of flipping out, so a few months away from the gym wasn't going to stop me from sticking the landing. I could feel my nervous system ramping up like a car turning over a few times before the engine finally fires.

If reading this makes you think, *Not again*, I need you to know you are not alone. I, too, was over my bullshit. Do you have any idea how annoying it is to live with an interactive comment section in your brain 24/7? My inner voice's trolling was ten times worse than any faceless avatar I'd come across online.

But then something unexpected happened. A second voice emerged.

I don't want to live like this anymore!

Said a small but mighty voice from a corner of my mind.

I stopped my forensic audit. The voice was right: I *didn't* want to live like this anymore. Call it my guardian angel, my higher power, my last shred of dignity, or my true self, but the new voice was tired of the abuse.

But before I could fully process what was happening, my inner demon fired back.

Well, then you should have gotten serious about dating sooner because beggars can't be choosers!

The little demon that had sprung from my breakup with Jack had morphed into something so demonic I was pretty sure that Satan himself was living inside me, and I wanted it to stop.

The new voice offered another thought.

Okay, so then I won't beg.

The demon all but screamed back.

But all of the good guys are taken! You're gonna die alone and everyone will pity you for being sad, lonely, and unlovable.

The dueling voices went back and forth for a couple of minutes before I realized that I'd really lost the plot. If anyone in my life ever spoke to me the way the demonic voice in my head spoke to me, I would cut them out like a cancer. So why was I continuing to give this demon free rein of my mind?

Because I didn't know how to make it stop, and when I tried to ignore it, the demon just got louder.

I decided right then and there that enough was enough. If I was able to heal my body from a mystery illness that took me to my knees, then surely I could heal myself from the evil forces that had taken hold of my mind.

The goal was clear: vanquish my inner demon, but the path forward was ambiguous at best. I put on my detective hat and started to investigate. I figured I should probably focus on the basics, the three W's: what, where, and why?

What was my inner demon saying?

I took out a sheet of paper and tried to write down every terrible thought I'd had about myself in nearly a decade. It read like the greatest hits of all my insecurities. I immediately noticed I was worried about being both too much and not enough. Ironic.

Looking at everything in one place made it easier to see that many of my negative thoughts were contradictory. It also made it easier to differentiate between facts and fears—and the majority of my negative thoughts revolved around fears. Plus, the sheer volume of terrible things I'd thought about myself felt too large to be true for someone who wasn't a sociopath, and sociopaths don't make lists of their insecurities. It's funny how being honest about your fears—writing them down or saying them out loud—somehow makes them feel less powerful.

Where were these demonic thoughts coming from?

I used the piece of paper from the first exercise and went line by line, fear by fear, and traced each one back to the first time I could remember thinking or feeling that way. For example, *You're not pretty enough to get the kind of guys you want*, was one of the demonic stories I'd told myself. So I tried to think back to the first time I could remember feeling ugly around a man I'd had a crush on. My mind drifted all the way back to high school, not to a boy but to my mother. I heard the genuine concern in her voice as she worried about the weight I'd gained in boarding school and immediately remembered the shame I'd felt around my new body.

My mind jumped to my freshman year of college. My childhood crush had asked me out on a date, and I was expecting an older version of the quirky surfer I knew to pick me up in the same vintage Mustang he used to drive when we were in high school. Instead, a clean-cut finance bro picked me up in a car where the doors flipped up rather than out. I never heard from him after that date, but I remember lurking on Facebook and feeling my cheeks turn red when I saw him surrounded by girls with fake boobs, toothpick arms, and teeth whiter than flavorless chicken at the cookout. Every photo of him featured a girl who looked like she'd just walked off a photo shoot. I remember thinking, *Ohhhh, right. I don't look like* that.

I wanted to go back in time and hug the younger version of myself who felt like she wasn't pretty enough for a second date. Suddenly I didn't feel like finishing the list of demonic thoughts because, wow—not fun.

So, I tried to think about the *why*.

Why was this inner voice hell-bent on tearing me down?
I wasn't immediately sure.
I took the next few weeks to revisit the origins of all my limiting beliefs, which is not for the faint of heart. Simultaneously, I started reading self-improvement books and listening to podcasts, anything to try to educate and uplift myself. I concluded that my inner demon was the result of a confluence of things: rationalization, protection, and unruly thoughts.

Many of my limiting beliefs grew out of experiences where my brain jumped to conclusions. Let's use the example of my childhood crush. I have no idea why we never went out again, but I imagine it had more to do with the fact that we'd grown apart. I was an eighteen-year-old art school weirdo with paint stains on most of my clothes, and he was a twenty-one-year-old young professional in a fraternity. Not to mention, I didn't even have fun on our date! But in the absence of a reason, my brain had tried to piece together a story that could be used for closure. I rationalized that we never went out again because I didn't look a certain way. *Woof.* And that became the story.

Then anytime my brain sensed remotely similar circumstances to my childhood crush experience, it would fire off alarm bells to protect me from getting hurt in a similar fashion. Just as we learn not to touch the sharp end of the knife after the first time we accidentally cut ourselves, our brains try to protect us from emotional hurts. But somewhere along the line, my brain went into overdrive. Instead of warning me once, my brain replayed these warnings on a loop.

Understanding that my inner demon was once a protection mechanism that had become dysregulated helped me feel more compassionate toward the voices that had been tormenting me for years. They weren't trying to ruin me; they were trying to save me from future pain. But by constantly reminding me of all the ways in which I was lacking, the voice (actually me) was hurting me more than anyone else ever could.

Many people will trace their limiting beliefs back to early childhood memories or parental dynamics. I used an example that was romantic in nature and from later in life, but you might realize that you have a fear of speaking up because when you tried to do that as a child you were punished.

Armed with this new awareness, I needed to figure out how to unwind the anxieties plaguing my mind.

Not to be *that* girl, but I am about to quote Ghandi so bear with me:
"Your beliefs become your thoughts,
Your thoughts become your words,
Your words become your actions,

Your actions become your habits,
Your habits become your values,
Your values become your destiny."

Or, as I like to say: Words are like spells so cast them wisely.

I did not want my destiny to be a repeat of the last couple of years, so I knew I needed to change my beliefs. But to do that, I needed to start smaller. I couldn't go back and rewrite history and I couldn't change my memory of certain events, but I could tweak the words I used to speak to myself.

Perspective is everything.

At the time, my outlook on love was bleak: I felt like the dating pool was a swamp filled with bottom-feeders, I didn't trust myself to make good dating choices (as evidenced by my past), and I seemed to only ever want the guys that didn't want me back. (This wasn't true, but it was how I *felt*.)

If you have ever found yourself thinking, *No one I like ever likes me back*, or *There aren't any good men left*, then it's unreasonable to think you're going to suddenly be able to believe something like, *Everyone I like always likes me back*, and, *There are so many incredible men just waiting to meet me*. I don't care how many times you stare at yourself in the mirror; if you don't believe what you're saying, the little voice in your head is going to call bullshit.

But! You might be able to wrap your head around this little tweak in thought.

It's <u>possible</u> that one day someone I like will like me back and I just haven't met them yet or *There could be an incredible man out there—I just haven't met him yet.*

Training your mind is like training for a marathon; you don't just wake up one day and run 26.2 miles. You start with one mile, and you build from there. Every time I had a negative thought, I stopped whatever I was doing and I sat with it. I asked myself where it was coming from and why it was warning me, and then I tried to subtly redirect the thought into something positive. The key being subtly. Remember, slow and steady wins the race here.

Inevitably, this process led me to confront feelings of pain, shame, regret and hurt. I started to understand that the mean voices in my mind were the neglected cries of my younger self. I'd spent years trying to tune them out or fight with those voices, but now that I was approaching them from a place of curiosity instead of judgment, they were getting quieter. I felt sorry for my younger self, the version of me who had nursed these wounds, and I was again reminded of how resilient I am.

Once I felt like I'd retrained my brain from thinking, *You're going to die alone,* to thinking, *You probably won't die alone*, I would move the dial another inch to thinking, *It's unlikely that you'll die alone*, and so forth. I kept recalibrating toward a more positive way of thinking until I found myself genuinely excited to start dating again. I believed tons of incredible men were dying to meet me. Instead of being sad when something didn't work out with a great guy, I would use the situation as evidence.

His existence is proof that great guys are out there.

Instead of focusing on losing someone I was into, I would remind myself that the loss meant I was on the path to finding someone even better.

Again, this rewiring of my thought patterns did not happen overnight. Sometimes my healing took one step forward and two steps back, but I kept going. And then something funny started happening. Not only did life feel more peaceful but also dating got easier. Something about me seemed to be clicking because I was attracting men, both on and offline. I was meeting guys at parties who would ask for my number, and I was getting hit on while I ran errands. Suddenly the world was full of viable options.

Great guys are everywhere, and they do want to date me.

This was how I ended up dating my next boyfriend. We met up at a coffee shop and talked for hours before I had to leave for another date with another incredible guy. (I am still friends with both men!)

My boyfriend and I lived together for two years before breaking up during the pandemic. Ultimately our lifestyles and relationship goals were not compatible, and we realized we were better as friends. Walking away from a good man is difficult if you don't believe other options are out there or that you deserve the love that you desire. So I'll bring it back to spells.

How you speak to yourself determines how you live. Words are like spells that you cast every single day, which means that you get to decide whether you are using your powers for good or evil. I took several months to "magically" change my life, but I can honestly say that altering my thoughts and the way that I spoke to—and about—myself transformed my life.

A FINAL GIRL'S GUIDE TO CASTING SPELLS

How you speak to yourself will determine the quality of your life, so speak to yourself like your biggest champion and not your biggest critic.

+Start with Awareness
Take a day and try to count all the times you say or think something negative about yourself. These instances might be as obvious as *That was dumb* or as subtle as *There's no point in dating 'cause all of the good men are already taken*. Write down every single negative thought you have in a day.

Alternatively, do this when you're triggered or spiraling. This will really show you the depths of your negative self-talk!

+Call it Out

Now that you're aware of how often you speak to yourself unkindly, you need to start calling it out. Continuing to track your negative self-talk can be helpful, or you might simply want to verbally say stop. Either way, the next time you have a negative thought, find a way to stop it. Maybe you want to clap four times or do three jumping jacks. Find something physical you can do to interrupt your thought as it's happening. Sometimes I tell myself, *Rory, this thought is not helpful, it's hurtful*, and that helps me to stop my spiraling. Other times I just say "stop" out loud. I have a friend who named her inner thoughts "Kevin." When she catches herself in a negative loop, she will say, "Kevin this is really unkind behavior; you've got to knock it off." Try some of these and figure out what works for you.

+Repattern the Thoughts

Someone told me you need to think seven positive thoughts to offset every negative thought you have, and while I don't know if it's a fact, it's a great reminder that negativity burrows deeper and faster than positivity. This is why this step is so crucial.

Look at the list where you've been tracking all your negative thoughts. Now actively reframe each one. For example, maybe you are struggling with money and you find yourself saying things like, *I'll never be able to afford that* or *It sucks to be poor*. I'm not telling you to convince yourself, *I am a millionaire, and I can afford anything*. However, you could tell yourself, *I'm not able to afford that now, but I am excited about being able to afford it in the future*. When that feels comfortable, adjust the thought to *I am going to be able to afford this because I'm changing my relationship with money*.

Always err on the side of possibility and positivity—because why not? Someone might try to argue that thinking glass half-full is unrealistic. I would argue that it *is* realistic to believe that when you change your life you change your circumstances and open the door to new possibilities. Why settle for negativity and "being realistic" when life is full of change and surprise? You're always a potential "yes," a meeting, an opportunity away from your life changing. You have no idea when you will run into the person of your dreams or when that perfect job opportunity might pop up. Stop playing it safe and small and allow yourself to believe in possibility. Plus, positive thoughts feel better. Even if it's a little delulu, I'd rather think thoughts that make me feel happy than thoughts that make me feel miserable.

+Close Out with Gratitude

Gratitude is one of the quickest ways to change your life. When the world feels bleak and you struggle to get out of bed, writing down a list of things you are grateful for can be a challenge, but trust me: This is one of those worthwhile challenges. Start with five things. They can be as broad as, *I'm grateful that I woke up today and I get to try being a human again,* or as niche as, *I am grateful for this pen and how it perfectly distributes ink.* Find ways and moments to tap into feeling grateful whenever and wherever you can. The ultimate hack is learning to feel grateful even in moments of pain and strife.

Thank you for this lesson.

Even though this is not what I would have chosen, I am grateful for the opportunity to grow.

In the same way that we are attracted to the familiar in dating, we are also attracted to the familiar regarding our emotions and thoughts. If you've spent your whole life shitting on yourself, finding flaws in the world around you, or accepting that you are unlucky, you will naturally feel more comfortable thinking these thoughts. Gratitude, possibility, and positivity might feel fake and foreign to you at first. But once you get used to gratitude and a positive mindset, these mentalities will become your new normal and what feels natural. Who would you rather hang around, Negative Nancy or Happy Hannah? So start a daily gratitude list, and once you've conquered five things, bump it up to ten.

I hope this helps you the way it helped me. Again, I didn't change my mindset overnight. I took months, working on it every day. But eventually I realized I was happier. And then one day I realized that my outer world was starting to reflect my inner world.

THE B STORY

♦

Every movie has a B story. In romantic comedies it's usually the plot of the funny friend (think Judy Greer or Kathryn Hahn's storylines), and in horror movies it's often where the themes of the movie get explored. And in my life, both are true.

While most of my A story has been directed toward my career, I feel like the theme of my life revolves around love. I often find myself coming back to the same questions: What do I love? How do I love? Whom do I love? How do I like to receive love? The nuances of these questions have taken me years to understand.

Coincidentally, my friends and family have played a large role in the B story of my life because they are the ones who have taught me the most about love. Through my platonic relationships, I've learned what it means to love unconditionally and to be loved unconditionally. Yes, romantic love is incredible and most of us want it, but my friendships and my relationships with family have added the most color and dimension to the pages of my story.

These are the people who buoyed me when I was drowning and celebrated me at my best. They're the ones who challenged me to aim higher and dream bigger and walk away from things and people that weren't healthy for me. Together we've taught each other how to be vulnerable and resolve conflicts and how to ask for what we need. I have grown with my friends, many of whom have known me for twenty-plus years.

So this is just to remind us not to neglect our friendships, because no movie is complete without a B story. It's easy to get wrapped up in lust, like, or love and bail on your friends because you think they'll understand, but that is shortsighted. Statistically speaking, you will not spend forever with the person you are dating. Even if you do end up married, that's one relationship out of the average of four to ten relationships most Americans will have before they get married. Your friends, on the other hand, are for life. At least, they could be.

Let this be my formal thank you to the supporting characters who make up the B story in the movie of my life. Without you, this movie would suck.

TIME IS RUNNING OUT

◆

The greatest gift a dating app has ever given me is my friendship with Nate, aka Nate the Neighbor. We matched on Raya in the spring of 2017 and exchanged messages for three months while he was shooting a movie in New York. He came back to LA, and on our first date, we realized that I'd bought the house next door to him. The moment we realized this, Nate looked at me and in all seriousness said, "I sure hope this goes well." We've been best friends ever since. I love him like a brother. And because we look alike and often unintentionally cockblock each other, I've started to say that we're siblings so that people don't think we're dating. It rarely works, but I'll keep trying. And for the record: No, we are not in love. Not even a little bit.

One day during spring of 2021, I was folding laundry while talking to Nate on speakerphone.

"I matched with another babe on Hinge. Colin's hack really works." Nate was catching me up on his busy dating life.

After we'd complained that Hinge was full of uggos, our friend Colin had taught us how to manipulate the settings to show us hotter people. Apparently, the tactic was working for Nate. (The hack no longer works or I'd share!)

Reflexively, I asked, "How old is this one?"

"Twenty-five, but my date tomorrow is thirty-three!" I think Nate could sense my judgment.

He went on to tell me about a babe he "hit it off with" at a party I'd bailed on. Then he said, "I'm worried she's young though."

I rolled my eyes. He knew she was young and wanted to couch it.

"What makes you say that?" I dutifully asked.

"She didn't get a lot of my references, and when we were talking about life and milestones, her answers made me think she was young."

This was not a hard problem to solve. "What's her name?"

A three-second google search revealed her age. "She's twenty-three."

After a brief silence, Nate said, "Shit. I think that's too young."

"Yeah, I feel like twenty years is a bit of a gap."

I continued to fold laundry as Nate lamented how cool and hot this girl was. I knew he hadn't asked her age, because he didn't want to know the answer. And I assumed he was going to go out with her anyway. But I was wrong. He really did think she was too young and didn't pursue her, but I didn't know that at the time, and in my irritation, I needed to get off the phone.

The agitation I felt was akin to having an itch on my back at the nail salon when both of my hands are wet with polish, or when I'm at the dentist and my mouth is filling up with spit but the tech hasn't seemed to notice and I'm literally counting down the seconds until I might choke on my own saliva. I suddenly wanted to crawl out of my skin and scream and break something. The rage surprised me. I told Nate that I was getting another call and then tried to channel my anger into folding the perfect underwear squares.

A couple days went by, and I found myself ruminating on my fury. The fact that I was still bothered by Nate dating a twenty-three-year-old was tripping me out.

Why do I care who Nate dates?

"Maybe you're starting to develop feelings for Nate?" Rhiannon asked over lunch.

That was for sure not it. If anything, his consistent attraction to younger women made me like him less. "Absolutely not."

"Well, you're not feeling triggered out of nowhere, so think about it."

I thought about it.

"I think it's resentment," I said.

The second the words exited my body, I realized that was it. Suddenly in my thirties, I felt a new kind of pressure, a pressure that most men evade until their late forties. Nate still got to fuck around and date for fun; meanwhile, I was starting to feel like an overripe banana that was never going to get picked. Society tends to consider a single woman in her forties a spinster. The assumption is that something must be wrong with her. Meanwhile, a single man in his forties is a bachelor who simply hasn't met "the one" who makes him want to settle down. The stigma surrounding single women feels like a curse.

"What do you mean?" Rhiannon asked.

"I just feel like I'm running out of time," I said. I wasn't resentful of Nate; I was resentful of the ticking clock I felt hanging over my body.

"To have kids?"

I could see that she was confused. "Yeah."

The truth is, I've always been able to punt the conversation about kids because I always had time to decide. My attitude has always been, *if* it happens, *if* I meet the right person, *if* my partner really wants them. Raising a child on my own has never appealed to me. (Shout out to single mothers everywhere; you guys are literally superhuman.) And I've never dated anyone I wanted to coparent with, so I've never really been in a position where I felt like kids *were* an option. But suddenly, I felt like I was running out of time.

"Well, I don't 100% know that I do, but I don't want to regret not having them," I said.

On the one hand, the world seems to be headed for environmental doom. Bringing a child into a world that might be fighting over clean water in fifty years feels crazy. But on the other hand, I can't imagine not having a family to celebrate holidays with twenty years from now. Family has been such a huge part of my life. I'm sad thinking about not having one of my own.

"If anything, I want to have the *option*," I said.

Even though in 1978 the National Institutes of Health randomly chose thirty-five to be the age for a "geriatric pregnancy," no really, look it up—thirty-five was an arbitrary number—many women still feel the stress of aging.[16] After I turned thirty, every doctor kept asking me if I was planning on having kids.

"Well, then you need to start dating intentionally," Rhiannon said.

"Exactly. Nate gets to waste time, and I have to start getting serious." The double standard felt unfair. I always thought I'd fall in love with the father of my child(ren), and he would be the one who made me want to be a mother. But that dream seemed to be dying with every passing year.

After lunch, I googled "celebrities who've had babies in their forties." I was temporarily calmed by the fact that Gwen Stefani had her youngest at forty-four and Halle Berry had a child at forty-seven, and then I remembered I was comparing myself to celebrities with endless amounts of money for surrogacy *and* donor eggs. The panic set back in.

A couple of weeks later, my anxiety had still not subsided, so I decided Rhiannon was right; it was time to get serious about who I was dating. No more fun guys. I needed someone who was responsible, financially stable, and mature enough to

---

[16] "Pregnancy Over Age 35: A Numbers Game | Your Pregnancy Matters | UT Southwestern Medical Center," n.d., https://utswmed.org/medblog/pregnancy-over-35/

have a kid. If I wanted to be able to meet someone, have time to fall in love and be a couple, *and* have kids, I would need to start *immediately*.

And that's when I had my light-bulb moment: divorced dads.

Never in a million years would I have dated a man with children in my twenties. The way I saw it, I had thousands of men to choose from so why would I opt for someone with that kind of responsibility. Being a parent means that your kids always come first—at least I think they should—and I figured that dating a man with kids would mean zero spontaneity, a lot of unchosen responsibility, and always coming last—none of which sounded cool to me.

Now in my thirties, I looked at dating someone with kids in a new light. I, perhaps naively, thought that dating a dad would mean that he was responsible, had his shit together, and could have more kids. Dating a dad would feel like riding a bike with training wheels; I could test the waters without committing to motherhood. If I liked it, then we could have another kid. And if I didn't, I could be the coolest stepmom on planet earth. Plus, I assumed that dating dads would mean that I was dating men who were more mature and emotionally stable.

Some of you might be shaking your heads, but I'm just trying to get you into the headspace that I was in when I expanded my age range on the dating apps. This was the logic that drove me to start dating dads. And boy, what a mistake that was.

ALIENS

The first time I noticed "it," I was washing my hands in front of my bathroom mirror and I did a double take. "Why do you look like that?" I said to the figure staring back at me.

I didn't recognize myself.

I leaned in for a closer look, "What the hell?"

It was as if someone had tweaked my face in Photoshop, slightly distorting all my features in a way that felt subtle yet malformed. I grabbed the flesh of my cheeks, hoping to snap myself out of whatever fever dream I was in, but it didn't work. I still looked *off*.

I chalked up my appearance to having an "ugly day" and assumed that I'd be back to my "normal" in no time. But a few days later, it was worse. I'd walk by a mirror and shudder. My own reflection kept catching me off guard. Something was amiss. I just couldn't pinpoint it.

Who are you? And why are you suddenly ugly?

My face looked unfamiliar, like looking in the mirror on mushrooms; I had turned into the grotesque version of myself.

The dissociation I was experiencing was jarring, not just visually but emotionally. To wake up one day and no longer recognize yourself is terrifying. I'd been in the same body for over thirty years, and while I'd gone through many transformations, changes were often imperceptible from day to day. And yet, overnight I'd somehow lost myself.

Whatever had hijacked my sense of self, I hated it. I felt like a prisoner in my own body, and I wanted out. I wanted to go back to normalcy, but I didn't know what was happening, so I didn't know how to stop it.

At first, I was worried I was getting an ME/CFS flare again but after a few days with zero additional symptoms, I decided it wasn't that. I turned to my friends. "Do you notice anything different about me?" I asked. Most people said no. One friend told me I looked thinner, but I'm pretty sure she just thought I was fishing for compliments.

I determined that I must be experiencing body dysmorphia, because rationally, I knew that this new repugnant version of me couldn't be what other people saw. Change doesn't happen that fast, and even if it did, the fact that I couldn't point out what was different suggested whatever was happening was mental. "Yeah, I think it's all in your head," my friend agreed.

Turns out, it was in my uterus. I was pregnant.

TRIGGER WARNING

A million books and articles share the joys of pregnancy and motherhood, but talking about the perils, and God forbid, the experience of not wanting a child is still taboo. However, I believe these topics are important. There's still so much shame and secrecy around abortions that I, despite feeling in-the-know, was largely in the dark. So this is a chapter dedicated to normalizing a different kind of pregnancy story. It is not to diminish anyone's desires or joys around pregnancy. I have a ton of girlfriends who loved being pregnant and some who have mourned their inability to get pregnant, and I support them all. This is simply *my* story, and these are *my* horrors. So if you feel like this topic might be triggering for you, I encourage you to protect your peace and skip this chapter.

◆ ◆ ◆

THE INVASION

Squatting over my toilet seat to take a pregnancy test felt oddly low stakes, because pregnancy wasn't on my radar. I didn't even think I could get pregnant, which doesn't mean that I wasn't careful. I was. But I need you to know that I was not nervous as I tried to pee on the tiny plastic strip between my legs. In fact, I was pretty sure that the fatigue and nausea I was experiencing were symptoms of an autoimmune flare.

So when I saw two blue lines screaming back at me, I about fainted.

I'm pregnant!

The fucking irony. I was six months into dating a divorced dad named Mike because the anxiety around my biological clock had led me to expand my age range and my preferences to include parents. But instead of jumping for joy and crying tears of happiness with my partner like I'd seen in movies and on social media, I was frozen with panic and dread.

I didn't want to be pregnant. In fact, I'd tried not to be pregnant, so everything about this was against my will. Suddenly, I felt violated.

No wonder my body felt alien to me; I'd been *invaded*.

All of my weird symptoms had a cause: the *it* growing inside of me—a collection of cells that, if left alone, *might* turn into a baby. All I could picture was an amoeba. It didn't feel like a baby; it felt like an *it*—an amorphous blob floating inside me, feeding off me, and draining me of vitality. I wanted to scream out, "I did not consent to this!" but that would have been pointless.

This should have been one of the happiest moments of my life, and instead, it felt like my biggest mistake. It felt like my HPV diagnosis all over again but *so* much worse. I felt tainted. While I have always believed in science and been openly pro-choice, this was never a choice I wanted to make. Personal and political beliefs aside, I was not immune to the societal stigmas that surround unwanted pregnancies and abortions. As if on cue, my inner demon shot up from the depths it had retreated to like a volcano awakening from its dormant state.

You're a slut and a fuck up and now no one will love you!

I found myself sitting alone in my living room, covered in molten shame and explosive disappointment.

I called Mike, but he didn't pick up and I didn't leave a message. *Hey, it's me, and I'm pregnant,* seemed like the kind of voicemail that, without warning, could lead to an accident on the freeway. I knew Mike didn't want any more kids; we'd already had that discussion. He already had his hands full with a pre-teen son and the cutest goldendoodle I'd ever seen. I wasn't looking forward to telling him that I was somehow pregnant, but I was looking forward to having some support—because this was easily one of the worst days of my life.

I thought about my friend Sarah, who was on her sixth round of IVF, and I felt incredibly guilty. She would have done anything to be in my shoes. For years, she and her husband had been trying to have a baby, and it felt unfair that they couldn't but I potentially could.

Then I immediately called my gynecologist. Even though conception had only occurred two weeks ago, I was already almost six weeks pregnant. I didn't realize that pregnancies are counted from the first day of your last period and not from the time you had the sex that resulted in the pregnancy. I had a thirty-two-day cycle, so by the time I realized I was pregnant I was on day thirty-five, which meant that I had five days to figure something out before the weekend made six weeks. I thought about all the women with longer menstrual cycles in states with six-week abortion bans and how terrified I would be if I were in Florida as opposed to California.

A medical abortion meant I could have pills delivered to my house within forty-eight hours, but a surgical abortion meant waiting an extra week. I wanted *it* out of my body as fast as possible, so I opted for the pills.

I never doubted my choice—and I still don't—but once I knew that I had a plan and the wheels were in motion, I allowed myself to wonder, *What if?*

What if things were different? What if Mike and I had been dating for six years not six months? What if we were madly in love and wanted to have a child together? How different would my life be?

I looked up my due date and mentally noted the first week in June. I thought about what would happen if I did nothing. Would I miscarry? Would I end up a single mother? Would Mike freak out, or would he do the right thing and help me raise a baby? I did not want to have a baby with Mike, a man I was still getting to know, but the mindfuck of dating dads, thinking they might be more open to having kids, and then getting pregnant with a man who definitely didn't want kids was not lost on me.

I wondered how Mike was going to react when I told him and if this was going to bring us closer together or drive us apart.

For a moment, I tried to pretend like my life wasn't mine but closer to Sarah's. How excited would I be if I were happily married and my husband and I had been trying for a baby? That thought made me sad. The distance between that life and where I was today felt oceans apart, and suddenly I was filled with regret—not for the abortion but for all the choices that had led me to this moment. I wanted to be excited. I wanted to be at a place in my life where this was the kind of news I documented for future home videos and mommy-and-me scrapbooks.

I realized that this might be my first and last time getting pregnant, so I spent the next forty-eight hours thinking about my life and all the choices that had led to this moment.

◆ ◆ ◆

THE ABORTION

My pills arrived in two bottles: mifepristone and misoprostol. I was supposed to take the mifepristone orally, twenty-four and forty-eight hours before I took the misoprostol. I was also told that I'd want to stay home and be comfortable because the second part "could feel like mild to really bad cramps." Historically, I have brutal periods, so I braced myself for the "really bad" option—but *nothing* could have prepared me for what was coming.

On an otherwise unremarkable morning, I held a tiny white octagon pill in my hand: the antidote. This was the pill that would block my production of progesterone, which is needed to maintain a pregnancy. I took a picture of the pill before I swallowed it, wondering if I should be more ceremonious about this process.

Several hours later, I felt relief but little else.

The next day, I woke up and cleaned my house before I got ready to clean out my uterus. I wanted one part of my life to feel organized, and, at that moment, my house was the only thing I had control over. Plus, it felt good to put effort into something and see immediate results. If only I could organize the rest of my life the way I'd organized my underwear drawer.

For the second medication, my nurse recommended vaginal insertion. Essentially, you want the pills to dissolve inside of you because that's how they get absorbed into the body. So I took three misoprostol pills, pushed them as far up as I could, got into bed, and didn't move.

And then I waited.

Fifteen minutes later, nothing had happened, so I tried asking Google for an ETA. Nothing makes you more aware of your lack of control than the unknown, and the internet did not provide me with much clarity.

So there I was, lying in bed waiting for one of the most taboo female experiences on the planet to start at any moment—an experience cloaked with so much shame that I, with all my medical knowledge, had no real idea of what to expect. And with every second that passed, I knew I was closer, which only added to my anxiety.

I was about thirty minutes away from a panic attack, when the cramping started.

It did, in fact, feel like period cramps. Which, for me, are awful—on a scale of one to ten, we're talking about an eight. I cranked up the heating pad, strapped it to my abdomen, and tried to distract myself with episodes of *Love Island* (the UK version, *obviously*).

About two hours later, I grabbed an ice pack to cool down my head. As I closed the freezer drawer, I proclaimed to no one, "I can handle this." The sensation was shitty and uncomfortable, but familiar. I knew I could tough this out for as long as it lasted, and I took solace in this epiphany.

I am going to be okay, I thought.

And then the abortion *actually* started.

Out of nowhere, I felt a sharp, searing pang above my right leg, just north of my hip bone. It was the kind of pain that made my mouth go dry and my eyes roll back. "Holy hell!" It felt like something stabbing me from the inside. As if the *it* had decided to fight back.

I tried to take a deep breath, but the skewering sensation was so intense that I found myself panting like an overheated dog. I tried to stay calm, but it was too late—my blood pressure was plummeting. I felt my sphincter muscles giving out, and I panicked: I was going to shit the bed, literally.

I wanted to get up, but the pain was so blinding that I couldn't move. I didn't know what to do. Fear hit me like an unexpected fist to the face.

Please don't let me poop myself! I begged.

With sheer will and a couple of shallow breaths, I swung my legs over the side of my bed, but as my feet hit the floor, my knees buckled. "Ooof." I hit the ground with a thud.

I wanted to curl up into the fetal position, pulling my knees so far into my body that they would punch through my pelvis, obliterating the source of my agony. Instead, I pulled myself up, reached for my heating pad, and yanked it out of the wall.

I'm going to need this, I thought.

With the heating pad in one hand, I braced myself against the bed, determined to make it to the bathroom. I'd only taken a couple of steps before dizziness washed over me like a wave rolling back before it comes crashing down. And down I went.

Walking was out of the picture, so I started to crawl.

In an instant, I'd been reduced to the most basic version of myself, a baby crawling on her knees. I wished I was religious. I wanted there to be someone I could pray to, someone to beg to make this stop. Even in my hysteria, the irony of this moment, of me on my knees, was not lost on me.

I made it to the bathroom just in time for my own personal Sophie's Choice: to shit or to vomit. I went with shit. I sat on the toilet with my legs pulled into my chest as far as I could while it felt like Satan himself was trying to exit my body.

The pain was a constant agony punctuated by intermittent waves of extreme torture. Every time a wave came, I risked barfing all over myself. I did my best to hold it in until eventually I turned around and vomit spewed out of me like an exorcism. I was no longer in control of my body; I was a helpless passenger at the mercy of the medicine and whatever was happening inside me. I pictured *it* with talons and shark teeth, wrestling with my insides in a bid to see who would come out the victor. I was pretty sure I was losing. I felt *it* gnawing and clawing away at my body, asserting its dominance over my meat suit.

The lights in the bathroom started to dim.

This can't be good.

This was immediately followed by a second, scarier thought.

Oh fuck, am I dying?

I woke up on the floor sometime later. The same torture that had caused me to faint had also jolted me back to reality. I was truly in hell.

When I realized what had happened, part of me wanted to call 911. The other part of me thought about how expensive it was going to be to ride in an ambulance to the ER and how they'd probably make me wait anyway.

I tried to negotiate with myself.

Five more minutes. You can last five more minutes.

I thought about all the moms I knew, and wondered if they had experienced this. Suddenly, I wanted *my* mom. I wanted her to hold me and to tell me everything was going to be okay. Yet I was grateful that I was alone. The burden of another person's presence would have been too much. More than anything,

I just wanted to know I wasn't going to die. No one had told me it would be *this* bad, and I was starting to worry.

Apparently, that's just what labor is like.

Are you fucking kidding me?

This was, hands down, the worst pain of my life. Worse than the 106-degree fever I had in Mexico when I vomited blood for two days, worse than when I tore my medial collateral ligament, worse than the dry sockets I got after having my wisdom teeth removed.

I've since been told that my pain might have been more extreme because I was trying to expel something so small, like the size of a poppy seed, but the mechanism of said expulsion was the same as labor.

I tried to count to a hundred but kept losing track around the thirties. I was being electrocuted in my uterus.

It's almost over. You can do this.

I kept trying to encourage myself, but at a certain point, I couldn't. My suffering was so bad, I was convinced something was wrong and that I was in trouble. I needed to call 911.

And then it hit me: My phone was in the bedroom.

Fuuuuuuck.

I'd never be able to get to my room. I wanted to cry, but the pain was so bad that I physically couldn't shed tears.

I somehow managed to plug in my heating pad. By this point, my top looked like I'd come out of a wet T-shirt contest in Cancun, and my sweatpants looked like I'd pissed myself. I was shaking and covered in goosebumps.

I pressed my face against the cold tile and let the heating pad sear my abdomen.

About an hour later, my contractions passed, and I was back to my eight-out-of-ten-level cramps, which felt like a goddamn vacation compared to what I had just been through.

I got back into bed a changed woman. I had survived, but I was not the same. I imagine this is how trauma changes people; it feels like harboring a secret no one else can fathom.

How would I ever properly express the terror or the pain I'd just endured? I couldn't wrap my head around it. How would I explain this to my friends? To Mike?

I shuddered.

The thought of Mike made me think of sex, which now felt inextricably linked to the harrowing experience I'd just been through.

I never want to have sex again, I thought.

Instinctually, I knew this feeling would probably pass, but for the foreseeable future, I was committed to celibacy.

What would that mean for my relationship? My mind started to race. Would we survive this? How would I tell him I was repulsed by the thought of sex?

Wait, why the fuck hasn't he called me back yet?

I stared up at the ceiling, a shattered version of my former self, wondering where Mike was. After all, he was just as responsible for this pregnancy, and yet I'd been the one to pay the price, literally and physically. I suddenly felt very far apart from him. I felt far apart from everyone. I guess secrets do that.

◆ ◆ ◆

THE AFTERMATH

In some ways, the aftermath was just as brutal as the actual abortion. I had to cancel all my plans because I was physically and emotionally exhausted in a way that prevented me from having normal conversations or pretending like I was okay. Only a handful of friends really knew what was going on; telling additional people took too much energy. Plus, when I did tell people, they would inevitably ask about Mike, who was still MIA—another twist I didn't see coming.

As days turned into weeks and I still hadn't heard from Mike, I was forced to face the fact that he'd ghosted me. Let me tell you, nothing makes you feel worse than being ghosted by the father of your potential child. It was mortifying. I'd handled and paid for everything and my body had endured intense trauma, and Mike couldn't even text me back.

I felt pathetic and ashamed but, unlike before, the demon in my mind didn't jump to my usual narrative of unworthiness. Mike's ghosting *did* trigger feelings of self-loathing but not for any of the reasons I was used to. Instead, the demonic voices in my head started to slut-shame me. Fun! As I recovered alone, imaginary conversations kept me company.

> *Did you hear what happened to Rory?*
> *No, what?*
> *She got an abortion.*
> *I mean . . . she does get around—like what do you expect?*

Or:

> *I heard Rory got ghosted by the guy who got her pregnant!*
> *Oh my god, can you believe her terrible taste in men?*
> *No, I'd kill myself—that's so humiliating.*

Apparently when one demon dies another one takes its place, and suddenly I was being harassed by an inner monologue that had found a whole new set of flaws to obsess over.

It's funny because, years later, writing out these thoughts seems silly. Not only did my friends react with compassion and understanding, but time has shown me that the call was coming from inside the house. Those demonic thoughts reflected my own hangups and internalized stigmas. Turns out you can intellectually be pro-choice and still not be immune to decades worth of anti-choice rhetoric.

Instead of trying to tune out those voices, I tuned in. I peeled back the layers of my anxiety and tried to understand where it was coming from. In doing so, I realized that the little demon in my mind wasn't torturing me with fears I had about myself but rather fears I had about how others would see me.

I was grappling with an overwhelming loss of control. Getting pregnant felt like something that had been forced upon me, and even though I chose to have an abortion, the experience itself had felt involuntary. I'd been at the mercy of a medicine that incapacitated me for about an hour, and I'd been in the dark about what was going to happen the entire time. While I'm grateful for the medicine, the lack of understanding about what to expect during an abortion set me up for failure. This lack of autonomy was probably compounded by the fact that Mike had ghosted me.

As a result, I was very selective when it came to talking about my abortion. I think that being careful about whom I shared my story with—and therefore who could have opinions about my choices—was a reaction to my lack of control around my pregnancy, my abortion, *and* being ghosted. I was so disenfranchised from my body and my life that I clung to one thing where I felt like I did have power: controlling my narrative.

I wanted people to know that I had been careful and that this situation was a fluke. Deep down, despite my own blind support of a woman's right to choose, I carried shame—shame that had manifested because we live in a world that continues to glamorize motherhood and condemn abortion. And again, I'm not dismissing motherhood, but I didn't grow up watching movies or television shows about women who are childless and happy; I grew up fearing that one day I could become an unloved, lonely, spinster. As time went on and I told more people, I found safe havens in unsuspecting places.

In the same way that pregnancy is both isolating and unifying, so is an abortion. They're both uniquely personal experiences. I felt deeply alone in the horrors of my pregnancy and subsequent abortion until I started talking about it with other women. Instinctually, I started by talking to strangers and acquaintances because that felt safer than talking to friends. If someone I barely knew judged me or made a harsh comment, it wouldn't hurt as bad as if a good friend did. But as I shared my secret I was embraced by a sisterhood who offered unwavering support.

This was how I discovered that the hair loss I was experiencing by the handfuls was a result of my abortion. I was at lunch with two friends and three women I didn't know when I looked down to see my shirt covered in hair.

"I've been losing hair at an alarming rate, and I have no idea why!" I said.

Each woman threw out a possible culprit before we moved on to another topic. An hour later, someone asked me what I'd been up to, and I honestly responded with, "Well, I had an abortion a couple months ago, so that sort of level-set my life in a way."

"Welcome to the club," one girl quipped. We'd only just met, yet she went on to tell me about the abortion she'd had in her twenties and how she was now a mother of three.

My friend Carolyn pointed at the pretty brunette sitting next to her. "Us too, babe." The pretty brunette chimed in, "Yup. Also, *that's* why you're losing hair!"

The table erupted. As it turns out, hair loss is a potential side effect of full-term pregnancies, miscarriages, *and* abortions, but no one had told me. We spent another thirty minutes talking about hair growth tips, and I was reminded of how powerful women are when they come together and share their stories. This love and support from newer friends helped me build the confidence to tell the other people in my life.

As time's gone on, I've become less precious about how and whom I talk about my abortion with—I mean, clearly. That's how I know that the shame I was carrying wasn't mine. I was holding on to opinions of people I don't even know or align with, but that's the power of societal stigmas. This is part of the reason why I've been so open about my experience. Regardless of whether you agree with abortion or if you've ever had one yourself, it's important to know that smart, successful, kind women get abortions. And statistically speaking, an estimated 60% are mothers who already have kids.[17]

While the event itself only lasted a couple of hours, the ripple effects from my abortion took months to resolve. I felt disconnected from my body and cut off from my sexuality for half a year. In the beginning, I couldn't even masturbate. My hormones took a full year to level out, and my hair took three years to grow back to its former iteration. When I hear critics talk about abortions like they're a frivolous decision made by a lazy or coldhearted woman, I shake my head. This perception could not be further from the truth. And again, while my experience was horrific, I am beyond grateful for my choice and I would still make it again.

A FINAL GIRL'S GUIDE TO ABORTIONS

I hope that no one goes through what I went through, but many of you reading this already have or will. So let me share some older-sister wisdom:

- You can absolutely get pregnant from pre-cum—trust me.
- Pregnancies get counted starting from the first day of your last period, not from when you have sex, which is what makes six-week abortion bans troubling, especially for people like me who have longer cycles.

---

17   James Studnick et al. "Estimating the Period Prevalence of Mothers Who Have Abortions: A Population Based Study of Inclusive Pregnancy Outcomes," *Health Services Research and Managerial Epidemiology*. (July 23, 2021), https://doi.org/10.1177/2333392821103499

- Emergency contraception, like Plan B, works mainly by stopping or delaying ovulation, when your body releases an egg. It also thickens your cervical mucus, which makes it harder for sperm to reach an egg for fertilization, where the combo forms a zygote before developing into a blastocyst. In some cases, emergency contraception can also help prevent implantation, when a blastocyst attaches to your uterine lining. Emergency contraception works best if you take it within seventy-two hours (three days) after sex. But if a blastocyst has already implanted to your uterine lining, it won't work; it won't end a pregnancy. You can buy emergency contraception over the counter, including online. TL;DR: if a blastocyst attaches before you take Plan B, you can still get pregnant.
- Implantation bleeding can sometimes seem like a period, so taking a pregnancy test is crucial.
- Medical abortions are incredible options, but everyone will react differently. Not knowing what to expect made my experience ten times worse.
- The worst part lasted about an hour; my friends have had similar experiences, but these instances are anecdotal.
- Some people experience very little pain when it comes to a medical abortion because, like I said, everyone will react differently.
- You can't control other people's opinions, but you can control whom you share your story with and how *you* feel about your choices.
- No one is entitled to know about your abortion.
- I am not haunted or traumatized by my choices.
- As time went on and my hormones leveled out, so did my emotions.
- Giving yourself grace and love is important.
- And remember, you are not alone.

GHOSTS

◆

You wanna hear a ghost story? Okay, gather 'round the campfire.

Twelve months after my abortion and Mike's disappearance, I walked into a hair salon for the first time. The girl who normally did my hair was on a sabbatical, and my roots were so grown out that my part looked less like a landing strip and more like the entire tarmac. So when my friend, who is a celebrity makeup artist, recommended a colorist named Lola, I booked with her immediately.

A few days later, I walked into a kitschy salon in the valley, where I was immediately greeted by a buxom blond with big blue eyes and a wild leopard-print dress. Lola had a raspy voice and an effervescent personality, and she talked a mile a minute. After we sorted out my highlights, Lola began peppering me with questions. When she inevitably asked me if I was single, I told her yes.

"Ooooh, are you dating anyone?"

I told her that I took a year off after getting ghosted by the guy who got me pregnant. Lola gasped, which felt like a reasonable response.

"Shut the fuck up. Girl are you *okay*?"

I laughed. "I am, yeah. *Now*. At the time it was brutal."

"What a piece of shit." I could see the wheels in her head starting to spin.

"You know what they say, rejection is protection. Could be way worse. I could still be with him."

Lola looked up from the highlight she was foiling and cocked one eyebrow. "I dunno. Rejection sent my ass to therapy for the first time at thirty-eight."

"Wait, really?"

"Oh yeah, this man *ruined* my mental health."

Obviously, I needed her to start at the beginning.

They'd met on a dating app at the start of the pandemic and hit it off immediately. Since there were mandatory lock-downs and people were scared of getting sick, their relationship turned exclusive early on. In fact, this guy was the only man Lola had ever introduced her daughter to.

"I thought I was dating my dream guy," she said.

About a year later, vaccines had started to roll out and restaurants were reopening in Los Angeles. Suddenly Lola was "too much" and "too needy" for this guy. He was pulling away but blaming his distance on Lola's behavior. Her boyfriend's sudden avoidance made her anxious, but anytime Lola tried to seek reassurance, he would tell her that he was feeling smothered and would disappear for a few days. Seemingly overnight, she went from being the perfect girlfriend to not being able to do anything right. Lola tried to be accommodating, but the distance chipped away at her confidence. Finally, she got the nerve to confront him about this behavior shift.

"He fucking ghosted me!"

"After a year?" I practically shouted.

At one point Lola thought he was dead. "*Then* I saw him post on Instagram." She let out a heavy sigh. "It really did a number on my head."

Lola spent weeks wondering what she'd done to cause him to treat her like this—a flawed train of thought. She found herself rehashing the days leading up to his disappearance, wondering if she had changed her behavior if it would have changed the outcome—as if it were somehow her fault!

"I kept trying to figure out when things shifted, and I drove myself insane."

Listening to Lola talk felt like walking down memory lane. I could hear the pain in her voice as she described the ways in which her boyfriend's ghosting had triggered a loop of endless self-criticism. I thought about my twenty-five-year-old self crying on my living room floor after Jack had broken my heart, and the inner demon that subsequently haunted me for years.

Ghosting is a shitty thing to do to someone because it leaves them in the dark, which makes processing the rejection harder. As humans, we are hardwired to fill in the gaps, find an explanation, and seek closure, and as a result people tend to assign meaning as to why they were ghosted. This often results in self-blame. We naturally want to try to understand someone's behavior, but personalizing it is an act of self-harm. (I should know!)

I did not have the wherewithal at twenty-five to look at Jack's actions and think, *Good riddance. This is not what I want from a life partner.* But I should have. Relationships are built on trust, communication, and mutual respect—none of which are shown when someone ghosts. No matter how perfect a person seems or how easy the relationship was in the beginning, ghosting reveals shortcomings that you don't want in a partner.

I wish I had seen Jack's exit from my life as a blessing, but instead I saw it as a consequence of my deficiencies. It birthed a demonic inner critic that gaslit me into believing I was hard to love and easy to leave. Internalizing romantic rejections became a habit that ate away at my dignity like acid on a weak stomach. At first, it's not dangerous, but as time goes on and hurts pile up, you're left riddled with ulcers. Eventually my inner monologue became untenable, and I was forced to face my inner demon head-on.

"Unfortunately, I know exactly how you felt—and it's traumatic."

I saw a flicker of self-consciousness flash across Lola's face. "Yeah, but I wasn't pregnant, so you had it way worse," she said, as if we were competing in the trauma Olympics.

"Oh, I wasn't even talking about *him*," I said.

And I wasn't. When Mike had ghosted me, I didn't beat myself up. In fact, I knew that his behavior reflected his own limitations and that I wanted nothing to do with him. Don't get me wrong: Being ghosted by the man who got me pregnant *sucked*, but I was way more concerned about how I fell for someone who would treat me like that than trying to understand the *why* behind his ghosting. I was done internalizing men's shitty behavior, but apparently I was not done attracting it. And *that* was terrifying. And problematic.

So I took the year to clean my slate and make myself accountable, not for the things that had happened to me but rather the patterns I'd repeated. I noticed some interesting themes. I had been over-investing in men who were less invested in me. The demonic voice in my head kept telling me that I needed to be better to be loved, and I kept finding myself in relationships that seemed to prove that inner voice right. I was routinely trying to win the affection of avoidant(ish) men instead of assessing whether they were even worthy of mine. Their inconsistencies felt like a challenge: If I could get them to love me, it would prove that I was lovable. Therefore, I saw breakups as rejections instead of what they really were: The universe trying to remove people from my life who were not good for me. Finally, I was able to step back and see that in order to change my love life, I was going to have to fundamentally change my belief system.

I needed to deprogram myself from deeply ingrained patriarchal narratives. Centering your life around men, wanting to be chosen, and fearing an "expiration date" are all manifestations of living in a world created by and for men. I know that sounds extreme, but many of our ideas about love and partnership stem from the relationship dynamics that prevailed in previous generations, and these dynamics no longer match the current world we live in.

As a single woman, you legally could not get birth control until 1972 (Eisenstadt v. Baird).[18] And you weren't able to get a credit card without your husband's approval until 1974 (Equal Credit Opportunity Act).[19] Financial freedom and bodily autonomy for women changed the power dynamics of dating and marriage because women were no longer dependent on men. Yes, straight women still *want* men, but they don't *need* men, and there's a big difference. In the fifty years since women have had access to their own credit cards, gender roles have shifted greatly, but relationship norms have not. Unfortunately, I consumed a lot of outdated dating advice that harkened back to a time when women's security depended on whether she was chosen by a man, and this advice warped my perspective.

Lola was almost done painting my highlights when I very earnestly said, "As crazy as it sounds, getting ghosted like that was a blessing."

She looked at me like I was, in fact, crazy, so I told her, "It blew up my life in a way that woke me up and jolted me into a whole new outlook."

After months of reflection, I now understood that I let my scarcity mindset dictate my dating choices. My fear of aging was a fear of becoming undesirable which led me to compromise on

---

18 Eisenstadt v. Baird, 405 U.S. 438 (1972).
19 Equal Credit Opportunity Act, Public Law 93-495 (1974).

my dating preferences. I never would have met Mike if I hadn't believed that I needed to settle in order to settle down. The irony is that I grew up with parents who'd met when they were forty, and they're still happily married today.

Yes, I have a biological clock that will at some point make having children the "traditional" way impossible, but that doesn't mean I can't have children or create a family at any age.

Mike was the wake-up call I needed and the silver lining of his ghosting was my growth. Relationships are built together as a team. Loving someone "better" will not get them to love you back, so I promised myself I'd stop doing that. I worked on reprogramming my limiting beliefs and recommitted to my standards. If I wanted to be adored, I needed to start acting like the prize. If you're the one who's always closing the gap, people can't pursue you. And if you're constantly putting men on a pedestal, they forget that you're also a prize. I needed to prioritize men who demonstrated effort and consistency as opposed to prioritizing them based on how much I liked them or what they *could* be.

At this point I was sitting under one of those retro hair dryers. It was heating up my head to help the bleach process faster.

"Maybe I would have gotten there without the ghosting, but I don't know," I admitted to Lola. "But take it from someone who's been there—you dodged a bullet!"

Lola looked at me sheepishly. "He apologized a few months later, and because I'm an idiot, I took him back." Before I could respond, Lola cut me off. "I know! I shouldn't have."

I told her I was just about the last person on earth who would judge her, "because I almost exclusively learn lessons the hard way."

Lola and her boyfriend got back together, and things were fine for about a month before he started to pull away again. The hot-and-cold nature of their relationship was hard on Lola's nervous system, just as my relationship with Dean had been hard on mine.

"I was so afraid to lose him," she said, "that I didn't realize every time we got back together it made me hate myself a little bit more."

Unfortunately I knew exactly how she felt.

One fateful evening, Lola texted her boyfriend to see if he was free, and he told her he was cooking dinner with his son. He sent a photo of their plates with the chicken he had made but forgot to disable the live feature. So, when Lola held her finger down on the photo, she saw a blond woman walking through the frame.

"That's how I found out he was cheating on me," Lola said.

This hair appointment was starting to feel like the 2009 romantic comedy *The Ghost of Girlfriend's Past*, except that I was revisiting all my worst ex's via another woman's story. The live photo fuckup felt eerily similar to how I'd discovered that Waldo was cheating on me. I immediately felt bad for Lola.

"Let me guess," I said. "You became obsessed with this girl."

Lola looked surprised. "How did you know?"

I laughed. "I told you, I've lived through every dating horror you can imagine."

The existence of this mystery woman sent Lola into a spiral. She began comparing herself, wondering what this mystery girl had that she didn't. Based on the photo, she'd determined the new girl was thinner, which unearthed a slew of insecurities. She was also convinced that the mystery girl had to be the epitome of cool—nothing like the needy, overbearing nag that her ex made her out to be.

Lola told her boyfriend to kick rocks, but she thought about him every day. So when he inevitably circled back, Lola didn't reject him.

"He texted me out of the blue, and I know I shouldn't have but I responded."

Guess she couldn't do it for ya huh? Lola had written.

In a fight for his love, she was determined to defeat this mystery woman, her new mortal enemy.

"I know it's super pathetic and I feel really bad about it now, but . . ." Lola's voice trailed off.

As time wore on and her boyfriend's bad behavior continued, Lola found herself consumed by jealousy and self-loathing. This was her rock bottom. She didn't want to continue down this stressed and spiteful path, so she found herself a therapist and began her healing journey.

I was lying with my head in the shampoo bowl so Lola could remove the foils from my head. She confessed, "At this point I'm grateful for her because I feel like I finally learned how to love myself." The existence of this other woman sent Lola on a self-love quest.

"Can you believe that loser still hits me up?" she asked.

I could. "Do you respond?" I asked.

Lola leaned over the shampoo bowl so she could make very serious eye contact. "I turn on my read receipts so that he knows that I've seen it, and then I leave him on read."

I laughed. God bless a petty woman.

Lola pulled out my last foil before another thought hit her. "I do miss his dog though. He had the cutest doodle I've ever met."

AND THAT IS WHEN IT HIT ME. "His name's not Mike, is it?"

I didn't even need her answer—because the way every stylist in the salon stopped what they were doing to look at us told me that it, indeed, was Mike.

"Because that is the man who ghosted me when I was pregnant," I said.

The salon went dead silent.

Lola walked out from behind the shampoo bowl and we locked eyes. I watched her studying my face, presumably looking for an indication that I was joking. I saw the exact moment she realized I wasn't. Lola looked like she was seeing a ghost come back to life. At this point, I already knew the answer, but I pulled out my phone and held up a photo of Mike. "Is this the Mike you're talking about?"

The salon erupted.

As you've probably gathered by now, *I* am the woman from the live photo. The person Lola hated was *me*. She'd spent months spiraling out over my relationship with Mike, which is pretty poetic considering how that storyline ended.

And yeah, for those of you keeping track at home: Third time's a charm. This is the third (and final) time that I was cheated on. Turns out that Mike was seeing Lola on and off the entire time we had been together. He'd ghosted me because they'd reconnected.

"I'm so sorry," Lola said.

She would continue to apologize for the things she'd said about me before we realized I was the girl from the photo. The situation reminded me of Hope and Waldo and how I'd hated her for months, only to meet her and fall in love with her as a friend. This hair appointment was turning out to be one of the most full-circle moments of my romantic life.

I tried to tell Lola that I didn't care and that I wasn't upset, but I could see that she didn't fully trust it. So I told her, "In the same way that I inspired *you* to get into therapy, you inadvertently did the same. And we are both better off because of it."

I explained that while I wouldn't want to repeat what happened with Mike, the situation forced me to take a hard look at my role in that horror and make positive changes.

"I'm better off today than I was a year ago, so you can stop apologizing," I said.

Call me delusional, but I don't think it's an accident that Lola and I met when we did. Neither one of us needed closure, but the truth was still validating. She got to see that I wasn't this super chill girl who got the better version of Mike, and I got to see how far I'd come. I'd grown a lot since my breakup with Jack, and I was hopeful that my last year of accountability and healing would set me up for a healthier future. I was right about a few things: The future was smoother, and closure often comes when you don't need it.

A FINAL GIRL'S GUIDE TO GHOSTING

FOR THE GHOSTS

Some people ghost for safety reasons, and I am not speaking to you. For everyone else, ghosting gives limp-dick energy.

First off, research shows that ghosting is psychologically harmful to the ghostee.[20] And anecdotally, I can confirm. So if you know it's going to be hurtful, why do it? I'd argue that you're either cruel or a coward, and both aren't chic. Ghosting is all about avoidance. But inflicting pain on someone simply because you're afraid of having an awkward or uncomfortable conversation is harmful and rude. People ghost because they want to avoid discomfort. That's not a main-character move! Ghosting is something the villain does, not the main character that we want to root for. But that's not the only reason why you shouldn't ghost.

Communication is the bedrock of every relationship. Even if you never want to see someone again, you should be practicing and improving your skills for the person you do want to end up with. Being unable or unwilling to communicate is not going to do you any favors in the long run. Dating helps you define who you are, what your communication style is, and what you

---

[20] Barbara C. Lopes and Rusi Jaspal, "Exposure to Ghosting, Gaslighting, and Coercion and Mental Health Outcomes," Partner Abuse, April 1, 2025, https://doi.org/10.1891/pa-2024-0031.

need in order to thrive. And ghosting robs you of these experiences and skills.

So yeah, don't ghost.

FOR THE GHOSTED

For those who have been ghosted, be grateful. I know that's a wild way to look at it, but being ghosted tells you *a lot* about what your future would have looked like with this person—because communication is the foundation of a good relationship. Plus, ghosting indicates character flaws that you don't want—and don't deserve—to deal with, like emotional immaturity, avoidant behavior, cowardice, or cruelty. I promise you, the sooner you see their exit as happening *for* you instead of *to* you, the freer you'll be.

Ghosting is very disenfranchising. So reclaim your power and remind yourself that you are in the driver's seat of your own destiny. Rather than focusing on the ghosting or the rejection, remind yourself that *you* don't want to be with a partner who ghosts. Remind yourself that this behavior is juvenile and not what you want from a partner or for your life.

That said, you are allowed to call out ghosting if it will help you feel empowered to move forward. You can send a text:

I've interpreted your continued silence as ghosting, which is admittedly disappointing because I expected better. That said, I wanted to wish you well, to close the loop here, and to ask that you respect this boundary moving forward.

This allows you to call out their behavior while also acknowledging that you are no longer interested. It also puts the kibosh on them trying to circle back in the future.

Be honest with yourself before sending a text like this. If you're secretly hoping to re-engage with this person, don't send this. If they respond and circle back and you allow it, you have essentially shown them that you are willing to break your own boundaries even though the only effort they've put in is replying to your text. In my experience, this only sets you up for future pain!

I still maintain that rejection is protection. What's meant for you won't miss you, and I firmly believe that the person of your dreams is not going to be the person who ghosts you. However, ghosting can conjure up negative thoughts and insecurities, and it's important to address them.

+First, Name It.
Are you spiraling over someone not texting you back? Are you being bogged down by negative self-talk? Are you obsessively checking to see if someone has watched or engaged with your social media? Are you catastrophizing someone's actions? Try to observe what feelings are coming up and what stories you keep repeating. Anxiety, unworthiness, shame? What are the demonic thoughts running through your mind?

Once you're able to identify what is coming up for you and you're able to write it down, talk to yourself like you would a best friend. Imagine it's not you but your friend dealing with these thoughts and feelings and start asking her questions about it. Where do you think these feelings are coming from? Where did these limiting beliefs come from?

+Separate Facts from Feelings.
Try to separate facts from feelings. If you've been ghosted, you might default to self-blame, but can you back that blame with facts? Can you prove that your inner demon is telling the truth? Or are these just fears and feelings?

+Detach.
Move your body, change your environment, and switch up your energy. Set your phone aside and do something offline that requires you to be present. Walk and listen to a podcast, paint,

cook, or go out with friends—anything that takes your mind out of the spiral and forces you to be present.

Remind yourself that you are enough, even with your flaws. Everyone deserves to be with someone who treats them with respect and kindness, and you do not want to have to beg for decency. Ask yourself: Would I want this relationship for my best friend? If the answer is no, then why are you settling for it? Start showing up for yourself like you do for your friends. Be your own best friend and see this person's disappearance as a blessing.

SERIAL KILLERS: THE SEQUEL

◆

Remember how I thought I was going to marry the "love of my life" but he broke up with me over the phone? Of course you do. Well, 364 days after that call, Jack celebrated his one-year anniversary with his new girlfriend, officially confirming that he did cheat.

But that's not all. There's one last twist!

Over a decade later, in the middle of writing this book, I discovered that I was actually the *other* woman. Dude, I know! As it turns out, when Jack had originally DM'd me to ask me out on a date, he had a full-blown girlfriend. When he moved back to LA and we started dating, he *still* had a full-blown girlfriend. Jack wasn't just a cheater—he was a pro!

And even though that woman is happily married with kids now, I feel sick when I think about how I unknowingly contributed to her suffering. I remember the heartbreak and all the tears I shed, and it kills me to think that I helped inflict the same pain on someone else. The way Jack discarded both of our hearts was cold-blooded, but like most serial killers, he had a pattern.

You may be balking at my comparison, but I'd argue that serial daters, cheaters, and womanizers are the serial killers of love. These are people who rip through victims, inflicting trauma with little remorse. The ripple effect of their actions goes beyond their ex's; hurt people go on to hurt other people who go on to hurt more people. Plus, the serial killers of love often have a signature. In Jack's case, he would lock in a new girlfriend before he got rid of his current girlfriend. This is a love crime. And while there's recourse for actual murderers (as there should be!), serial heartbreakers get off scot-free. Think about it: I can't damage your car without expecting repercussions, but I can waste the best years of your life and damage your spirit and there's nothing you can do about it. The ones who are left bleeding out on their living room floors are just expected to get over it and move on.

You might think the lesson here is to trust no one, but that couldn't be further from the truth. The lesson is to develop even more trust in yourself. Like I wrote in the first chapter of this book, the number one asset in every final girl's arsenal is a healthy mindset, which is impossible to cultivate without self-love and self-trust.

In the same way that you can't prevent being in the wrong place at the wrong time, you also can't prevent yourself from experiencing the pitfalls of love. Odds are, you will have your heart broken, ideally not by a serial cheater, but it will hurt all the same. It's almost impossible to experience love without also experiencing loss. Knowing that, I don't think the lesson is to walk into relationships with your dukes up. No, the lesson is to love freely and bravely and cultivate a strong enough foundation that you can survive the aftermath of anything thrown your way.

As with many things in life, when it comes to relationships, all you can control is how you handle the circumstances set in front of you. Shit happens, but it's how you deal with that shit that will define who you are and what your future looks like.

This is why you need a plan for handling rejections both big and small. How are you going to ensure that you bounce back better instead of feeding that little demon inside your mind?

Regardless of the circumstances regarding your breakup, deciding to see your ending as a new beginning will change the way you heal. Being mindful of your thoughts and the messages you are repeating to yourself is critical to your well-being. When it comes to neuroplasticity, it's widely accepted that high repetitions are needed to create new neural pathways.[21] Would you rather that pathway reinforce the idea that you are worthy of the kind of love that makes you feel safe and seen, or do you want to ingrain the idea that you're never going to find someone as amazing as your ex? The choice is yours.

You might take solace knowing that regardless of how dirty someone does you, you still have the power when it comes to *how* you heal. Our thoughts become our reality, and your mindset will determine your future. Heartbreak can act as an anchor that drags you down or a spring that catapults you forward, but only *you* decide which one it is. Never forget that you have agency in how you move forward.

Sometimes I wonder how my life would be different if I'd known back then that Jack was a serial cheater. I ignorantly thought that Jack left me because he didn't love me enough or that he left me for something better. I didn't realize he had a history with infidelity and lying. As a result, I internalized a lot of stories that weren't true and weren't meant for me, and I carried those stories into my future relationships. I'm sure there's a Jack (or Jill) in your life, and it's worth thinking about the stories you have around that relationship and whether or not you want to keep holding on to them.

---

21 Jessie Agrimis, "Principles of Neuroplasticity: Repetition Matters — NeuroLab 360," NeuroLab 360, December 23, 2021, https://www.neurolab360.com/blog/principles-of-neuroplasticity-repetition-matters#

Now, with the benefit of hindsight and many lessons learned, here's what I would do differently if I got dumped tomorrow:

A FINAL GIRL'S GUIDE TO HEALING

- I would allow myself to feel terrible instead of trying to push through the pain.
- I would flag any and all negative thoughts that bubbled up and I would write them down and share them with someone I really trusted. By sharing those secret demonic thoughts, you immediately weaken their grasp on your psyche. I would allow my trusted circle to help me parse out facts from fears.
- I would practice giving myself the love that I wanted from my partner.
- I would establish a new routine to help me build structure but also to build self-trust with myself.
- I would write out a list of short- and long-term goals, and whenever I felt down, I would look at that list and I'd pick something that I could work toward. That way, when I felt down or anxious, I could channel that energy into something that would lead to a sense of accomplishment.
- I would find a way to give myself closure.
- I would remind myself every day that life is happening *for* me and not *to* me and that even if I don't understand it now, one day I will see why this was practice for something better.
- I would make sure to center myself and not my ex. Instead of thinking about them and wondering how they were doing or if they were hurting the same way I was, I would channel that energy into obsessing about myself. I would invest in my health, passions, other relationships, and goals.

- I would remind myself every day that I am worthy of the love I desire and just because it did not work out this one time does not mean that it will *never* workout.

That's what I would do if my fiancé abruptly ended things without giving me closure. It would be hard and hurtful, but I know that I'd not only heal but I would bounce back better. I'm sharing this so you can bookmark it or rip out the page and use it as a guide should you find yourself lost in the fog of heartache.

Importantly, I need you to know that at this point I am grateful that Jack cheated on me. If he hadn't, I would not be the person I am today—and I love who I am. My ending with Jack gave me the opportunity to start over, dream big, and trust that life was going to get better for me; and it did. If we had gotten married, I never would have written this book, because I don't think I'd even be a writer. Our breakup inspired me to take a risk, to share my story, and to write my first screenplay, a move that ultimately launched me into a new career.

My only regret is that I internalized even the smallest bit of self-doubt, which is why I want to drill this into your brains: What is meant for you won't miss you. The quicker you can accept and believe that, regardless of how tragic this loss is now, the better off you'll be. The situation will ultimately push you to grow and evolve in beautiful ways. Look for the silver linings!

Let's say you've been married for twenty years, have three kids, and discover that your husband (or wife!) has been leading a double life. Overnight your world blows up and you must start over again. I would say the world is giving you a second chance to change things up and pivot into something even bigger and better. Yes, it's going to hurt—change requires discomfort—but in the end, you must trust it will be worth it. Remember, if you do not believe you will make it to the end of the movie, you won't.

Unfortunately, none of us will make it out of this life unscathed; I fear that is the price of being human. The best we can do is channel our inner Sally Hardesty and commit to becoming the hero of our own story.

I admit that I have no idea what jump scares might be headed my way, but I'm confident in the arsenal I've cultivated over the years. I know that I can survive anything, and I want you to feel the same way. So allow me to share a few of my tips in Act III.

ACT III: THE AFTERLIFE

LESSONS LOOKING BACK

◆

Having been to hell and back, I have the privilege of hindsight, so now it's time to put it to use. Acts I and II were about my romantic journey and the lessons I collected along the way, so Act III is about looking back at what I've learned and how I would do things differently.

DICKSAND

Blame movies, the news, or my overly active imagination, but I've lived with a general sense of anxiety about being stuck in the action sequence portion of my life since I was about twelve. Look, you never know when you'll be in a car that 360s off a bridge and lands in water, leaving you with sixty seconds to escape before it sinks, or when you'll find yourself outrunning a knife-wielding sociopath hell-bent on filleting you like a fish. I've spent a lot of time mentally preparing to be the Neve Campbell of my life's franchise. So, it should come as no surprise that I grew up obsessing over quicksand.

Knowing that at any moment I could step down and the ground beneath me might crumble into a pit, slowly sucking me into its hungry mouth, is a burden I have carried for years. It's also a great analogy for what dating is like: You never know when your #soulmate will turn out to be a soul sucker. Which brings me to "dicksand." Unlike quicksand (which I recently learned is nothing like it's portrayed in the movies and is almost impossible to die from), dicksand is 100% real and will absolutely bury you. In fact, I think it's the number one enemy of love.

So what the fuck is dicksand? It's a catchall term for any type of romantic relationship that keeps you in limbo and wastes your time. Sometimes it's a one-night stand that "dickmatizes" you (against your better judgment) into a year of no-strings attachment, and other times, it's a six-year relationship headed nowhere. These relationships trap you with their potential—like at any moment you could turn a corner and things would be perfect—but that potential is never realized. And before you know it, you're waist deep in dicksand, missing out on other romantic opportunities.

Dicksand is the relationship equivalent of falling in love with "perfect" jeans that don't zip up, but you buy them anyway because you've convinced yourself that the pair will fit like a glove when you lose five pounds. Those jeans were never going to work, because if you lost the five pounds—which I have historically never done—the jeans might zip but the butt would sag. So those jeans sit in your closet taking up space, and over time, they just make you feel bad about the fact that you bought them in the first place. Maybe we don't share the same shitty shopping habits, so let me put it this way: Dicksand is the ever-present excuse(s) for holding onto the relationship a little bit longer, making it harder to extricate yourself in the long run.

There is no greater horror than exiting a relationship and realizing you voluntarily wasted your own time—but that is exactly what dicksand does to you. Lucky for you, I've experienced the four types of dicksand: textual relationships, thrill rides, treadmill relationships, and chronic breakups. And I can personally attest that they will all waste your time and leave you feeling stuck. So consider this your warning!

◆ ◆ ◆

TEXTUAL RELATIONSHIPS

I'd been "seeing" Bryan for three and a half months when photos of him and his pint-sized normcore girlfriend popped up on my Instagram feed. It was the day after my birthday—which I'd spent anxiously checking my phone for a birthday message that never came—when Bryan decided to hard launch his new girlfriend Jessica and their apartment in New York.

I'd seen Bryan on December 16 when I'd given him a stack of books and an embarrassingly long love letter. My birthday is December 18, but he was fully MIA for that. Then on December 19, this man showed up on the 'gram with a whole ass girlfriend, living in another state on the opposite side of the country. Either Bryan had fallen in love in two days, or I had been royally played.

I marched myself over to my friend Lila's Beachwood Canyon bungalow, and she promptly poured me a glass of rosé. I began to lay out, in excruciating detail, the facts of my case (i.e., breakup).

Bryan and I had met at a Labor Day wedding, where we hit it off talking about politics, film, and the best cigarettes (Benson & Hedges). He looked like Jacob Elordi preparing for the role of a "moody intellectual with a casual drug problem," which is to say that Bryan was tall, dark, and handsome, but also thin, brooding, and chain-smoking. Even though he was by far the hottest man at the wedding, I had zero interest in him because he was, admittedly, fresh out of a relationship and also because I was actively trying to fuck David Blaine.

"Like the magician?" Lila looked confused.

"Mmhmm," I said in between sips of wine. "My friend took me to his show, then introduced me afterward, and he has swagger."

Instead of going home with the top illusionist in the world, I started a romance with Bryan, an entirely different type of illusion.

The day after the wedding, Bryan asked for my number, then immediately asked me out on a date. However, he was leaving for the East Coast in two days and wouldn't be back for three weeks. And thus began our flurry of messages, memes, and voice memos.

"How long did you guys date again?"

"Three months-ish."

"Ish?" Lila asked.

"He was getting out of a pretty serious relationship, so we were going really slow because he was still in a dark place."

"So you weren't exclusive?"

"Apparently not." I took a large swig of my rosé for dramatic effect. "But he reassured me. His exact text was, 'I would let you know if I thought I was being unfair to you.' Call me crazy, but I think concealing a secret girlfriend is pretty unfair."

"Hold up." Lila said. "He reassured you via text?"

"Yeah," I said, ignoring the judgment in her tone. "He also told me that I'm the kind of girl he sees himself marrying one day."

Lila raised one brow before asking me, "How many times did you and Bryan actually go out?"

I was quiet. The answer was technically two dates, four if we wanted to include two hangs at my house, and five if we wanted to include the night we met, but even I thought five was a stretch.

"I'm not a math wizard, but four dates in three months?" Lila said, cringing. "If he liked you so much, why wasn't he trying to be with you?"

I regurgitated a laundry list of reasons: He was in between jobs, in between apartments, and—my personal favorite—he told me he was trying to get his life together to be ready for a girl like me. Of course, these were all his excuses, but I had bought into them like an eager investor in one of those pyramid schemes. And like most people investing in bad business models, I'd been had.

My eyes welled up.

"Babe, how are you this distraught?"

"I liked him! And I actually thought that he was trying to get his life together to be with me."

I wiped a tear away, and Lila comically poured herself some more wine.

In the beginning, Bryan was borderline obsessed with me, but I liked it. In a world full of left swipes and double taps, his unambiguous interest was attractive. Every night, over text we traversed everything from childhood stories to present day fears and future goals. What started off as a flicker of interest quickly exploded into a wildfire of attraction, threatening everything in sight. We would talk for hours (like five) about his weird love of cilantro or how I got the tiny scar on my pinky finger.

I soon found myself prioritizing conversations with Bryan over work and real-life dates. It was like an episode of *Black Mirror*, where I found myself controlled by the dopamine release I'd get every time my phone dinged with a new text. I can feel some of you judging me right now, and I fully get it, but I also know that plenty of you reading this are nodding your heads like, *Fuck girl, I have sooo been there.*

Lila was not having it. She didn't care that I'd seen Bryan the moment he got back to LA or that he'd shown up with a bottle of wine and refused to have sex with me "because he wanted to be respectful." The ninety-nine photos, twenty-three videos, hours of voice memos, and pages of messages meant nothing to Lila. She wanted to see action.

"You were in a textual relationship."

Her words stung, but she was right. A textual relationship is exactly like it sounds: a relationship revolving around your phone or computer. It's fueled by a constant stream of communication: memes that become inside jokes, intimate morning selfies, voice memo stories, Facetime phone sex. Textual relationships cultivate a false sense of intimacy and trust in a short time. You know what it *isn't*? A relationship built on shared experiences and unfiltered moments.

In a lot of ways, these digital relationships are like body pillows comforting us in the cold winter of singledom, a place to project all our relationship fantasies without the stickiness of an in-person romance. Sure, I knew Bryan in real life, and we had hung out, but 90% of our time together was spent on the other side of our phones. Bryan repeatedly told me I was "the sweetest," and that meeting me was the highlight of his year, but for all I know, he could have been taking a giant shit when he told me I was his "dream girl." I didn't really know Bryan; I knew the version he was projecting through his phone.

As Lila tried to hide her judgment, I became increasingly embarrassed.

Why am I this upset? I thought.

In the past when I'd dated someone for a couple of months and it didn't work out, I'd delete, mute, block, and keep moving on with my life, but textual romances can be some of the hardest relationships to get over because in a lot of ways you're falling in love with yourself.

As great as Bryan might be, I had really fallen for the fairy tale I'd created in my mind. I liked how witty I was with him and how he saw me as beautiful and funny and kind. Whenever I was headed out, I would pop a pic on Instagram and eagerly wait for him to respond.

Looking good [heart-eyes emoji].

Of course, I only posted the very best-looking photos of me. If I was lounging around at home when Bryan requested a selfie, I would quickly replace my ratty sweatshirt for a cute but casual top, add a couple of swipes of mascara, find my light, and snap tons of photos before selecting my favorite. I'd even subtly edit out a zit or two.

"Dream girl," he'd respond, before calling me a **"natural beauty."**

Sure, the photos of me were real, but with my best foot forward and not what Bryan would have seen had he been with me in the moment. Technology provides a barrier that allows us to conceal the parts of our lives we wish to avoid, and that is not how real relationships work. In the way that Instagram is often the highlight reel of our lives, textual relationships are also curated affairs. Regardless of how "real" I was with Bryan, I was in the driver's seat, instinctually dodging around the potholes and obstacles of my life's story. And so was he.

Through the lens of Bryan's phone, he saw me the way I wanted to see myself. I was lost and stressed and wanted to pour my energy into a new relationship rather than deal with the mess that was my life at that moment. He provided me with an escape, and an excuse to waste my time—and boy did I.

When I saw the photo of Bryan and his new girlfriend in their place in New York, I didn't reach out. In fact, I didn't do anything. I continued to watch them parade their love via every social media platform as if I were just another follower. It took time for me to see my relationship with Bryan for what it was because it felt so real to me. It also hurt knowing it was one-sided. While I was falling for Bryan, he had been falling for Jessica.

If I could take things back, I would have told David Blaine that I'd drive him to the airport. I'm kidding! I'd knock some sense into the Rory of yesteryear. While I think what Bryan did was shitty, the person I want to shake is me.

Stop waiting! Stop deflecting! You're wasting your time!

And I was. I'd built Bryan up to be someone that he wasn't, and I did it at the expense of my own well-being. If you find yourself making excuses or holding on to the future version of a relationship, stop. You're in dicksand and you're wasting your time. Stop valuing the potential of what a relationship "could be" over how it actually *is* in the present moment and start judging romantic partners based on their actions, not their words.

If I had done these two things, I would have realized that Bryan was not making enough effort to warrant the amount of energy I was giving him. I would have saved myself months! As a general rule of thumb, actions > words, always. So yeah, textual relationships = huge waste of time!

◆ ◆ ◆

THRILL RIDES

Derrick was considerably less cute than the rest of the men on my summer 2017 roster. From a distance, he had it going on, but up close, Derrick had dark bags under his eyes that looked like he hadn't slept in fourteen years. They were so distracting that I barely noticed his venti-size forehead carved with wrinkles. He also looked like he'd walked out of a J Crew catalog, making him about 99.9% preppier than the rock 'n' roll guys I was used to. He wore rolled-up khakis with loafers and collared shirts. He was persistent though, and I was feeling lazy, so I gave him a shot. But once we slept together, I went from apathetic to insatiable overnight. What dark bags? The only thing I could see through my heart-eyes was potential.

Anatomically, Derrick and I were a match, but he was also a master of angles. He was able to get his body low enough on the bed that it simulated edge-of-bed sex except that both of his hands were free which was especially fun for my clit. Together, even missionary felt less vanilla and more Rocky Road. I was so dick-whipped that when Derrick asked me to be his girlfriend after three weeks, I almost said yes. Thankfully I had the wherewithal to tell him we should take it slow. I was clear that I wasn't seeing anyone else but that I didn't want to rush into anything.

A few days later, I noticed that Derrick and Clara, one of my best friends, had started following each other on Instagram.

I thought it was strange that this friendship had never come up in conversation, so I called Clara.

"How do you know Derrick?"

"Who?" Clara never knows who anyone is, and I love that about her.

"Derrick Brown. You follow each other on IG."

"Oh, *that* guy. We matched on an app, and he's been up my ass ever since, why?"

"He's the new guy I've been seeing."

Derrick was on tour when I confronted him about this, and he responded by closing his computer, thus ending our Facetime. LOL.

The emotional rollercoaster of those three weeks reminded me of the time I'd gotten stuck on an actual roller coaster: Rascal's Revenge. Boy, did that ride truly get its revenge.

I climbed into a small two-seater car and pulled the lap bar down as tight as it would go. The ride looked like a giant W with a loop in the middle. We shot backward before slowly clanking our way up to one of the peaks until we stopped. At first, I thought the pause was for dramatic effect, but after about thirty seconds, I realized something was wrong.

Is this really happening? I thought.

This was the kind of thing that only happened in movies.

So there I was, suspended face down, 150 feet in the air, like I was looking through the face cradle on a massage table, except not only was there no table, there was also no floor. I was high enough that the people below look like ants. I watched as park employees scurried around in a panic, trying to figure out what to do. Eventually, a voice boomed over the loudspeaker, something about a mechanical error but that also (ha ha!) the emergency release lever was stuck.

After more chaotic scrambling, an employee scaled the metal ladder welded onto the side of the ride. Upon reaching the top, he breathlessly explained that our only option was to climb, one-by-one, down the same ladder.

I might actually die up here. I thought.

My hands were slick with sweat as I white-knuckled the safety bar keeping me from free-falling to my death.

I held my breath as passengers at the front climbed out and onto the little tin platform and started down the ladder. My turn drew near, and I questioned all the life choices that had led to this moment. Whatever fun I might have had on this ride, the enjoyment was not worth what was happening now. Sure, fewer than five people a year die on roller coasters.[22] But the experience taught me that machines, which are fallible, are operated by people—who are also fallible. So regardless of safety statistics, I decided from then on I would care more self-preservation than the adrenaline surge I got from thrill rides.

Thankfully though, before my turn to climb down the ladder, the emergency release started working, and we rolled slowly down the track. I don't remember a single thing after exiting that ride, but I've never been back to that theme park.

I swore off roller coasters altogether. After my traumatizing experience, prioritizing never being in that situation again—over gaining a quick thrill—was easy. But I have had numerous Rascal-style experiences with men, and it's never stopped me from getting back on their rides. Derrick is a prime example.

About nine months after our dramatic split, I found myself late-night booty texting Derrick from a bar we used to frequent. I knew the text was a bad idea, but I swore to myself, *It's just sex. You're never going to date him again.* An hour later, Derrick was swimming in apologies, and we embarked on the beginning of our "second try." I realized, not long after, that I was back in the same sinking boat: He was good in bed but bad for

---

[22] A R Pelletier and J Gilchrist, "Roller Coaster Related Fatalities, United States, 1994-2004," Injury Prevention 11, no. 5 (October 1, 2005): 309–12, https://doi.org/10.1136/ip.2005.008425.

my head. Derrick was by far the jankiest roller coaster I'd ever ridden, and I was grateful when a better ride came along.

They say that good dick imprisons you, and I personally believe that's because it's about as rare as dry panties during a Ryan Gosling movie. I tolerated Derrick because after Chris I was in an era of my life where sex and my satisfaction felt like a priority. I'd reached a place where I would rather have orgasms with a lying loser than be sexually starved with a great guy. In my mind, I knew dating Derrick again was a bad idea, but I had been dickmatized, so I had little control.

I lost a lot of time and probably missed out on meeting someone better because I was stuck riding "Derrick's Revenge" when I should have braved the rickety escape ladder. Instead of wasting emotional real estate on an unworthy partner, I should have invested in better vibrators.

Learning to own my pleasure has been one of my most freeing experiences, and it released me from the sexual circus I felt trapped in. Prior to my sexual awakening, I kept buying tickets for rides hoping they were safe, fun, and well operated, and I kept finding myself in terrifying, Rascal-style situationships. Dating Derrick was like riding the worst roller coaster at the saddest carnival, but the element of danger made it all the more exciting. You've got to be careful with those thrill rides because you can waste a lot of time whipping around the same tracks, and sooner or later you're going to develop terrible whiplash.

◆ ◆ ◆

TREADMILL RELATIONSHIPS

Treadmill relationships—unlike the other subsets of dicksand—can run for several years, but no matter how many miles you log with your significant other, you'll never actually get off the machine. Much like it sounds, a treadmill relationship can be defined as any type of partnership that isn't going anywhere. This can look like a toxic cycle or a relationship that's mediocre—or maybe even great—but that never progresses forward into something *more*. I, of course, have been in both kinds.

Let's start with the toxic relationship. Y'all remember Marcus, my zombie? I was convinced that Marcus was my soulmate even though we would brawl all the time, like two cage fighters 'roided out and ripping each other apart. Then we'd make up, and it was like falling in love for the first time all over again. We really put the *fun* in dysfunctional.

I loved him like a security blanket that was so old it couldn't be washed without destroying it. Its frayed and tattered edges might have been covered in dirt, but at least it was familiar and felt soft and warm. Marcus and I were the *tread* in treadmill, repeating the same toxic loop until finally it wore me out. I'd finally realized that my security blanket was more of a biohazard.

Years later I found myself giving advice to a friend in a similar relationship. I told her, "You shouldn't measure a relationship by how good the good times are; you should measure it by how bad the bad times are." I don't know if I could have heard this back when Marcus and I were twenty, but it would have saved me a lot of time and spared me so much drama. I also think about the people I missed out on during this on-and-off relationship and how I was never fully available because I always felt like Marcus and I were going to get back together.

Those fiery, toxic relationships might be fun in the short run but the more times you repeat a cycle, the more normalized bad behavior becomes. It's a slippery slope, my friends.

A less tumultuous example of a treadmill relationship was my time with a guy named Scott. Six months into dating, I *knew* he wasn't "my person" but I didn't want to break up, because Scott and I had so much fun together. Part of why I didn't see a future for us was part of what made him endlessly entertaining: He did not live in reality. Scott was a trust-fund party boy with a heart of gold, but I also couldn't trust him to keep my plants alive if I went out of town. Responsibility? He'd never met her. And yet, some of my favorite memories are laughing with Scott until the wee hours or the morning.

We were together for a year and a half, which would not have been a problem—except that I was looking to find the person I could spend the rest of my life with. Call me crazy, but I'm pretty sure staying in a multi-year relationship with a guy you don't see a future with is not how it's done.

Sure, I could argue that I was living in the moment or hoping Scott would grow into the man I wanted him to be, and both of those things might be a tiny bit true, but it's probably more accurate to admit that I liked our life together and I didn't want anything to change. Even though I knew that Scott and I were going nowhere, I was comfortable running in place. I wasn't ready to get off the treadmill. Deep down I longed for new sights and fresh air, but the fear of the unknown and running alone kept me from getting off the treadmill and leaving the proverbial gym.

There's an aptly named business theory called the "sunk cost effect" that describes peoples' continued investment into things that aren't working. Like "throwing good money after bad," the sunk cost effect theory hinges on the principle that people are so averse to loss that they will often continue to sink money into failing ventures simply to avoid the pain associated with failure. Treadmill relationships are basically the romantic equivalent of the sunk cost effect: The longer you linger in one, the harder it is to let it go. I stayed with Marcus and Scott because I didn't want to face the loss of either of those relationships.

The longer you stay in something that isn't going anywhere, the closer you'll find yourself in the middle of nowhere. Treadmill relationships may feel safe because they're comfortable or familiar, but at what cost? Ultimately you have to ask yourself what's worse: committing to something that isn't right for you and regretting it later or wiping the slate clean and starting over. If you don't want to settle, then don't settle. The sooner you get out, the sooner you can heal and meet someone better. And there is someone better!

◆ ◆ ◆

CHRONIC BREAKUPS

I broke my arm as a teenager, but my last breakup hurt *way* worse. The pain was so excruciating at times that I thought I might die from heartache. It was brutal, and yet I quit him cold turkey. I didn't reach out, I rarely checked his social media, and anytime my mind drifted to thoughts about my ex, I redirected my attention. Yes, I grieved, and I allowed myself to feel my feelings, but I did not indulge my impulses, and I maintained a strict healing protocol. We had a clean break, and as a result, I healed and moved on. But that was very different from how I handled my breakup with Greg.

The first time I stepped on a skateboard, I fell flat on my face. My second time on a skateboard, I was kicking it to a friend and somehow managed to launch myself into a backflip, before kissing the concrete.

Next thing I knew, I was sitting in a large beige room with my legs dangling off a gray-green table reminiscent of an ironing board. It was cold and smelled like old people with a hint of industrial cleaning supplies. I clung to my left arm as I surveyed the giant x-ray machine sitting next to me. It felt like a tiny fire had started deep inside my forearm before spreading out to my fingers.

Suddenly, a wiry man with scrubs and a white coat walked in with my father.

My dad put his hand on my back. "How're you holding up?"

I put on a brave face. "It hurts pretty bad, but I'm okay." I noticed a familiar metallic taste in my mouth as my eyes welled up. I gulped hard, determined not to cry in front of my dad's colleague. The man in the white coat held up my x-rays as if they would mean anything to me.

"You broke your arm, but it's not bad," my dad explained. "We are gonna get you into a cast though, so that it heals properly."

Hot tears rolled down my face. Something finite about the diagnosis made me cry. Once the doctor made it official, I knew I had a long healing road ahead of me, and it was overwhelming.

My arm hurt the most on the day I broke it and in the immediate weeks after (just like my heart hurt the worst on the day that my ex and I broke up and in the immediate weeks after). I wore a cast for months, which made my day-to-day life tricky, but slowly my arm began to hurt less and less until eventually the bone healed.

The thing about fractures, whether they're hairlines or full-blown shatters, is that they need to be properly addressed and then given the time and rest to heal. Otherwise they just continue to re-break and you run the risk of a chronic issue. A wound is considered chronic if it has not healed significantly in four weeks or completely in eight weeks, and while some breaks might take longer, the key is forward progress. Emotional breaks (aka breakups) are no different.

I am a firm believer that no contact after a breakup is the emotional equivalent of a cast. This includes blocking or muting on social media, not scrolling through photos, and resisting trips down memory lane. Setting boundaries around communication, having a plan for recovery, and taking the time and space to heal without seeing your ex helps you bounce back faster. Going no-contact might hurt more in the beginning because it's understandably hard to go from talking to your "person" every day to suddenly not at all, but I wholeheartedly think it's the healthiest way to heal. I mean, I've tried the other way.

Greg and I only dated for a couple of months before we broke up, but you would have thought we'd been together for sixty years. In my weak defense, this relationship came after Dean, so I was fragile and unwell. I monitored Greg's social media like I was a P.I. going so far as to set up a finsta (a fake Instagram account) where I could monitor everyone he was liking and following. I justified this batshit behavior by telling myself that it would help me move on once I saw that Greg had. But it did the opposite. He was always at the forefront of my mind, and consequently I was always finding a reason for us to talk. I thought about him just as much post-breakup as I had when we were dating. Each little interaction chipped away at any of the healing I was doing until the crack in my heart looked like the Grand Canyon. If you're rolling your eyes or shaking your head, I should warn you: It gets worse.

In a particularly low and delusional moment, we hooked up. It was the final blow that shattered my already tattered heart. I didn't even love this guy, and our breakup took me longer to recover from than any of my long-term boyfriends. As I wallowed in the hurt, unable—or simply refusing—to move on, I took what started as a clean break and turned it into a chronic ailment. I tortured myself, and it didn't have to be that way.

Imagine if I had refused a cast in the hospital the day I'd broken my arm and instead kept jumping back on (and falling off) the same stupid skateboard? There's no way I would have done that! My arm would have ended up mangled. So why did I do this with my emotional health? Unlike with broken bones, we don't have doctors who can set our broken hearts and outline the steps for us to properly heal—we have to be our own advocates. We have to be the ones to metaphorically set our own casts and maintain our boundaries for proper healing.

Whether it's been three weeks or three decades, breakups hurt. And while we might not be able to control whether a relationship ends, we do have the ability to create excellent aftercare. Keeping a past relationship alive in your heart is a lot like keeping food in the refrigerator past the expiration date: At first, it's not a big deal, but slowly the food starts to rot and eventually the whole fridge smells like garbage. A mourning period is normal, but holding on to an ex long enough that you isolate yourself from reality, making everyone suffer the consequences of your decomposing fridge, is not.

In terms of dicksand, a chronic breakup is one of the more horrifying ways to waste your time. Don't make excuses like I did—just confront the situation head-on and heal so that you can move on to someone better. Trust me, the alternative is scary.

In conclusion, dicksand will waste your time and hold you back from getting what you want. It's sneaky, so you have to stay vigilant or else one day you could wake up and realize you spent years of your life in dead-end relationships. And no one wants those kinds of regrets. Speaking of regrets, be careful with skateboards.

SLUTS GET CUT

◆

"**D**eath by Sex" is a famous trope in horror movies where "sluts" die first. As with Tina in *Nightmare on Elm Street*, Lynda in *Halloween* and, all the opening couples in *Friday the 13th*, we see that sex is a classic recipe for death. Conventional horror movies and conventional dating advice are similar in that they both pedestal virginity—if you want to survive the horror movie or make it to the altar, you can't give *it* up. Those are the rules.

But who came up with those rules?

If you look at popular dating books from the last couple of decades, they are rife with misogynistic "advice" for women about withholding sex as a tactic to get men to respect them but also fall in love with them. For example, *Not Your Mother's Rules* features a rule (and chapter) dedicated to not sleeping with a man before you're in a relationship so that you don't become another "notch on his belt."[23] The rationale is that guys

---

[23] Ellen Fein and Sherrie Schneider, *Not Your Mother's Rules: The New Secrets for Dating* (Grand Central Publishing, 2013).

only want girls who are "hard to get" and women who "value themselves". Their words, not mine.

In *Why Men Love Bitches,* there's an entire section of the book dedicated to sex called "The Candy Store" where the overarching principle is no free candy—aka don't give it up.[24] They assert that men won't see you as "worthwhile" if you don't make them wait. Conversely, men will see you as more attractive and more valuable if you make them wait as long as possible to have sex.

First off, what the actual fuck?

Second, I despise this kind of advice. What does it say about men and the standards we have for them if they don't see women as fully realized individuals without taking sex off the table? Does no one think it's insane that we've collectively accepted the notion that men can only fall in love with women if they are tricked into it by short-term celibacy or gameplaying? Give me a break.

And what does it say about women? By this logic, the most valuable thing a woman brings to a relationship lies between her legs. I'm sorry, but this is antiquated AF.

Chastity has its roots in religion, but more specifically, in the *control* of women. Have you ever noticed that there's a wild double standard when it comes to sex? If a man sleeps with a bunch of women, he's considered a playboy, desired, or "the man," but if a woman sleeps around, then she's loose, easy, slutty, or has low self-worth. Words like *slut, whore, thot,* or *run-through* are all derogatory terms used to insult or degrade women for doing the same thing that men get praised for. We don't even have negative words to describe a male "slut."

Have you ever wondered why this is? I sure have. And all roads lead back to the oppression of women. I realize this might sound hyperbolic, but hear me out. If you look at the last

---

24 Sherry Argov, *Why Men Love Bitches: From Doormat to Dreamgirl — A Woman's Guide to Holding Her Own in a Relationship* (Simon and Schuster, 2002).

hundred years of women's history in America, you will see that whenever women have gained significant freedoms, these gains have always been met with resistance in the form of slut shaming or revoking bodily autonomy.

In the 1920s, when women were moving to big cities and gaining independence and dating became a thing, there was The American Plan: a federal act that allowed the government and civil servants to arrest, detain, and imprison women on "suspicion of lewd behavior."[25] There was a problem with STI's amongst soldiers in WWI, so the government enacted the Chamberlain-Kahn Act, which gave police officers and government agents the power to detain any woman they thought could have an STI. Eating alone, changing jobs, or walking without a chaperone were considered suspicious behaviors that could lead to a woman's arrest. Punishments ranged from reform schools for women who didn't seem ladylike, to forced hysterectomies and months in prison without due process. Naturally, this disproportionately affected the poor and women of color. America had an STI problem with soldiers, but everyday women paid the price.

Similarly, birth control was legalized for single women in 1972, and women were finally allowed to get credit cards on their own in 1974 (Equal Credit Opportunity Act). These were monumental moments for women's independence. Not long after, Ronald Reagan ran and won on a platform of conservatism. His "traditional family values" campaign marked the beginning of a conservative backlash, with an emphasis on restricting reproductive health care.[26]

One might argue that the current push for abortion bans and reproductive health restrictions is a reaction to the #metoo

---

25 Scott W. Stern, "America's Forgotten Mass Imprisonment of Women," HISTORY, June 30, 2025, https://www.history.com/articles/chamberlain-kahn-act-std-venereal-disease-imprisonment-women.

26 "Radio Address to the Nation on Family Values," Ronald Reagan, (December 20, 1986), https://www.reaganlibrary.gov/archives/speech/radio-address-nation-family-values.

movement and the gains women made against the normalization of sexual violence. Either way you slice it, women's liberation, and more specifically sexual liberation, is a threat to the patriarchy because it challenges gender norms and undermines our system of male dominance. Men have historically had control over women, and whenever that shifts, a trackable reaction follows.

So, how does this relate to horror movies?

Horror movies have often been used to explore the fears and repressions of various generations. With the damsel-in-distress trope and the men-terrorizing-women trope, the horror genre has always been steeped in patriarchal gender norms. In fact, Carol Clover, PhD, the woman who coined the term final girl, noted that for horror movies to be successful, the surviving character needed to be female because the person needed to experience terror, and audiences have a hard time accepting men who show fear.[27] Male audiences are more apt to connect with the killer than they are to a scared male lead, and for a movie to be successful, the filmmakers need audiences to align with and root for the survivor. Hence the creation and proliferation of the final girl.

Many of the original final girls were seen as morally superior compared to the other female characters who ended up dying. Unlike their friends, these women abstained from sex and drugs and other "bad" behavior. Final girls always withheld sex like the aforementioned dating books advised.

But that was then. Recently, there have been a slew of "slutty" final girls, and it speaks to the changing times. And yet a lot of dating advice remains stuck in the dark ages. So much has changed in the last fifty years, and the advice we give to women (and men) around sex needs to change as well.

Personally, I dislike any sort of advice that suggests women need to wait to have sex because if they "put out" too soon, men

---

27 Carol J. Clover, "Her Body, Himself: Gender in the Slasher Film," Representations 20 (1987): 187–228, https://www.jstor.org/stable/2928507.

won't be interested. Anecdotally, that advice has also not been true for *me*. Many of my long-term boyfriends (who aren't mentioned in this book because they aren't *monsters*) are men I had sex with on the first or second date. Conversely, I've waited to have sex and it's blown up in my face.

In my experience, men seem to know when they like you, and they're either available or they're not. It's as simple as that. So much time and energy gets devoted to figuring out how to tell if a man likes you, and I just want to say: It should be obvious. If it's not obvious, it's probably a no. A lot of times men will give us the answer, but we won't like it, so we'll spend weeks and months trying to change it. I've never managed to trick an unavailable man into falling in love with me by withholding sex, just like I've never been able to turn off a man who did like me because we had sex. I think the bigger question is, Why is so much advice focused on teaching women *how to be chosen* instead of teaching women *how to choose*?

When it comes to dating advice no one knows the "rules," because there *are no rules*. You need to come up with your own rules. You need to figure out your own set of dating principles based on your own ideals and do what feels right for *you*. Don't listen to me (or anyone else); follow your own standards. If you don't feel comfortable having sex until you know you are the only person your partner is seeing or sleeping with, then you should honor that and reject casual sex. Conversely, if you want to have sex on the first date and you know that it won't hurt your feelings if you never hear from them again, then your rules will look different. As long as you are in alignment with your values, you will move through the world with confidence, and that will attract the type of person you're looking for. It's when you aren't acting in alignment that things get a bit wonky. We can sense when people are faking it, and that goes for pretending to be casual about sex when that's not how you feel.

Either way, I implore you to question the origins of your beliefs around sex. Most women I talk to know that having sex is not morally wrong, and yet they still feel bad if they don't "hold out." I have friends who still blame themselves when something doesn't work out with a man because they slept with him "too soon." And to that I would say, too soon for *whom*? Who led you to believe that there is a right and a wrong time for sex? Who created this arbitrary timeline and where is this story coming from?

One of the best things I ever did for my dating life was get honest with myself about sex so that I could establish my own set of rules outside of the conventional bias I was raised with. I realized that casual sex was something I could enjoy and not regret if I went into it without any expectations. If I found myself on a first or second date thinking, *This is my dream man* or *Maybe he can be my date to this wedding in three months,* then I knew I had to pump the brakes on sex because I had hopes and expectations. This rule requires me to constantly check in with myself and make my decisions based on how I'm feeling. If I suspect that I'll be disproportionately upset if a relationship fizzles after we hook up, then I abstain from sex until I feel more secure.

To be clear, I'm never holding back because I think doing so is going to change the outcome of a relationship; I am holding back to protect myself. When I pump the brakes on sex, my actions are about *me* not *them*. I am not abstaining to attract the person; I am doing it as an act of self-care and a way to mitigate my anxieties. If I am already excited about a person and we add intimacy to the mix, I know I'll be at risk of diving in too fast, ignoring red flags, putting them on a pedestal, etc. My actions are not about trying to get a man to like me more; they're about self-regulating so that I can show up as the best version of myself.

Again, this is *my* compass that I have developed through trial and error and lots of introspection; you will have to figure out what works for you. But the only time it's too soon to sleep with someone is if it is too soon *for you*. You have just as much right to enjoy pleasure as men do, but it needs to be on your own terms. Whether you want to wait three months or three hours, as long as you're not playing games, I fully support your timeline.

Remember, sex has been weaponized against women for years. Developing a sense of sexual agency and an understanding of your personal boundaries arms you with a protective shield. In a landscape as horrific as the modern dating scene, every final girl needs her own protection!

BODY COUNT

"What's your body count?"

If you're over thirty, you may or may not know what I am talking about. A person's body count does not refer to how many people he or she has murdered, but rather to how many sexual partners they've had. It's the modern version of "what's your number?" And it's *fuuuuuuucking* lame.

There's something inherently sick about equating past partners to a pile of dead bodies, and it reeks of double standards. Reducing a person down to the number of people they've had sex with is immature at best and misogynistic at worst. And, yes, men can be victims of misogyny as well.

The only people who will ask you about your body count are people who are insecure about your answer. I assure you that any man confident in his masculinity isn't asking a woman about the amount of men she's slept with before him.

If a man is worried about how many people you've slept with, I promise you, you can do better—and you should. Do not settle for a guy who sees your value as something that can fluctuate depending on how many people you've had sex with. You're not Bitcoin, for God's sake!

If someone ever asks you your body count, consider it an immediate red flag, and I suggest you abandon this romantic prospect as fast as humanly possible. If you insist on ignoring my advice, then try these responses:

"I'm sorry, are you sixteen? I didn't know anyone seriously asked this question after high school?"

"I lost track after I hit 3K."

"With a gun or with a knife?" And when they are inevitably confused, you could just say, "Ask stupid questions, get stupid answers."

"That's a super unattractive question. I'm going to give you the benefit of the doubt and pretend like you didn't ask that." Then change the subject.

As a warning, your date my respond by saying they want to know your body count because they're worried about STIs and want to know if you're "clean." While I love a conversation about sexual health, this is obviously *not* the way to have that conversation. And please, stop using words like *clean*!

If you want to ask about someone's sexual health, do that. Simply say, "Before we get too heated, I'd love to talk about sex." Then, if it were me, I'd use the moment as an opportunity to ask about when their last STI panel was, what kind of protection they want to use, and what they're into. I think the sexual health conversation is a great time to talk about boundaries, turn-ons, and turn-offs. It's sexy *and* informative. Plus, if someone can't handle a conversation *about* sex, I know that I'm probably not going to enjoy the actual sex. (But that's just me.) This would also be the moment to disclose if you do have any STIs and how you've navigated this with previous partners.

TL:DR: If they ask you your body count, run!

FUNERALS

Everyone breaks up.
Unless you happen to be that one in a billion who marries their first love and dies in a freak accident at the *exact* same time as your partner, you're going to go through a breakup of some sort. Whether it's "till death do you part" or "it's not you, it's me," having a plan for the end could be the difference between moving on and enduring prolonged psychological damage. Enter: the romantic funeral.

When most people think of funerals, they think of death—which makes sense. Even before Homo sapiens, Neanderthals had deliberate post-death rituals. What I'm saying is as long as there's been life, there have been traditions around death. And for good reason. Funerals provide a sense of closure and a way to comfort those in mourning. Every culture has their own funeral rites because they're a vital step in the grieving process.

I was less than ten when my grandmother died. It was the first time anyone in my world had passed and my first experience with mortality. I vaguely remember speaking at her funeral, but mostly, I just remember being sad. A few years later, at fourteen, my first friend died. Magnus was one of those freakishly smart kids—he literally had the second highest math scores in the state of California—that everyone, including parents, loved. His untimely death was a tragedy in the truest sense of the word, and our entire school went into mourning.

His funeral had so many people in attendance that the church didn't have enough room for everyone, and the overflow spilled into the parking lot. People made posters, playlists, and shirts to commemorate his life. Everyone expressed their sadness in different ways, and I took comfort in knowing I wasn't alone in my sorrow. It was a dark time, but I felt a strong sense of community. Having the space and structure to grieve made it possible for me to process that kind of loss at such a young age.

I would argue that breakups are a kind of death. In some circumstances, you do lose that person entirely, whether you need a clean break, they ghost, or one party does something so hurtful that you have an unspoken agreement that you'll never talk again. In other circumstances, the "death" is the loss of the life you shared with your partner. Outside of losing your best friend and the person you talked to everyday, breakups force you to let go of the future you thought you were building together and the person you were becoming in that relationship. The part of you that had invested deeply in another person is now left untethered. Suffice to say, breakups can trigger the same level of grief as an actual death.

But don't just take my word for it. Helen Fisher, PhD, a biological anthropologist, studied people who had recently been dumped and found that the same parts of the brain associated with addiction were activated post-breakup.[28] In other words, romantic rejection can lead to the same types of pain, cravings, and withdrawals caused by alcohol and drugs.

In 2011, Ethan Kross, PhD, and the University of Michigan conducted a study on heartbreak to test whether heartbreak

---

28   Helen Fisher, "Dumped!" New Scientist, February 14, 2004, https://www.newscientist.com/article/mg18124345-300-dumped/.

would light up the same parts of the brain as physical pain. The researchers divided participants into two groups. The first half were exposed to physical pain, and their reactions were measured via MRI. Meanwhile, the second group, having recently been dumped, were asked to recall specific experiences or memories while looking at photos of their ex. Their reactions were also measured via MRI. The study found that the brain networks that activated when people experienced severe physical pain also activated when the second group talked about their breakups.[29]

Then there's broken heart syndrome, or takotsubo cardiomyopathy, which is a medical condition that can, in rare cases, lead to death. This is a real physical condition where intense emotional stress causes your heart muscle to suddenly weaken. It can feel just like a heart attack, with chest pain and shortness of breath, even though there's no blocked artery.[30] So if we know that heartbreak can lead to unbearable anguish and physical harm, why is it often minimized?

Once, after a particularly brutal breakup, I sent a mass email out to my friends because the thought of having to tell everyone individually made me want to run into oncoming traffic. At first my friends were supportive and rightfully concerned about my well-being, but after a few months, they moved on from the topic. Four months out and no one was asking me how I was doing anymore. It's not that I have bad friends—quite the opposite. It's that the general sentiment around breakups is "time heals all wounds, and you'll get over it." (I am guilty of this too!)

Societally, we treat heartbreak as if it's a trivial thing that everyone should be able to bounce back from. After all, it's just

---

29 Ethan Kross, et al., "Social Rejection Shares Somatosensory Representations with Physical Pain," *Proceedings of the National Academy of Sciences* 108, no. 15 (March 28, 2011): 6270–75, https://doi.org/10.1073/pnas.1102693108.
30 Joseph Assad et al., "Takotsubo Syndrome: A Review of Presentation, Diagnosis and Management," Clinical Medicine Insights Cardiology 16 (January 1, 2022), https://doi.org/10.1177/11795468211065782.

a breakup, right? If a loved one dies, you're expected to skip exams, cancel plans last minute, and take time off from work, but that same grace is rarely extended for heartbreak. Maybe for a divorce, but people tend to project their own opinions about how fast someone should be able to recover from romantic loss based on their own biases. The irony is that the lack of societal support for the heartbroken tends to compound one's pain, making healing even harder. Lacking encouragement and care will prolong your grieving and healing process.

Breaking up is life-altering, and the hill I'm willing to die on—pun intended—is that treating a breakup like a death will help you heal better. That means establishing rituals and routines for the end of relationships just as we do for engagements and weddings and baby showers. We should approach endings with the same fervor with which we approach beginnings. The next time you find yourself in the throes of heartbreak, throw yourself a romantic funeral.

I am not the first person to propose this. A quick google search will show you articles as far back as 2008 discussing romantic funerals. But I *am* trying to make them more popular. I'd never heard of a romantic funeral when Jack broke my heart. It wasn't until several years later, after Waldo, that I stumbled into my first "funeral."

My first romantic funeral happened by accident. I found out Waldo was cheating on me a couple of weeks before I found out that Hooters was offering a "Shred Your Ex" special on Valentine's Day. If you came in with a photo of your ex and shredded it, you'd get a free order of wings. What started off as a funny joke on the group chat turned into an all-girls Valentine's Day celebration of my jilted heart.

The lead-up to Valentine's Day meant constant texts on our group thread. Funny memes, jokes, and words of support flooded my phone. Several single girlfriends decided they wanted to join in, and suddenly our Hooter's trip became more than a moment to reclaim my singledom but also a way to reclaim Valentine's Day itself.

I fired off a few photos of Waldo, asking the group to pick which one I should destroy.

"ALL OF THEM," wrote Heather.

Despite living in New York for most of our friendship, Heather always seemed to be in LA anytime I was going through a breakup. By this point, she'd seen several monsters and was eager to help put Waldo behind me. I made the trip to Kinkos and printed out a small stack of photos, giving me plenty of options.

We decided to dress up. I wore all black—minus a dark-blue mini skirt—and my girlfriends did the same. Then, we trekked to the Times Square of Los Angeles, Hollywood and Highland, and walked into Hooters. An adorable waitress with bouncy hair and very short shorts walked us to a circular high-top. I placed the photos of my shitty ex face down before ordering a margarita "with salt, please."

When it came time to order, I presented our waitress with my photos, and she directed me to a booth in the center of the restaurant. I felt a surge of adrenaline, and suddenly, my palms were sweaty. My friends looked at me, concerned. I didn't realize the entire restaurant was going to be involved in this. *Whoops.* I swallowed hard and made my way to what looked like a kissing booth refurbished with broken hearts. Before I could stop to process what was about to happen, another waitress rang a loud bell, grabbing everyone's attention.

"Shred. Your. Ex!" she cheered.

And then, in front of approximately fifty strangers, I held up a photo of the man who did me dirty and I ripped his face in half.

The room erupted in cheers and whoops. And in that moment, I felt seen. None of these people knew the details of what I'd been through, but they all understood my pain. Heartbreak is one of the most universal experiences on the planet. I felt supported and encouraged, and for a brief moment I was excited about moving on with my life. I wanted to look back on this day and laugh. Granted, I was still obsessed with Hope and my healing process would be complicated, but that moment in Hooters propelled me forward.

"Your *free* wings," the waitress said as she presented me with a basket full of chicken tendies.

I took a bite.

My girlfriends held up their margaritas. Then Heather made a toast. "To Waldo, for showing you who he *really* is and not wasting any more of your time!"

"I'll drink to that," I said.

We clinked our glasses and spent the remainder of the night gabbing, gossiping, and reflecting on my breakup over baskets of fried food.

And let me just say, there's something about *free wings* that just tastes better. But more importantly, being surrounded by my girlfriends reminded me that life is about so much more than romantic love. This accidental and unconventional Hooters funeral helped me bookend my relationship, gave me perspective, and inspired me to move on. When your community shows up for you, it's easier to see that there's more to life than having a boyfriend.

Coming to terms with a breakup, especially if it wasn't your choice, can be hard, but to move on, you *have* to let go. Unlike a physical injury where your body spontaneously heals itself, heartbreak requires you to be in charge of your own healing. If left undirected, your mind will try to make sense of things you don't understand by ruminating and making up narratives. Our brains are designed to keep us safe by replaying memories of things that hurt us so that we don't do them again. This is great if the lesson is about not touching a hot stove, but it's less great when you've been cheated on. So give your relationship a death certificate, complete with a cause of death. Name the pain so you can give yourself closure and let go.

I think of the romantic funeral as the first step to accepting your new reality. It's your way of saying to yourself—and to God, the universe, whatever you believe in—that you are ready to embark on your healing journey. It's an event to mark the end of one thing and the beginning of the next, while also providing you with support from your community.

HOW TO THROW A ROMANTIC FUNERAL

Okay, so you want to throw a funeral, but you don't know where to start. Fear not, I've got you. First off, you can make this experience whatever you want it to be, so use my suggestions as just that—suggestions—and make this moment into what will serve you and your healing the best.

+WHO
Depending on how long the relationship was and how badly it ended, maybe you want an intimate gathering or a total blowout. Regardless, surround yourself with people who genuinely love you and want to see you win. You can send out an invitation for "The Death of [insert you and your partner's name]" or "RIP our Relationship."

+WHEN
I recommend you give yourself a couple of weeks post-breakup to let the shock wear off and figure out exactly what you want to achieve moving forward. Planning a funeral will, ideally, help take your mind off your grief, so it's a nice distraction, but you also want it to be far out enough where it'll actually benefit you.

I think two to four weeks is a sweet spot, but again, you should follow your gut on this.

+WHERE
This is where you get to really figure out how you want to celebrate the end. Do you prefer an intimate gathering at home? A private room at a restaurant? Does your funeral start at your place and end up at a karaoke dive bar scream-singing till 2 a.m.? Or maybe you end up smashing things at one of those rage rooms or sweating it out in a massive dance party. Either way, consider the *what* as you plan your *where*.

+WHAT
A funeral, duh! This is where I challenge you to think about *how* you want to celebrate. Do you need something small and intimate or wild and raucous? Think about the ways in which you can use this event to both close out one chapter and set you up for the next. Think about the ways in which your network can help support you. Do you need help packing up all the things that remind you of your ex? Maybe part of your funeral process is asking your friends to remove the physical triggers that make you think of your former love and storing them in a safe space out of sight.

Use the funeral to prepare for the future and the inevitable obstacles your brain will throw at you. For me, I'd want to come up with a mantra, something I could repeat to myself when my toxic narratives start to creep in. We all replay the greatest moments from our relationships, so maybe take time to write a list of the unpleasant memories you have from the relationship. Ask your friends to chip in if you feel comfortable. Then, when your mind inevitably runs wild and tries to replay all the good times, you can reference this list and ground yourself back in reality.

Again, customize the event to you to and make sure it meets your needs. And for those of you feeling overwhelmed by grief, here are some ideas:

FUNERAL SUGGESTIONS

- Give yourself closure—come up with a reason for the breakup, even if you weren't given one. *Because I deserve someone better* or *because I want to be with someone who loves me the way that I love them* are good places to start.
- Acknowledge the pain you're feeling. Since we live in a culture that doesn't properly acknowledge the agony of heartache, you need to do that yourself. It's okay to say, *This break up isn't what I wanted, and I'm devastated.* But then cap it. Don't spend the whole night dwelling, because again, moving on means letting go, and this is the first step in hopefully doing that.
- Have a guest book and ask your friends to write you messages for those days when you're feeling down. You could also do this with a jar. Have everyone write notes of encouragement on little pieces of paper, crumple them up, and throw them into a jar. When you need a pick-me-up, pull out a note.
- Write a eulogy (a letter) to your old relationship, and share it or burn it.
- Change something about your living space to give yourself a "fresh start."
- Ask your friends to make toasts with their wishes for you moving forward.
- Get a jar (or use the same one from above) and have everyone write down their favorite movies, podcasts, books, or TV shows, and the next time you find yourself feeling sad or aimless, pull a suggestion out of the jar. Afterward, connect with your friend and tell them what you liked about their suggestion.
- Do something that brings you joy. Dancing, laughing, face masks, or bar hopping—whatever it is, make sure you enjoy it to remind yourself that happiness exists

outside of your relationship. Give yourself that dopamine hit!
- Maybe it's fun to dress up like it's an actual funeral, or maybe you want to theme it. Get creative with the dress code. Who doesn't love a good theme night?
- Make sure to thank the people who showed up for you. Breakups are hard on everyone, not just the person feeling heartbroken. Your community will appreciate the acknowledgment.

ROMANTIC FUNERALS WITH YOUR EX

What if you want to have a funeral with your ex, like conscious uncoupling? This won't be for everyone, but assuming you want to stay friendly or you don't have hard feelings, I think it's a lovely option. In that case, I would recommend you come up with a date together, then go no-contact in the meantime. If it were me, I'd choose three to four weeks. Decide if you want this to be a private thing between the two of you or if you want to invite your community to join you. Personally, that feels more apt for long-term relationships or marriages, but again, this is *your* ritual.

Start off by celebrating the good. Highlight the things you loved about each other and the ways in which you both grew. Be grateful for the time you shared together. Also, feel free to express your grievances or get clarity on the things that might still be hurting you. Acknowledge the pain you're both carrying. Cry it out. Give yourselves the closure you wish you'd gotten in past relationships, even if you need to ask for it. Be sure to discuss the process of moving forward and establish any boundaries you might need. Then wish each other well.

Above all, remember you will be okay. The thing about endings, regardless of whether we want them, is that they automatically provide new beginnings. If you can look at your pain as a starting point and commit to using it to catapult you forward, I promise you your life will not only be okay; it will be better. Be the phoenix that rises from the ashes, and don't let yourself be distracted by embarrassment, shame, or disappointment. Like I said, everyone breaks up—you are not alone.

THE GRAVEYARD

◆

A fun way to make sure someone stays "dead" is to put them in your graveyard. This works best for situationships, people you might regret texting in a moment of weakness, or people you're worried might try to circle back.

So the next time you're ready to cut ties with a fuckboy or a toxic ex, take screenshots of anything you want to remember before changing their name in your phone to this: [three tombstone emojis]

Then delete your text thread with them, and voilà: you've officially killed them off.

As you add more people to your graveyard, knowing who is who will be impossible, meaning you won't be able to contact them, and you also won't know who they are if they try to contact you.

This is how you can protect yourself against zombies rising from the dead asking you, **wyd**.

If you do end up getting a **"hey"** text, you can ignore it or reply:

I don't know who this is, because you're in my graveyard, which means that you've been digitally laid to rest but wish you the best! RIP!

Note: Emojis are copyrighted, so I wasn't able to use the original screenshots. The images above are recreations (by Chris Stewart) of two Instagram Stories I posted. The first story was a screenshot of a text I received, and the second was a screenshot of my graveyard.

THEY ALWAYS COME BACK

◆

At the end of *Scream*, after Gale shoots Billy (aka Ghostface), she hands the gun to Sydney Prescott, who promptly shoots him again before saying, "They always come back." It's a reference to the popular horror trope where monsters seemingly come back from the dead, and it is a catchphrase in the sequel. It's also a popular dating trope. The idea that exes, cheaters, situationships, and let's be real, *men*, will always circle back.

I'm here to dispel "they always come back" as a flex.

Look, I have no doubt you're amazing and the type of person that someone would regret leaving—I really do. However, "they always come back" is not a reflection of how great and desirable you are; it's a reflection of how selfish your ex is and how weak they think your boundaries are.

If they've left you, hurt you, or done you dirty, then they've already shown you that they didn't value what they had when they had it, so what makes you think they're going to value it now? It's true that some people change, but most don't. Most just hit a point where they're lonely and feel like having a warm body or quick validation and they go with the path of least resistance. That's not romantic; it's sad.

He's back because he thinks he can come back and you'll let him—do not prove that man right.

You've seen this movie before, pick a new one.

SCORCHED EARTH

♦

After you've thrown a funeral, you might be tempted to jump into another relationship or slip back into the dating pool, but I would caution against it. Sure, there's the old saying, "In order to get over someone, get under someone else." But I genuinely believe that's ill-advised. Assuming you read these chapters in order, you can see that I often "got back out there" largely to my own detriment.

Instead you need a fallow period. Long before over-tilling and toxic chemicals, our food came from sustainable farming. Not to go on a tin-hat tangent, but this is why older generations had more nutrient-dense food and fewer diseases. They had better food because they had better soil. And much like crops, we all need fertile ground for healthy relationships. This brings me to fallow periods.

A fallow period is a dormant or inactive segment of time. Authors have fallow periods in between books, and directors have fallow periods in between movies. But in keeping with our land metaphor, I am referring to the time when soil is allowed to lay idle for restoration. Let's say you have an acre that you want to grow food on. You might think that you can grow back-to-back crops on it, but you'd be wrong. The land needs time to replenish and restore nutrients; otherwise your crops won't be as robust.

A fire-fallow, or the slash-and-burn method, is a type of agricultural system in which the plants are cut and burned because the ash provides a nutrient-rich layer to help fertilize crops. After those crops are harvested, the land is left fallow for regeneration.

In the context of your love life, this means giving yourself time to get back to your baseline, regain your strength, and prepare for the sequel. Personally, I love the image of everything burning to the ground and starting over, using the ashes of what *was* to nourish *what's to come.*

Every time I rushed the period between an ending and a new beginning, I paid the price for it. When Jack the Ripper broke my heart, I needed a full year before I was ready to even *think* about dating someone else. I waited until my heart had been fully rehabilitated before venturing into a new relationship, and as a result, I ended up with Chris who was kind and loving and generous during our breakup. Our breakup was mutual and amicable, so I thought I was fine to hop into my relationship with Waldo, but look at how that played out. Not only did that relationship end with a perverse twist, it also paved the way for my devastating relationship with Dean. *Shivers.*

In fact, I encountered many of the monsters in this book because I didn't allow myself a proper fallow period. Depending on the situation, I'd wait a couple of weeks or months, and then I'd try to "get back out there." And like clockwork, I'd have my ass handed to me. *Why did I always rush this part of the healing process?*

I wasn't doing it consciously, but looking back, I was always eager to meet someone new because I was terrified of sitting alone with myself. I kept running toward my next love interest because I was running away from my own pain, and worrying about another romantic prospect was a lot more fun than searching inward and dealing with my inner demons. It's hard to sit with feelings of loneliness or self-doubt, but that's what you need to do to process those emotions. You can't keep shoving those feelings down; eventually they have to come out.

Your baggage might look different, but it's normal to want to avoid it. Before you jump into your next relationship, I'd challenge you to look inward and ask yourself if you're avoiding inner work. Otherwise you might find yourself alone at Halloween Horror Nights with a "mid" dude that you're not even that into.

I also think singledom needs a hard rebrand. There's a stigma around being single, especially if you're an older woman. We need to change that for future generations. We can do that together by refusing to assume that someone who is single is lonely, unhappy, or not actively choosing to be single. We can stop pitying those who are unmarried, and we can start celebrating platonic milestones in the same way we celebrate romantic milestones. And I think we should—because celebrating single life is an act of resistance.

I realize that many of the people reading this book want to fall in love and get married, myself included. However, that does not preclude me from pointing out that single women threaten the fabric of the patriarchy, which is what our whole world is built on. This is why a single bachelor in his forties is seen as someone who is picky, creating the illusion that he's more desirable, but a single woman in her forties carries the stigma of being unpicked and unwanted. I fully support your dreams of a white wedding and your desire for partnership, but I also want to encourage all of us to help improve the PR around single life, because fearing singledom only encourages women to settle faster.

Plus, being single *can* be awesome. I realize I've spent a lot of this book running from singledom, but as I have explained, I was just running from myself. Once I handled my bullshit, I realized that there are endless benefits to being a party of one. When you're happy being solo, you'll find that sticking to your boundaries and not settling for less are easier. When you're not afraid of being alone, you'll make relationship choices from a place of power, not desperation. If you're happy with your life, a partner becomes the icing on the cake instead of the cake itself.

But don't just trust me. Let's turn to the ultimate final girl, Laurie Strode from *Halloween*. There are thirteen movies and several timelines in the Halloween franchise, but there's a reason why we don't see Laurie (Jamie Lee Curtis) every day. She's recuperating in between each movie. Babe, you're no different than Jamie Lee Curtis. You've got to give yourself time to get your strength back up so you can go out into the world, face down the demons, kick ass, and get the love that you deserve. And if, God forbid, you get a little banged up along the way, you have time to heal emotionally and mentally so that you walk into the sequel without any of the residual hangups from the first movie. After all, you might be able to outrun a monster, but you can't outrun the monster inside of you.

If I've managed to convince you that you do need a fallow period, your next question is probably, *How long should my fallow period be*? Conventional wisdom says half the time of your relationship, but I don't know who came up with that. If you've been together ten years, waiting five years seems crazy. And conversely, I've had three-month situationships that have taken me a full three months to recover from. There's no one size fits all when it comes to how long you should wait, because it's not about *time*; it's about *you*—I know, that's an annoying answer. Instead, let's ask ourselves some questions.

QUESTIONS TO ASK YOURSELF BEFORE YOU START DATING AGAIN:

- Would you get back together with your ex if they wanted to?
- If you found out that your ex was dating or in love, would it bother you?
- When memories of you and your ex or your past relationship pop up, do you feel hurt, angry, or sad?
- Do you still check your ex's social media?
- Do you think about your ex more than once a week?

If you answered yes to any of these questions, you're not ready to date (and you're not over your ex). Do yourself and romantic prospects a favor and stay single. No one wants to be used as a human Band-Aid. You gotta heal on your own! When you can look at the past in a more neutral fashion and you don't still feel the pain, you might be ready.

- Do you feel like your life would be better if only you had a significant other?
- Do you often wonder what parts of you are to blame for still being single?
- Do you have an emotional urge to date?
- Are you scared that you're running out of time before you're undesirable?
- Do you romanticize past relationships because you dislike being single?
- When someone you find attractive doesn't match with you on a dating app, do you take it personally? Does it hurt your feelings or get you down?
- If you've gone on less than three dates with someone and it doesn't work out, will you spend weeks wondering why?
- Do you find yourself getting attached to dates very fast and then feeling bad if it doesn't work out?

Maybe a scab has formed over your initial heartbreak, but you have some deep healing to do before you're ready to really get back out there. You might be looking to fill a void and grab some validation, but instead, resist the urge and reflect inward. You need to face down those inner demons, those voices that tell you, *You're too much, you're not enough, everyone always leaves you, you're never the one who gets chosen.* These are your insecurities flaring, and they need to be addressed. You've got to get to a point where small rejections feel more like a stubbed toe and less like a broken bone before you get back out there.

Remember when Chad told me: "I feel like you just want *a* boyfriend and not that you necessarily want to date me"? It took him saying that out loud for me to realize that one, he was right, and two, he could feel it. The people you're dating will feel your desperation, and they will feel your insecurities even when you are fighting for your life to conceal them. Plus, the longer you put off healing and the more infected those wounds get, the worse you'll feel and the harder it will be to recover.

If you're truly over your ex, you're doing the inner work, and you're generally happy with your life—then yeah, go ahead and get back out there. As a general rule, when you start to question if you even *want* to date because dating will mean changing your habits to accommodate someone else and you love your life as is, that's when you're ready.

Scorched earth is part of the healing process. Allow yourself to burn it all down, lay low, and rebuild so you can love better later.

MAYBE I'M A MONSTER TOO

When I think about some of the monsters I've encountered, I regret not being absolutely feral.

For example, I dated a guy in high school who, in a fit of rage, tried to punch me in the face. Thankfully, I ducked and he missed. But from that moment on, I refused to acknowledge him until graduation when, per tradition, all the senior girls got together to write the "senior song." I made sure our entire female senior class sang about his shrimp dick as we held up our pinkies for size. (Technically it was the size of my middle finger, but it's still the smallest dick I've ever seen in person.) Was that an *insane* move on my part? Yes. Do I regret it? No. In fact it feels like just the right amount of shaming that should come from trying to deck a woman.

Unfortunately, that's about it for my revenge résumé. I've always felt like happiness was the ultimate revenge, so I've been one of those girls who tries her best to glow up and move on. I haven't always been successful, but my priority has always been peace of mind rather than revenge.

And yet, I'm sure I'm the villain in someone else's story. We all are, right?

Whether warranted or not, there's probably a man who curses my name when he hears it, a therapist who thinks of me as being the problem, or someone I've inadvertently hurt. I mean, I fell asleep with my date in the living room!

And, it's not like I'm claiming to be a perfect angel who never fucks up.

There was the time I stopped seeing a man after two dates because he had an incurable cancer and I couldn't stomach the thought of watching him die. He didn't know that though; I told him I'd reconnected with an ex and I wanted to see where it went. (Joke's on me because that man is still very much alive.)

Conversely, I let a man think I was dying so he would dump me and then ran into him six months later at a festival. In my defense, he mistakenly thought my autoimmune thyroid disorder was fatal, and rather than correct him, I decided it would be easier to let him think I was leaving earth and not just leaving him. I know! *Not* my finest work. So yeah, maybe I'm a monster too.

Then again, I've never cheated, ghosted, or taken advantage of someone, and I've always tried my best to end relationships with kindness and care. When I really stop to think about the most monstrous things I've done and the person I've treated the worst, it's *me*.

In this book alone, I've self-abandoned, spiraled, silenced myself, ignored my instincts, minimized my feelings, and betrayed my true desires. I've always wanted real love and partnership, but I've settled for less on so many occasions—because the dick was good, or *less* seemed better than being single, or I felt like this person was the best I could do at that time. I've gaslit myself to the point where I lost touch with my intuition and I've spent way too much time wondering if a man likes me instead of wondering if *I* like me.

After reading about my endless hours of self-evaluation, you must be wondering how this happened. And the answer is simple: In every single terrible instance, I let fear win.

My inner demon—or monster if you will—runs on fear. And so does yours.

Picture a little demon living inside your brain. That demon holds a core belief (or three) that's holding you back in life. Every limiting belief is reinforced by fearful thoughts and self-destructive actions. I like to imagine my inner demon emanating rays of negativity into my brain. Those rays become thoughts like, *See, I never get the guy I want* or *There's no point in trying, because I never win.* The problem with these demonic thoughts is that they cloud the way you see the world.

Our brain is made up of a web of complex systems that work together. For a long time, scientists believed that the limbic system—including structures like the amygdala, hippocampus, and hypothalamus—was the primary part of the brain responsible for memories, learning, emotions, motivation, and our autonomic nervous system.[31] According to this classic view, the limbic system attaches significance to our emotional experiences, which in turn influences future behaviors. For example, if you have an intense emotional experience, like a breakup or a betrayal, your brain will take in a ton of sensory information to store the memory to protect you from similar experiences in the future.[32]

However, more recent neuroscience, especially the work of Lisa Feldman Barrett, PhD, suggests an alternative theory. Lisa argues that there is no one emotional center in the brain and that, instead, emotions and beliefs are constructed using whole-brain networks like the salience network, default mode network, and regions like the insula and prefrontal cortex, which work together to predict and interpret sensory information based on past experiences. Under this logic, a painful break up doesn't

---

31 Cleveland Clinic Medical Professional, "Limbic System," Cleveland Clinic, December 19, 2024, https://my.clevelandclinic.org/health/body/limbic-system.
32 Srdjan D. Antic, "Limbic System," *Limbic System*, n.d., https://meds371s.uchc.edu/Antic%20limbic%20text.pdf.

get categorized by the limbic system; it becomes a part of a conceptual system that your brain uses to shape your beliefs and make predictions about future romantic situations.[33]

Either way you slice it, both models help explain confirmation bias, a phenomenon where people interpret, remember, and favor information that confirms their preexisting beliefs. In other words, your brain will prioritize things that align with your beliefs and goals. Barrett's theory attributes this to our brain's predictive coding system, and traditional neuroscience links this to sensory gating.[34] At any given moment, our brains are taking in too much information to process it all, and sensory gating acts like a filter, sorting what is and isn't important based on our individual belief systems so it can focus our attention accordingly. But here's the catch: You can influence what the system deems important. Whether you're a traditionalist or a Lisa Feldman Barrett fan, both concepts suggest that through new learning and new experiences we have the power to reshape what our brain prioritizes.

Let's say you believe that you need to lose twenty pounds in order to be loved or think you need to make a certain amount of money in order to be able to get the kind of girl that you want, well your brain will quite literally filter out information that contradicts those ideas, thereby highlighting and reinforcing your negative convictions. So you will think you're getting proof that confirms your fears, even if you don't want those things to be true! *This* is why having a handle on your thoughts and your beliefs is so important.

For a long time, I believed that true love was rare and hard to find, and life kept confirming this. My brain probably filtered out people and examples that would contradict this belief and

---

33 Lisa Feldman Barrett, *How Emotions Are Made: The New Science of the Mind and Brain* (Houghton Mifflin, 2016).
34 Howard C. Cromwell et al. "Sensory gating: A Translational Effort from Basic to Clinical Science. *Clinical EEG and Neuroscience*, no. 2 (April 2008): 69–72, https://doi.org/10.1177/155005940803900209.

instead directed my attention to evidence that affirmed this negative perspective. Your brain wants to prove you right. Let me say that again: *Your brain wants to prove you right.* So why not let it work to prove you right about good things?

To reprogram your brain, you have to change your core beliefs, which is easier said than done. Hopefully the chapter on spells got you thinking about your thoughts and the way that you speak to yourself—because you will need that introspection to rewrite your personal narrative.

The first step to fighting any monster is knowing what you're up against. Ask yourself how your inner demons show up in your day-to-day life. Are you numbing yourself out, and if so, when and in what kinds of situations? Notice when you feel the most insecure or upset with yourself. What patterns precipitated these moments? How do you speak to yourself and what are the stories you keep repeating? Take a forensic look at your life: Look at your thoughts and behaviors and work backward.

- Maybe you identify that you hold people at an arm's length.
- Maybe you notice your inner monologue is constantly critical of your body.
- Maybe you realize you have a pattern of always rushing into relationships.

Once you've identified the behaviors—which I like to picture as the rays emanating from the demon—you can figure out what core belief they're coming from.

- Holding people at arm's length is a way to ensure that you never get hurt.
- Worrying about body image is rooted in a fear that you

aren't enough or lovable as you are.
- Rushing into relationships can be a result of fearing loneliness or hurt. By quickly locking down a relationship, people seek validation to avoid the feelings associated with being vulnerable.

Keep pulling back the layers of these fears to reveal the core negative belief (aka your inner demon).

- If you hold people at an arm's length, ask yourself if you resonate with a fear of abandonment. Are you scared that the people you love always leave?
- If you find yourself obsessing about your image not measuring up, you might have a core belief that love is conditional and that unless you look a certain way you will be unlovable.
- A pattern of urgency and jumping into relationships might be tied to the belief that there's a finite number of good mates out there. Does a scarcity mindset resonate with you at all? Or maybe it's a fear of being alone and the belief that you're not enough on your own.

You will have to find the limiting beliefs that resonate the most with you. The important part is that you do the work to identify them; you cannot tame what you cannot name. You need to understand what kind of monster you're up against.

My inner demons grew out of a handful of limiting beliefs:

- Good love is hard to find.
- Love is conditional.
- My romantic judgment can't be trusted.
- I'm running out of time to find a partner.

Once I was aware of my limiting beliefs, I pushed up my sleeves and prepared for a battle of epic proportions: me vs. the monsters in my mind. But in a cruel twist, the more I tried to resist the urges of my inner demons, the harder they persisted. As it turns out, you cannot kill those fuckers by ignoring them or silencing them. You don't overcome the darkest parts of yourself by fighting or avoiding; instead, you have to learn to love your inner demons, and in turn, to love yourself. (Such a mindfuck, right?)

The good news is, once you identify your fears and call them out, it's like turning on the lights in a dark hallway, making the fears less scary. Next, pretend you're making a documentary about yourself and the life of your inner demons and try to figure out their origin story. Really investigate where these limiting beliefs came from and map out all the ways in which life has seemingly proved them to be true. Understanding *why* you hold the fears that you do is helpful when practicing self-compassion. This is deep work, so be patient with yourself. Healing takes time. But you *can* heal.

To change your life—and to stop being a monster to yourself—you need to change your thoughts and your core beliefs. You can do this by tracking and changing your thoughts (as outlined in the "Spells" chapter), by seeking out books, people, and experiences that affirm or support your new truth, by repeating affirmations that challenge your old limiting beliefs, and by visualizing positive outcomes and the life you want to lead. Think of it as giving your brain new (positive) data in order to reshape the way it sees the world. Instead of imagining all the ways in which a relationship could blow up in your face, start imagining what your dream relationship would feel like. Put yourself in situations where you practice the feelings associated with your new core beliefs.

If your thoughts become the walls of the house that you live in, then your beliefs are the foundation. It's up to you to decide whether you want to live in a haunted house or your dream home. Change your perspective, and you change your life. I know that sounds overly simple and too good to be true, but in reality it's a lot of hard work. And even when you manage to diminish one demon, there will always be another.

Singledom, relationships, marriage, motherhood, and divorce all bring their own set of fears and demons. As we evolve as people, so do our limiting beliefs. What holds you back when you're twenty-one and single might not be what holds you back when you're married with kids at fifty. I mean, it could be, but the point is we will constantly be collecting new demons, new fears, and new baggage. So the inner work never ends.

Now when I notice self-destructive behaviors, unproductive thoughts, or new anxieties, I repeat the process. I try to name the demon and figure out where it's coming from and why. Then I give myself the same compassion and love I would if I were a friend. (Be your own best friend!) I speak to myself the same way I'd speak to a child who needs to be comforted. I love myself despite my flaws and fears, and in doing so, I ease the grip that my inner demons have on me, forcing them to retreat to the dark place where they reside.

In many ways, this book is dedicated to the monster in me. My inner demons were the connective tissue tying me to the horrors in each of these chapters.

I'm not saying this to absolve the men who have wronged me, but rather to highlight the power in accountability. Introspection and accountability are two of the greatest assets a final girl can possess. Sure, I could blame the men whom I've dated, but the reality is that *I* dated them. No one forced me into those relationships. And look, I couldn't see some of the twists and betrayals coming, but I could have avoided plenty of monsters had I been better to myself.

Blaming others robs us of the opportunity to learn and grow from our pain—and what is life if not an endless lesson in growth. Look at the ways in which you, too, have been a monster, not only to others but also to yourself. Relationships, especially romantic ones, act like a mirror reflecting back to us the parts of ourselves that need work. Without accountability and self-reflection, you're doomed to continue making the same mistakes. Trust me, I know; I've lived it. And you've read it, so hopefully you can see the patterns too.

This has been my journey, but ideally my lessons can help illuminate the winding path that is your journey. Perhaps you can learn from my mistakes. Regardless of whether you are single or partnered, remember that the world is already full of horrors; the least you can do is stop being a monster to yourself.

Be your own best friend instead.

FINAL GIRLS

It's not surprising to me that you, dear final girl, have made it to the last chapter of this book. After all, you are a survivor.

I have good and bad news for you.

The bad news: There will always be a sequel. The horror never actually ends; it just changes and evolves because life is hard, and love—in all its forms—is complicated. You are absolutely going to meet someone you adore, and you'll exit the "hell" of single life. Unfortunately, every phase of our romantic lifespan has its pitfalls. Relationships are hard work. Marriage isn't all unicorns and rainbows, just like raising kids isn't a walk in the park. The more you love someone, the greater your risk for pain and heartbreak. And no one is coming to save you.

- If you don't know your own self-worth, people will shortchange you.
- If you don't speak up and advocate for yourself, the world will gladly silence you.
- If you don't strive to stay open and soft, life will harden you.
- If you don't believe that love is out there for you, you will never make it out of the haunted house.

You are the heroine of your own story, and you don't need saving. You might feel like you do at times, and you'll have incredible supporting characters along the way, but you were cast in this role with all the tools that you need to survive. And whenever you feel like you're ready to make a mad dash for the exit sign, remember that there is no one else on earth quite like you. The odds of your being born were one in four *trillion*—you are quite literally a statistical main character. So don't forget to act like it.

No matter how many ghosts, zombies, vampires, or demonic clowns you encounter, trust that you are equipped to handle whatever comes your way. (If I can do it, then why can't you do it? You can.)

I know you're probably wondering if I ever found love, and the answer is yes. If you think I'm going to tell you about a guy, I'm not. It doesn't mean that there isn't one; I've just realized that he's not the most important love of my life. *I am.* And I don't mean that in a selfish or egotistical way. I say that as someone who loves partnership. However, the quality of love I have in my relationships, both romantic and platonic, is directly proportional to the love I have for myself. When you start loving yourself the way you want a partner to love you, you'll show up as a better wife, friend, mom, and citizen of the world.

I get that everyone loves a happy ending, and I promise you, I am constantly writing mine. I could tell you that I'm engaged or married now, and maybe that would give you more solace, but the truth is my story has nothing to do with *your* journey. It might be inspiring to see someone who has been through the trenches reach the proverbial finish line, but all you need to know is this: As long as love exists, it can exist for you too. As long as you keep believing that it's out there for you, you will find it. And in the meantime, do your best to enjoy the ride.

You only have so much time on earth, so what is the point of being miserable?

If you're in a relationship and you're unhappy, make a change. Get out or fix it, because one day your partner won't be there and you will have wasted the one thing you can't ever get back: time. If you're single and unhappy, remember that this could be the last time you're single for the rest of your life. Do you want to spend your last single days complaining and feeling sorry for yourself, or do you want to live it the hell up? Only you get to decide. Similarly, ask yourself, if I had the partner of my dreams right now, how would I be living? Start living *that* life. Don't wait for someone else to start building your dream life!

I can confidently tell you that the only relationship you won't regret over-investing in is the relationship you have with yourself. So take the opportunity to start showing up for yourself the way you show up for others. Start romanticizing yourself the same way you idealize your crushes. Be your own knight in shining armor. If horror movies have taught us anything, it's that you can't rely on someone else coming to your rescue. Falling in love will not save you—there will always be new jump scares.

Again, I don't say any of this to be depressing or glib. I believe that love is beautiful and worth fighting for, and I know that it's out there for you. Yes, *you*. I just want to arm you with the kind of mindset that will get you through whatever horror is thrown your way.

They say that the definition of crazy is doing the same thing over and over and expecting different results, but in the pursuit of love, I disagree. I think it takes guts. It takes genuine bravery to keep getting back up and walking down the same haunted hallways you've been terrorized in before. If the price of love is loss, then the most romantic thing a person can do is say to that inner voice, the one that carries all their past romantic pain, that this time might be different—that *this* time might just end with "till death do us part." Because if there's anything a final girl needs to survive the third act, it's hope and trust in herself.

To final girls everywhere: You inspire me—keep going.

X, Rory

WORKS REFERENCED

Agrimis, Jessie. "Principles of Neuroplasticity: Repetition Matters." *NeuroLab 360*, 23 Dec. 2021, www.neurolab360.com/blog/principles-of-neuroplasticity-repetition-matters.

Antic, Srdjan D. "Limbic System." *Limbic System*, University of Connecticut Health Center, n.d., https://meds371s.uchc.edu/Antic%20limbic%20text.pdf.

Argov, Sherry. *Why Men Love Bitches: From Doormat to Dreamgirl — A Woman's Guide to Holding Her Own in a Relationship*. Simon and Schuster, 2002.

Assad, Joseph, et al. "Takotsubo Syndrome: A Review of Presentation, Diagnosis and Management." *Clinical Medicine Insights: Cardiology*, vol. 16, 1 Jan. 2022, https://doi.org/10.1177/11795468211065782.

Baer, Drake. "Heartbreak Looks a Lot like Drug Withdrawal in the Brain." *The Cut*, 17 Feb. 2017, www.thecut.com/2017/02/why-heartbreak-getting-dumped-feel-so-bad.html.

Barrett, Lisa Feldman. *How Emotions Are Made: The New Science of the Mind and Brain*. Houghton Mifflin, 2016.

Bedera, Nicole. *On the Wrong Side: How Universities Protect Perpetrators and Betray Survivors of Sexual Violence*. University of California Press, 2024.

Cleveland Clinic Medical Professional. "Limbic System." *Cleveland Clinic*, 19 Dec. 2024, www.my.clevelandclinic.org/health/body/limbic-system.

Clover, Carol J. "Her Body, Himself: Gender in the Slasher Film." *Representations*, no. 20, 1987, pp. 187–228. *JSTOR*, www.jstor.org/stable/2928507.

Cromwell, Howard C., et al. "Sensory Gating: A Translational Effort from Basic to Clinical Science." *Clinical EEG and Neuroscience*, no. 2, Apr. 2008, pp. 69–72. https://doi.org/10.1177/155005940803900209.

Eisenstadt v. Baird, 405 U.S. 438 (1972).

Equal Credit Opportunity Act. Public Law 93-495, 1974.

Fein, Ellen, and Sherrie Schneider. *Not Your Mother's Rules: The New Secrets for Dating*. Grand Central Publishing, 2013.

Fisher, Helen. "Dumped!" *New Scientist*, 14 Feb. 2004, www.newscientist.com/article/mg18124345-300-dumped/.

Foster, Olivia. "It Takes Just 11 Weeks to Get Over a Break-up (but Divorcees Need 18 Months to Move On)." *Mail Online*, 19 Jan. 2015, www.dailymail.co.uk/femail/article-2916925/It-takes-just-11-weeks-break-divorcees-need-18-months-on.html.

Garcia, Michael Ray, Stephen W. Leslie, and Anton A. Wray. "Sexually Transmitted Infections." *StatPearls*, StatPearls Publishing, 20 Apr. 2024. *NCBI Bookshelf*, www.ncbi.nlm.nih.gov/books/NBK560808/.

Herbenick, Debby, et al. "Women's Experiences with Genital Touching, Sexual Pleasure, and Orgasm: Results from a U.S. Probability Sample of Women Ages 18 to 94." *Journal of Sex & Marital Therapy*, vol. 44, no. 2, 5 July 2017, pp. 201–12. https://doi.org/10.1080/0092623x.2017.1346530.

"Infographic: Debunking 'Lesbian Bed Death.'" *Kinsey Institute Blog*, 27 Oct. 2022, blogs.iu.edu/kinseyinstitute/2022/10/27/infographic-debunking-lesbian-bed-death/.

Kim, Jane J., et al. "Human Papillomavirus Vaccination for Adults Aged 30 to 45 Years in the United States: A Cost-Effectiveness Analysis." *PLOS Medicine*, vol. 18, no. 3, 11 Mar. 2021, e1003534. https://doi.org/10.1371/journal.pmed.1003534.

Kross, Ethan, et al. "Social Rejection Shares Somatosensory Representations with Physical Pain." *Proceedings of the National Academy of Sciences*, vol. 108, no. 15, 28 Mar. 2011, pp. 6270–75. https://doi.org/10.1073/pnas.1102693108.

Kyejo, Willbroad, et al. "Cervical Vasovagal Shock: A Rare Complication of Incomplete Abortion Case Report." *International Journal of Surgery Case Reports*, vol. 97, 25 July 2022, article no. 107455. https://doi.org/10.1016/j.ijscr.2022.107455.

Lopes, Barbara C., and Rusi Jaspal. "Exposure to Ghosting, Gaslighting, and Coercion and Mental Health Outcomes." *Partner Abuse*, 1 Apr. 2025, https://doi.org/10.1891/pa-2024-0031.

Love Island. Season 3, produced by Mandy Morris, et al., CBS, 7 July–15 Aug. 2021.

Markowitz, Lauri E., and John T. Schiller. "Human Papillomavirus Vaccines." *The Journal of Infectious Diseases*, vol. 224, no. Supplement_4, 18 May 2021, pp. S367–78. https://doi.org/10.1093/infdis/jiaa621.

McQuillan, Geraldine, Deanna Kruszon-Moran, Laurie E. Markowitz, et al. "Prevalence of HPV in Adults Aged 18–69: United States, 2011–2014." *NCHS Data Brief*, no. 280, National Center for Health Statistics, 2017, www.cdc.gov/nchs/products/databriefs/db280.htm.

Nacul, Luis, et al. "How Myalgic Encephalomyelitis/Chronic Fatigue Syndrome (ME/CFS) Progresses: The Natural History of ME/CFS." *Frontiers in Neurology*, vol. 11, 11 Aug. 2020, https://doi.org/10.3389/fneur.2020.00826.

"Once in a Lifetime." *Ally McBeal*, created by David E. Kelley, written by David E. Kelley, Nicole Yorkin, and Dawn Prestwich, directed by Elodie Keene, season 1, episode 15, Fox, 2 Feb. 1998.

Pelletier, A. R., and J. Gilchrist. "Roller Coaster Related Fatalities, United States, 1994–2004." *Injury Prevention*, vol. 11, no. 5, 1 Oct. 2005, pp. 309–12. https://doi.org/10.1136/ip.2005.008425.

"Pregnancy Over Age 35: A Numbers Game." *Your Pregnancy Matters*, UT Southwestern Medical Center, n.d., www.utswmed.org/medblog/pregnancy-over-35/.

Reagan, Ronald. "Radio Address to the Nation on Family Values." *The Ronald Reagan Presidential Library & Museum*, 20 Dec. 1986, www.reaganlibrary.gov/archives/speech/radio-address-nation-family-values.

Snyder, Blake. *Save the Cat!: The Last Book on Screenwriting You'll Ever Need*. Michael Wiese Productions, 2005.

Stern, Scott W. "America's Forgotten Mass Imprisonment of Women." *HISTORY*, 30 June 2025, www.history.com/articles/chamberlain-kahn-act-std-venereal-disease-imprisonment-women.

Studnick, James, et al. "Estimating the Period Prevalence of Mothers Who Have Abortions: A Population Based Study of Inclusive Pregnancy Outcomes." *Health Services Research and Managerial Epidemiology*, 23 July 2021, www.ncbi.nlm.nih.gov/pmc/articles/PMC8312161/.

Waltz, Margaret, Anne Drapkin Lyerly, and Jill A. Fisher. "Exclusion of Women from Phase I Trials: Perspectives from Investigators and Research Oversight Officials." *Ethics & Human Research*, vol. 45, no. 6, 1 Nov. 2023, pp. 19–30. https://doi.org/10.1002/eahr.500170.

ACKNOWLEDGMENTS

Holy shit . . . there are so many people to thank.

First off, my family. Thank you for your unconditional love and unwavering support. Mom and Dad, the love that I grew up with made me think that fairy tales were real, and that is remarkable. You guys are the gold standard, always and forever. I realize that reading about some of this stuff was not ideal, but you still supported me anyway. No one has championed my creativity more than you and Cass. As I've said in this book, the three of you have taught me more about unconditional love than all of my romantic relationships combined. So, thank you, thank you. I love you.

To all my friends who let me go MIA for months because I was writing, editing, or panicking about this book, I love you all so much. Even at the depths of my heartache or the lowest lows with my health, I have always had incredible friends who have made life better—and funnier.

My worst fear is trying to list everyone and accidentally forgetting someone, then having to live with that error, in print, for eternity. So, I'm not going to name people individually, but I'm pretty sure you know who you are. THANK YOU for being the kind of friend who would make the acknowledgments of a book. Aside from ending global warming or world hunger, my wish for people would be to have a friend group like mine. I love you guys. Thank you.

Thank you to my agent Claire Harris for believing in me and never giving up on this book, even when it meant losing out on money. You are such a real one.

Thank you to my editors Rea Frey and Jennifer Chesak. You both made this book better than it ever would have been. I am forever grateful for the ways in which you pushed me to be a better writer.

Sophie Flack, you were an early champion of what would become this book. Your edits and guidance gave me the confidence to make this book a reality. Thank you.

Meredith and Benielle, thank you for reading every draft, even the very early ones. Would I have written this book without you guys? Unclear. You have really been my day one's on this book and I am extremely grateful.

Myles, thank you for taking my photo and for always taking my photos and for being my friend.

Elaine York for layout and formatting. Daniel for your eye and for helping me at the last second.

Nick, Sophie, Elio, Gabrielle Stone, Cassen, Emma, Jesse, Nola, Akilah, Judy, Amy, Daniel, Babs, Benni, Nikki, Helen, Sabina, Sarah, Sarah, Kassaundra, Tara, Amanda, Hillary, Scout Sobel, Marissa—thank you for your advice, your notes, or your recommendations (and in some cases, all three). You guys helped me make this book. And while it's not a baby, it still takes a village. Thanks for being a part of mine.

The following is a list of people and things that have made my life better, which indirectly (or directly) made this book better:

Low-dose Naltrexone, Dolly Parton, Two Bunch Palms, Ghia, red light therapy, Robyn (specifically "Body Talk"), hojicha, Wednesday Addams, South Korea for all of your skincare, Breegan, Whole Again, Australian red licorice, iS Clinical cleanser, the Hitachi Magic Wand, people who rescue pets, the LA Philharmonic, Camp Smith, Kodak Ultramax, Botox, Drew Afualo, sleeping in, OSEA, Stevie Nicks, crispy tacos, Nora Ephron, Etsy witches, Gisèle Pelicot, and like twelve different brands of sunscreen. Beyond grateful for all the above.

And, lastly, the elephant in the room: This book would not exist as it does today without a ton of people rejecting me. LOL.

To the dudes who broke my heart—are you guys good? Why the hell are you still reading this? I mean, thank you, but unhinged to be reading the acknowledgments. To be fair, your rejections *did* make me grow as a person and they led to the creation of this book, so thank you. Genuinely. But also, I do hope some of you are blessed with daughters. To the former reps who didn't "get it" and to the publishers who passed because I didn't have enough followers, I also thank you. Those rejections made me double down. Y'all deepened my conviction and forced me to sharpen this book in ways I never thought possible. I love this book, and because of your rejections, I got to make it on my own terms. So, THANK YOU.

Okay wait, there's one more person I want to thank. Me! I love you, girl. Thank you for never giving up, on love and on yourself. I hope we keep making the future Rory proud. xx

Photo: Myles Pettengill

ABOUT THE AUTHOR

RORY UPHOLD is a multi-hyphenate creator, performer, and accidental dating anthropologist. She began her writing career in music as a songwriter before transitioning into television, where she's developed and sold original shows to your favorite networks. Rory lives in Los Angeles, where she hosts a podcast and regularly shares snippets of her life on social media.

@icouldbeblonder

@roryuphold

www.ingramcontent.com/pod-product-compliance
Lightning Source LLC
Chambersburg PA
CBHW020533030426
42337CB00013B/828